How to Do *Everything* with Your

Digital Camera

Third Edition

Dave Johnson

McGraw-Hill/Osborne

New York   Chicago   San Francisco   Lisbon
London   Madrid   Mexico City   Milan   New Delhi
San Juan   Seoul   Singapore   Sydney   Toronto

W9-ABT-983

McGraw-Hill/Osborne
2100 Powell Street, 10th Floor
Emeryville, California 94608
U.S.A.

To arrange bulk purchase discounts for sales promotions, premiums, or fund-raisers, please contact **McGraw-Hill**/Osborne at the above address. For information on translations or book distributors outside the U.S.A., please see the International Contact Information page immediately following the index of this book.

How to Do Everything with Your Digital Camera

890 CUS CUS 0198765

ISBN 0-07-223081-9

Publisher	Brandon A. Nordin
Vice President &	
Associate Publisher	Scott Rogers
Acquisitions Editor	Megg Morin
Project Editor	Jenn Tust
Technical Editor	Dave Huss
Copy Editors	Marcia Baker
	Emily Rader
Proofreader	Paul Medoff
Indexer	Valerie Robbins
Composition	Tom Anzai
	Allan Shearer
Illustrator	Bert Schopf
Series Design	Mickey Galicia
Cover Series Design	Dodie Shoemaker

This book was composed with Corel VENTURA™ Publisher.

For Newt
1987–2000

About the Author

Dave Johnson writes about technology from his home in Colorado Springs, Colorado. He's editor of *Mobility Magazine* and senior editor at *Handheld Computing*. He also writes a weekly electronic newsletter on digital photography for *PC World* magazine. In addition, he's the author of two dozen books that include *Robot Invasion: 7 Cool and Easy Robot Projects, How to Do Everything with MP3 and Digital Music,* and *How to Do Everything with Your Palm Handheld* (the latter two with Rick Broida). His short story for early readers, *The Wild Cookie,* has been transformed into an interactive storybook on CD-ROM. Currently, he's writing *How to Do Everything with Your Digital Camcorder* with Rick Broida and Todd Stauffer. In his spare time, Dave photographs wildlife—particularly wolves, tigers, and sharks—and is a scuba instructor.

Dave started writing professionally in 1990, before anyone had a chance to talk him out of it. Prior to that, he had a somewhat unfocused career that included flying satellites, driving an ice cream truck, loading bombs onto B-52s in a remote region of Michigan, stocking shelves at a New Jersey Quick Check, teaching rocket science, photographing a rock band, and writing about space penguins. He's still not playing bass in a psychedelic band, but at least he's found steady work.

Contents

Acknowledgments

Thanks to all the great folks at Osborne who are always fun to work with—especially folks like Megg Bonar and Jenn Tust, who, it turns out, is also a Kristin Hersh fan. Finally, let me thank all the selfless models who posed for me as I shot picture after picture for this book—including Kris, Evan, and Marin.

Introduction

Welcome to *How to Do Everything with Your Digital Camera*. This is not your typical book on digital photography—I wrote it to answer all the questions I had about digital cameras and photography techniques when I was starting out. I've been a photographer for about 20 years, and in that time I've read a lot of books and magazines about the art and science of photography. I figured that this was a good time to write a book that would hopefully explain it all in the space of a few hundred pages.

A tall order, I know.

Nonetheless, I know what it feels like to have a new digital camera and search fruitlessly for the answers to seemingly obvious questions. I've read too many books that make passing references to "control your depth of field with the aperture" without explaining what either the aperture or depth of field actually is. Or mention that you need a lot of pixels to print an 8×10-inch picture without ever telling you how many pixels you actually need.

So when I wrote this book I mapped out all of the things I thought you might need to know. I started at the beginning and decided to cover photography techniques like lighting, composition, and close-ups. Hopefully you'll find that the book walks you through the key steps of using a digital camera—from working with memory cards, to file formats, to editing images on a PC, to printing, and finally, to sharing your images.

The world of digital photography is changing fast. It's just crawling out of its infancy, so it has a long way to go before digital is as common—or easy to use— as a 35mm point-and-shoot camera. But this is a great time to purchase and use a digital camera, and I hope that some of my enthusiasm for the digital medium comes through. I love the freedom and flexibility that a digital camera gives me; armed with my Olympus e-20 or a Sony DSC-F717 Cyber-shot, I can take pictures without worrying about buying film or using it before it expires. I can instantly preview my work and download just the images I want to keep. And I particularly like the fact that I can print 8×10- or 13×19-inch enlargements exactly the way I want without trying to convey imprecise instructions to some tech in a photo shop. I've even used a digital camera underwater when scuba diving, and that, too, is a whole new and exciting world of photography that is made dramatically easier through the use of digital cameras.

I wrote this book so that you could sit down and read it through like a novel if you'd like to—but I realize few people will actually do that. If you're looking for specific information, I've organized the book so topics should be easy to find. Part I kicks things off with the basics of using your camera. I begin by explaining how to shop for a digital camera and how to operate the most common controls on digital cameras. From there, I delve into stuff you need to know no matter what kind of camera you have—stuff like composition, lighting, close-ups, and how to take advantage of the special features on your camera.

Part II of the book is about getting the images from the camera into your PC. I talk about how to use file formats like JPG and TIF, and how to care for the memory cards that come with your camera. For those of you who want to scan traditional film prints into your PC, I've dedicated a chapter to selecting and using a scanner.

I'm guessing that most of you will be keenly interested in Part III—at least that's one of the most exciting parts for me. This is where you can learn how to edit digital images as if your PC were a sort of digital darkroom. Sure, there are simple techniques in here like how to crop and resize images, but I also write about cool special effects—adding text, changing images so they look like they were painted, and even creating Hollywood-style "bluescreen" effects.

Finally, the book ends with Part IV, a few chapters that explain how to print and share your images. I tell you exactly what you need to know to get great results—like optimizing your printer, using the right paper, and calculating how large you can print your image based on how many pixels it has. Then you can learn how to share your images—on the computer screen, in e-mail, on the Web (even without programming), and in devices like Palms and digital picture frames.

You will find special elements to help you get the most out of the book:

■ **How To**   These special boxes explain, in a nutshell, how to accomplish key tasks throughout the book. You can read the How To box for a summary of what the chapter is explaining at-large.

■ **Notes**   These provide extra information that is handy for trivia contests but isn't essential to understanding the current topic.

■ **Tips**   These tell you how to do something a better, faster, or smarter way.

■ **Sidebars**   These talk about related topics that are pretty darned interesting, but you can skip them if you prefer.

■ Within the text, you'll also find words in special formatting. New terms are in italics, while specific phrases that you will see on the screen or need to type yourself appear in bold.

Want to e-mail me? You can send questions and comments to:

cameraquestions@bydavejohnson.com.

My web site is located at **bydavejohnson.com**, and you're welcome to visit and check out other books or my photography anytime you like. I also write a free, weekly e-mail newsletter for *PC World* magazine called Digital Focus. You can subscribe to Digital Focus by visiting pcworld.com and clicking on the newsletters link. Each week I offer digital photo and editing tips, answer readers' questions, and award prizes to reader-submitted photos. Join—it's a blast!

Thanks, and enjoy reading the book!

Part I

Your Camera

Chapter 1

Welcome to the Future

How to…

- Navigate around your digital camera

- Distinguish between point-and-shoot and professional camera features

- Pick a camera resolution based on print size

- Conserve battery power

- Tell the difference between a digital and an optical zoom

- Shop for a new digital camera

- Choose gear and accessories for a digicam

This chapter is called "Welcome to the Future," and I mean it. I'm convinced that digital photography is, for most people and in most situations, the best way to take pictures. And the technology just keeps getting better all the time.

With a digital camera, it's possible to take photos and review them instantly—while they're still stored in the camera—to see if they turned out the way you like. From there, you can transfer them to a computer and easily crop them to size, adjust color and brightness, even perform special effects on them if you want to, and then print the final result to exactly the size you like for a frame in your living room. Then you can take the same picture and e-mail it, post it to a Web site, display it on a TV, or show it to friends from your handheld organizer. The beauty of digital imaging is its immediacy and versatility—just try to do those things with a 35mm or Advanced Photo System (APS) camera.

So if you've recently bought a digital camera, congratulations—I think you've made the right choice. In this chapter, we'll take a quick look at your camera and at digital cameras in general. And if you're still shopping for your camera, flip to the end of this chapter, where I tell you what to look for when you head off to make your purchase.

A History Lesson

When I was a kid, my dad bought a darkroom kit so he could develop his own photographs. I clearly remember that box, and how it sat, untouched, on top of a hall closet. For years. Why did my dad never get around to setting up his darkroom? In a nutshell, it was just too much trouble.

Darkrooms require, well, darkness. You have to have a room that you can dedicate to the task and trust that people won't come barging in while you're developing film (or hang their wet bathing suit in there when you're not watching).

And then there are the chemicals. Film processing is all about using nasty, toxic chemicals that, if you were running a business, would get the attention of OSHA. When I worked in the space launch business, I'm sure that some of the rocket fuels we used weren't as frightening as the chemicals that home darkroomers routinely expose themselves to. Who wants to muck around with that stuff?

Oh, yeah—and it isn't all that easy, either. Black-and-white processing isn't really brain surgery, but working with color film is tough. It's not a hobby you can master in a few weeks, to be sure. And the whole point of having your own darkroom is so you can get better results than the corner store delivers, right?

No wonder my dad never got too far with his darkroom kit.

These days, digital photography gives you the same flexibility as those old chemical darkrooms—the ability to brighten or darken an image, crop it down to generate a better composition, and print enlargements in a variety of sizes—but without the chemicals, without the steep learning curve, and without dedicating a part of your house to nothing but photography. How did we get here?

A Slow Evolution

These days, some digital cameras can compete with the best 35mm SLRs in terms of resolution and image quality. Obviously, it hasn't always been this way.

When you consider the first digital cameras that debuted in the early 1990s, it's a miracle that anyone used them at all. The first models you could buy for under a grand included the Logitech Fotoman, Kodak DC40, Apple QuickTake 100, and the Casio QV-10. They were strictly for gear-headed early adopters that bought them just to try out the nascent field of digital photography. They certainly weren't particularly useful, since they offered poor image quality, limited resolution, and substandard optics. Early digital cameras generated low-resolution images, like 376×240 and, later, 640×480 pixels—not even enough to fill a computer screen when set to the lowest Windows resolution. That was if you could figure out how to get the images out of the camera and into your PC.

Those early digital cameras typically had plastic lenses, and the light sensor that captured the image was a component called a Complementary Metal Oxide Semiconductor (CMOS) chip. CMOS chips were popular because they were cheap and required very little power, but they created horribly fuzzy pictures. Charge Coupled Devices (CCDs) cost a small fortune in comparison, so CMOS chips found their way into many of the first cameras. See Figure 1-1 for an example of the difference between an image taken with a CMOS chip (on the left) and a CCD (on the right).

CMOS is making a comeback—the technology has improved dramatically, and some new cameras with CMOS chips work as well as CCDs and cost less to boot. Since some of the best professional cameras on the market now include CMOS sensors, don't ignore a new model just because it has a CMOS sensor.

In the early days, VGA resolution (640×480 pixels) established itself as the first real standard size for digital images. Digicams came equipped with CMOS or CCD chips capable of capturing 640×480-pixel images, which was ideal for display on a computer screen, posting on Web pages, or e-mail, but you couldn't really print such a picture. On a typical inkjet printer, you'd get a photograph that measured just three inches across.

Then came *megapixel*. "Mega" means million, and the term simply refers to the maximum number of pixels the camera can capture. A megapixel camera can create an image with a million pixels—for example, 1000×1000 or 860×1200, or any other pixel dimension that multiplies out to about a million dots of information. The first megapixel cameras raised the bar for everyone. Like owning last year's laptop with a slow processor, no one wanted to own a VGA camera. That started the race we're still in the midst of today.

FIGURE 1-1   Older cameras with CMOS sensors (left) typically offered lower image quality than those with CCDs (right).

FIGURE 1-2   More megapixels means more resolution, which is handy for changing the composition of your picture through cropping, as well as for making good-quality prints.

Today, most digital cameras capture anywhere from 2 to 5 megapixels, with 6-megapixel cameras tempting photographers as well. And it doesn't end there. Some high-end cameras capture even more pixels—we're starting to see pro-level cameras with 12 million and more. Why the fuss over pixels? Well, as I alluded to earlier, the more pixels you have, the sharper your image is, and consequently the larger it can be printed. If you'd like to print a digital photo at 8×10 or larger, for instance, a VGA or one-megapixel camera simply won't cut it—each pixel would be the size of a postage stamp. Take a look at Figure 1-2. On the left is a detail from a picture taken at 640×480 pixels. On the right is the same detail, but it's cropped from a 3.3-megapixel image. As you can see, the smaller image has fewer pixels to work with, and that's why it looks so grainy. Obviously, you need lots of pixels to print pictures at a large size, and that's why each year we see ever larger-resolution digital cameras hitting store shelves.

The Future of Digital Cameras

And there's no end in sight, at least for a while. The goal of most camera manufacturers has traditionally been to elevate the resolution of digicams (shorthand, of course, for digital cameras) to what you can already get from an ordinary film camera. But not all film cameras are the same, and serious photographers always want more resolution. More resolution—or more pixels per picture—allows photographers to blow up images to larger sizes and to crop images and enlarge just one small section of a photo without sacrificing image quality as well. Some medium- and large-format cameras, for instance, shoot negatives so large that you can make the print take up a billboard. That's impossible with any consumer-grade digital camera made today. But it won't be impossible for long, since better digicams come out each year.

On the other hand, most folks never make prints any larger than about 8×10 inches, and that means a 3- or 4-megapixel camera is good enough for them. But if you want larger pictures—like 11×17 or 13×19 (well within the ability of some consumer-priced wide-format inkjet printers)—you need more pixels. Or, you might want to change the composition of a digital image by cropping away a lot of unwanted pixels, and then print the resulting image as an 8×10. You'll need to start with a larger image, such as a 5- or 6-megapixel, to get good results. See? The whole issue of resolution can get a bit complicated.

These days, quite a few affordable digicams can generate 6-megapixel images. Photographers consider that an important number because that's the resolution generally associated with 35mm cameras. It's hard to pin down the exact resolution of 35mm SLRs because it varies depending on the choice of film, lens, and lighting conditions, but somewhere in the neighborhood of 4 to 6 megapixels is a good estimate, especially if you're talking about a snapshot taken with a point-and-shoot camera with ISO 400 film.

Unlike film cameras, digital cameras have no resolution limits. All 35mm SLRs use the same size negative, but digital camera resolution can go up each time a new model packs more pixels onto the CCD. So while it would be great to take a wall-sized picture with your 35mm SLR, that's simply impossible, even if you go out and buy a more expensive camera. 35mm slides and negatives are far too small; if you enlarge them, the grains start to become readily visible once you get past 8×10-inch prints. The only way to get larger prints is to start with a larger negative, and that means switching to medium- or large-format photography—an entirely different kind of camera.

So what's next? With digital high-end cameras already breaking the dozen-megapixel mark, it looks like the next big innovation might be higher-quality sensors. A company called Foveon, for instance, has introduced a sensor that triples the image quality by capturing data for red, green, and blue at every pixel. In ordinary digital cameras, it takes three pixels to measure the full range of color information. When I wrote this book, the only camera with the Foveon chip was the Sigma SD9, a 10-megapixel digital SLR (with an effective resolution of about 3 megapixels) that sells for about $1,500, but it may be just a matter of time before it shows up in many cameras, especially if it proves to be a smart technology that genuinely improves image quality.

FIGURE 1-3   Point-and-shoot digicams promise great results without a lot of effort or expense.

In the meantime, we're seeing another trend in digital photography: an effort to satisfy traditional film photographers. Right now, the most common kind of digicam is the point-and-shoot model, like the Nikon CoolPix 5400 in Figure 1-3. Point-and-shoot digital cameras appeal to casual and even some advanced photographers. They look like 35mm point-and-shoot models and automate most of the features needed to take pictures.

But Single-Lens Reflex (SLR) digital cameras are getting more popular all the time. These cameras are aimed at serious photographers. Models like the Nikon D100 (in Figure 1-4) and the Canon D60 feature interchangeable lenses, powerful flash units, and a wealth of manual controls. In a nutshell, they work and behave just like SLRs from the film world.

If you have a trusty old SLR and want a digital camera that's just like it, this is a good time to be getting into digital. Only a few years ago, the prices of these pro-oriented cameras were $5,000 and beyond. Right now, I can find the Canon D60 for $1,500 and the Nikon D100 for $1,400 by shopping at www.pricegrabber.com. Olympus sells the e20n, a clever SLR-like camera that offers professional controls but doesn't include interchangeable lenses, for less than $1,000. In the first edition of this book, when such cameras were still selling for $5,000, I predicted that within two years they'd sell for $2,000. I was right. And now, in just the year since I wrote the second edition of this book, the price of these SLR-style digital cameras has dropped by $500 to $1,000, while the resolution and features have gone up. As digital

FIGURE 1-4 SLR-style digital cameras offer lot of resolution, plus plenty of advanced photographic control.

cameras get ever more popular, we'll see more of these SLR-style cameras that give photographers all the power and flexibility of SLR cameras with the immediacy of the digital medium, and their prices should drop rapidly.

So prepare for more dramatic price drops in the future. In fact, this table shows how digital camera prices, on average, have plummeted in the past few years:

	Under 1 Megapixel	1–2 Megapixel	2–3 Megapixel	3–4 Megapixel	4–5 Megapixel	5–6 Megapixel
Jan 1999	$839	$663				
Jan 2000	$716	$461	$885			
Jan 2001	$141	$377	$532	$815	$1,733	
Jan 2002	$85	$264	$345	$556	$805	$1,982
Jan 2003	$71	$193	$310	$477	$725	$1,066

Features, Gadgets, and Goodies

No two digital cameras are the same. Each camera maker is known to some greater or lesser extent for implement-specific kinds of features—such as interchangeable lenses, swivel bodies, and movie recording features. If you cut through all those goodies, though, you'll find that most cameras share many of the same fundamentals. Let's start at the top and cover your camera's fundamentals.

The Optical System

At the heart of every camera, no matter how it stores its images, is an optical system, as you can see in Figure 1-5. Most digital cameras have two distinct viewfinders— an optical one and a digital one. In most cases, the optical viewfinder is composed of a glass or plastic lens that shows you your subject directly—it's just a plain window that lets you see through the camera to the other side. But there are exceptions. In addition to the common "window" viewfinder, you might have a camera with a true TTL (through-the-lens) viewfinder—also referred to as an electronic viewfinder. It mimics what you'd see in the large liquid crystal display (LCD), and in general it's preferable. You'll find it in pricier cameras.

The digital viewfinder is a large LCD display that reproduces what the camera's CCDs are actually seeing.

Which one should you use? Whichever one you like. You'll get better results, though, if you understand the difference between the two. The majority of digital cameras are point-and-shoot designs. With a point-and-shoot, you do not actually see what the camera sees when you look through the optical viewfinder. The optical viewfinder is a parallax-inducing viewfinder, a popular low-cost mechanism that dates back almost all the way to the invention of the camera itself. No doubt you have a point-and-shoot camera lying around the house with just such a viewfinder.

Lens ———▶

Optical viewfinder

Digital viewfinder

FIGURE 1-5   Almost all digital cameras rely on an optical system that includes both a viewfinder and an LCD display.

FIGURE 1-6   The optical viewfinder and the camera's lens don't always see exactly
the same thing, especially when close-up to the subject.

When taking pictures from a distance, the optical viewfinder and lens see
essentially the same thing. Close-up to your subject, though, they clearly see two
different things (as you can see in Figure 1-6). The concept of parallax—and what
it means to your photographs—is discussed in detail in Chapter 5.

The digital viewfinder, on the other hand, shows you exactly what the camera
sees, and thus is the most accurate gauge of your potential photograph. You
won't want to use your digital viewfinder all the time, though. For starters, it
uses a lot of power, and you can get more mileage out of your camera's batteries
by using the optical viewfinder instead. In addition, the LCD display can be very
difficult to see in certain lighting conditions, such as outside in mid-afternoon.

 *Some cameras allow you to turn off the LCD display to conserve
power. Leave the display off most of the time to get more battery life.*

Power Systems

It shouldn't surprise you terribly to learn that your digital camera takes batteries.
Many—but certainly not all—digital cameras rely on a standard set of AA batteries
or their rechargeable equivalents.

An increasingly common practice is for manufacturers to design cameras around
special lithium ion battery packs. The advantage is that the batteries are much smaller

TTL Viewfinders

As I've already mentioned, not all cameras are rangefinders with parallax-inducing viewfinders; some have TTL (through-the-lens) optical systems. These TTL viewfinders trace a light path through the lens, which means they show you exactly what you're going to photograph (see the following illustration). They come in especially handy with zoom lenses. While digital SLRs like the Nikon D100 have an electronic TTL viewfinder, some more affordable cameras—especially those from Sony and Olympus—include this feature as well.

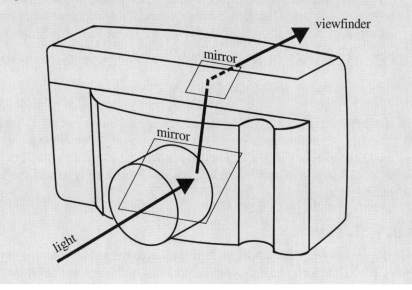

than a foursome of AAs, meaning the camera can be much smaller. You can see the size difference between the battery compartments of an Olympus C-5050 and a FujiFilm F410 here:

On the downside, you can't just pop in ubiquitous AA batteries when the cells run dry, which means you need to keep one or more spares on hand. I personally don't care for these small cameras with unusual batteries, but your mileage may vary—if you want a really small camera, you might not mind the inconvenience of the odd batteries.

Power management is discussed in more detail in Chapter 6, but for now, heed this sage advice:

- Insert batteries according to the diagram on the camera body—make sure you align the battery's positive and negative ends correctly.

- Don't leave batteries in the camera for an extended period of time. Some kinds of batteries may leak when fully discharged, and if that happens, your camera can be ruined.

- Don't mix and match fresh and used batteries or different kinds of batteries.

- When you can, run your camera using AC power.

That last bullet is particularly important. Some digital cameras come with their own AC adapters, while for others it's an optional accessory. Check the camera body for an AC adapter connector. If you can connect the camera to a wall outlet, especially during image transfers to the PC, you can significantly extend the length of your battery's life.

Memory Storage

Think of the memory in your camera like film. Memory cards store your digital images for you. The more memory your camera has, the more images it can store. Chapter 8 includes an in-depth discussion of the various memory formats available, but for now suffice it to say that your camera most likely includes a memory card with some memory capacity (such as 16MB or 32MB) that, when inserted into the camera, stores images. When it's full, you can remove this card and insert another card for additional storage. You can use the connection cable that came with your camera to transfer images to the PC, or use a memory card reader that sits on your desktop and accepts memory cards (see Figure 1-7) as if they were little floppy disks.

There are five major kinds of memory cards in use today:

- SmartMedia
- CompactFlash
- Memory Stick (and its new big brother, Memory Stick Pro)

FIGURE 1-7   There are five main kinds of memory cards in use today, and your digital camera accommodates one or more them. Readers, like the 6-in-1 device shown here, can read your memory card like a floppy disk, eliminating the need for cables.

■ Secure Digital (commonly abbreviated SD), along with its little brother, MultiMediaCard (MMC)

■ xD (Extreme Digital)

NOTE   *How many images you can fit on a memory card has nothing to do with the kind of memory card. All that matters is the resolution of the images and the memory card capacity.*

In addition to each of those, a few cameras—specifically Sony Mavica cameras—use a recordable CD for storing images. Only very inexpensive or old digital cameras do not include removable storage at all. Such cameras rely exclusively on the memory that's built into the camera to store images.

Camera Controls

Perhaps the most subjective of digital camera features, the controls are also among the most important. I can't really tell you which is best; you need to experiment with a few cameras to see which you like the best. Try handling cameras in the store whenever you can.

Flash control

Eyepiece diopter
control

Optical
viewfinder

Menu navigation
controls

Macro mode

LCD display
(digital viewfinder)

FIGURE 1-8   Most of these controls are common to all digital cameras.

Digital cameras typically feature one of two distinct control systems: on-body buttons or dials plus onscreen menus. Figure 1-8 shows some body controls, such as a diopter dial (for adjusting the eyepiece to your personal eyesight), a shutter release button, and zoom controls. The onscreen menu (seen in Figure 1-9) is commonly

FIGURE 1-9   Digital cameras use a series of menus in the LCD display to operate the more advanced or less frequently used features.

FIGURE 1-10   The star symbol is sometimes used to indicate a resolution control.

used to adjust less frequently used controls, such as resolution settings, exposure compensation, and special effects filters. That's not always the case, though, as you can see in Figure 1-10. This camera uses buttons to change the resolution without resorting to a menu system.

You need to take the time to review your camera manual to find out how to operate all your camera controls. Without knowing how to operate your camera, you can't really learn to take great pictures.

The Upgrade Race

Do you need to get a new camera next year just because the megapixel bar has been raised—or some other cool new features have surfaced?

No, you don't. Just like your desktop computer, a digital camera isn't obsolete just because a new model came out with more memory or horsepower. It's only obsolete when it no longer does what you want it to do.

Take me, for instance. Although I get to see and play with a large number of cameras every year, I stuck with what you'll surely consider to be an ancient model—an Olympus D-620L, released early in 1998—for almost three years before switching to a different camera. I liked this camera because it has an electronic TTL viewfinder and an excellent macro mode.

The downside? It captured a mere 1.4 megapixels. That's so Twentieth Century. It was OK, though—I used the camera to take photos for books, magazines, and Web sites, when I rarely needed a resolution much beyond the 1.4 megapixels it could provide. I didn't *need* more pixels, so I stuck with the camera. These days, I use the 5-megapixel Olympus e20n—already almost two years old—and it'll probably make me happy for another year or two.

The bottom line? Find a camera you like and stick with it. Digital cameras are a costly investment, and they won't "pay for themselves" in film savings if you replace them every year or so with a newer model.

Choosing Your Own Digital Camera

If you haven't yet made your digital camera purchase—or if you are planning to upgrade—you're in luck. The field has never been more crowded with excellent choices, and as I mentioned earlier, technology advances keep making these cameras better each year.

Even though the camera field is evolving all the time, the basics really don't change. The next few sections cover the most important elements to consider when shopping for a camera.

Resolution

First and foremost, figure out how much resolution you need. This should be the very first decision you make, since it determines what cameras you will be evaluating. Use this handy little guide to decide what megapixel range you need:

Megapixels	Print Size
Sub-megapixel (VGA)	Onscreen only (Web, e-mail)
1 megapixel	3×5-inch prints
2–3 megapixels	5×7-inch prints
3–4 megapixels	8×10-inch prints
5–6 megapixels	13×19-inch prints, prints from small cropped areas of the original image

Remember that even if you choose a 6-megapixel camera, you can set it to capture lower-resolution images—even a mere 640×480 pixels—making your camera quite versatile. Or you can capture a high-resolution image and reduce its size on the PC in an image-editing program. (I explain how to do this in Chapter 12.)

The higher the resolution, the fewer pictures you can store at a given time, so there is a bit of a trade-off. If you buy a camera with too little resolution, though, you can't ever add information to a picture, and trying to "blow it up" to print beyond its ideal size will generate a pixely, grainy mess.

Optics

It is a camera, after all—not a computer. Don't forget to weigh the optics carefully. Your camera's optics should be made of glass, not plastic, and multiple "elements" help keep everything in sharp focus through the camera's entire zoom range.

Also consider what kind of pictures you want to take. A fairly wide-angle lens is good for landscapes, indoor shots, and general-purpose photography. If you want to take portraits or wildlife shots, a longer reach is important. But take a look at the specs for a digital camera—what the heck is a 9.3mm lens? Is that wide-angle? Who knows? That's why most digital cameras also advertise their focal length in "35mm equivalents"—in other words, if this digital camera were a 35mm camera, its 9.3mm lens would give you the same picture as a 50mm camera, for instance.

Making sense of all this can be a pain. Worse, there's no one formula you can use to convert digital camera local lengths into 35mm equivalents. That's because the focal length of a traditional 35 mm camera lens is based on the size of the film, which in the case of a digital camera is the sensor. Because the sensor varies in size, there's no industry-wide consensus on standardizing the size of the CCD in all cameras. So, your best bet is to check out the 35mm equivalency figures on the camera box or on the manufacturer's Web site. I've also concocted a formula you can use in a pinch to convert digital camera focal lengths to their 35mm equivalents. Since CCD sizes vary, this is only an approximation. In the following formula, AFL is the actual focal length of the digital camera's lens, usually a small number like 5mm or 10mm:

$$35\text{mm equivalent focal length} = AFL\ /\ .19$$

So if the camera has a 6.5mm lens, for instance, you can run it through this handy little equation and determine that it will work like a 35mm lens.

Choosing a Zoom

Of course, very few digital cameras come with a fixed–focal length lens. The focal length is a measure of how much the camera magnifies the image, and zoom lenses let you zoom in and out of a scene for the perfect composition. In general, the greater the zoom, the better. You'll commonly see 2x, 3x, and perhaps even 5x zooms on

FIGURE 1-11   Zoom lenses are popular because of their flexibility when composing pictures.

digital cameras. With some simple finger pressure, you can use your camera to go from a normal or wide-angle view to telephoto. The effect of a 4x zoom is apparent in Figure 1-11, taken with the Olympus e-10 at both ends of its zoom range.

Beware, though, of a camera's digital zoom. While optical zooms move the lenses around to actually magnify the image, a digital zoom simply grabs a block of pixels in the middle of the scene and processes them to make the image look enlarged. Since the result is pixely, I suggest that you ignore digital zoom ratings when evaluating a camera and just look at the optical zoom ratings.

Memory

The more memory your camera holds, the more pictures you can take. It sounds simple, but don't forget that cameras come with all different kinds of memory solutions. In general, I'd say it doesn't matter a lot whether your camera uses CompactFlash, SmartMedia, Memory Stick, Secure Digital, or xD memory— the only things to consider are cost and capacity:

- **Capacity**   If you only want to carry a single memory card on a long trip and store a huge number of images, a CompactFlash digital camera is your best choice. You can get CompactFlash cards in capacities well beyond 1GB (imagine a thousand 2-megapixel images). Other memory formats top out around 512MB, and the nearly extinct SmartMedia card holds just 128MB. Of course, you can also buy several memory cards and carry spares, which is usually cheaper than buying one really huge card. Me? I tend to carry a 512MB and a 128MB CompactFlash card for my camera when I shoot away from home. I have other tricks to avoid running out space, which I'll talk about in Chapter 8.

■ **Cost**   The various memory card formats play a lot of leapfrog when it comes to price, so you might want to shop around for memory cards before you commit to a specific camera. Of course, the newest memory card formats (I'm looking at you, xD) cost a bit more than the more established memory cards, like CompactFlash.

Flash

Almost all digital cameras come with a built-in flash. The real issue is how well the flash works. Check to see what the maximum range of the flash is and if it works when the camera is in macro, or close-focus, mode. You might also want a flash with special features such as these:

■ **Red-eye reduction**   This mode preflashes the subject to try to minimize reflected light from the pupil known as *red eye*.

■ **Force/fill**   Force, or fill, flash is used to reduce shadows outdoors or in otherwise adequate lighting when the flash might not fire.

■ **Rear curtain flash**   This mode fires at the end of a long exposure. It comes in handy at night so that light trails precede the main subject, illuminated by the flash.

Some cameras also come with sync ports or hot shoes that allow you to connect more powerful, external flash units.

Special Effects

Since digital cameras are part computer, they can be programmed to do some neat tricks that were inconceivable with traditional 35mm cameras. Few of these effects are necessary; in fact, I'd choose a camera based on solid features such as the zoom, lens quality, and overall handling before I looked too hard at whether the camera included a video mode or sepia tint. Nonetheless, these are some of the effects you may see:

- **Panorama mode**   This feature takes wide screen–style images either by automatically cropping the top and bottom off an image or by letting you stitch together several pictures to create one oversized one.

- **Movie mode**   Some cameras can capture short, low-resolution video clips as well as still images. Don't confuse this with real, high-quality digital video, though—the results are strictly for Web pages.

- **Tint modes**   With special settings, you can take black-and-white or sepia-tinted stills. Remember, though, that you can achieve the same effect in an image editor on the PC after the picture is taken, so you aren't losing anything if your camera lacks this feature. In fact, I'd say it's better to start with a full-color image; that way you can do whatever you like to it later and always have the high-quality original to fall back on.

Transfer Mechanism

Getting images out of your camera is just as important as taking the pictures to begin with. If you like to view your freshly shot images on a television or want to record them, slide-show style, directly to a VCR, CD, or DVD, then you should definitely consider a camera with a video-out port. Using an ordinary composite video cable (also called an RCA cable), you can connect the camera to a TV, VCR, or some other video display unit.

For computer connection, I recommend a Universal Serial Bus (USB) cable. USB-capable digital cameras let you transfer images painlessly, especially compared to the more traditional (and now virtually obsolete) serial cable.

Some cameras include even more convenient solutions, like adapters that accept the removable media card and connect to the computer directly. The advantage with these devices is that you can transfer images without draining the camera batteries, and transfers are often easier to do because you avoid using arcane transfer software and instead just drag and drop images from a folder on the Windows desktop.

Gear You'll Need

Every hobby has its accessories. I sometimes joke that my dive buddy only became interested in scuba diving after she discovered that scuba gear was a whole new way to spend money.

While there's no doubt some truth to that, it's also true that there are some things you really need to buy to accompany any activity, and digital photography is no exception. Here's a short shopping list of things you might consider buying as you get more into shooting digitally:

- **A camera**   It goes without saying that you need a camera, but don't rush into the purchase. You can even use a 35mm camera to begin with, and then scan the images into the PC for editing and printing. If you've read the previous sections of this chapter and decided what features are important to you, you can shop like a pro.

- **An adequate PC**   Crunching data to process digital images takes a bit more horsepower than you might be used to when working with Word or Excel. I suggest using a PC with a 1-GHz processor and no less than 256MB of RAM. If you want to work with really big images—6-megapixel, for example—then consider 512MB or even 1GB of RAM. You might be surprised to learn that more memory is generally more useful than a faster processor.

- **Batteries**   Digital cameras are power hogs. If your camera uses AA-style batteries, I highly recommend buying two sets of rechargeable batteries because they'll pay for themselves before you can say "alkaline." If your camera didn't come with an AC adapter, I suggest you buy one from the camera vendor's accessories store so you can power the camera when you're transferring images to the PC or displaying images on a TV.

- **Memory**   Buy the biggest memory card you can afford, or a combination of two cards each with reasonable capacity. The measly 16MB memory card that came with your camera won't last a day when you're on vacation, so having a 128MB, 256MB, or 512MB card is almost essential. A spare card, if it's in the budget, can keep you going when you fill up your main card far away from your PC.

- **Image editing software**   Your camera probably came with some rudimentary image editor, but it may not be up to the task. Try a few out, and buy the image editor that you like best. I typically use Paint Shop Pro 8 (from www.jasc.com) and Adobe Photoshop Elements 2 (www.adobe.com), for instance.

- **Printer**   Get a good color inkjet printer and premium photo paper—see Chapter 15 for details. Don't skimp on this step—when the time comes to print your pictures, why bother having a good camera, this book, and taking the time to improve your photo skills if you're going to print pictures on a budget printer with lousy paper?

■ **Tripod**   If you want to extend your photography into the world of close-ups or long-range telephoto images, a tripod is a necessity. It needn't be large or heavy, since most digital cameras are significantly lighter than their 35mm counterparts.

■ **Lenses and filters**   The time may come when you want to take pictures—such as extreme close-ups, wide-angle shots, or extreme telephotos—that are beyond the range of the lens that came with your camera. Likewise, you might want to reduce glare or add other special effects to your images. If that's the case, you want lenses and filters for your camera. You may not need them right now, but consider them an advanced purchase for later on.

■ **Camera bag**   Choose a bag that lets you arrange your camera and accessories in a way that they're protected from theft and damage, but easy to use when the time comes to shoot a picture. Look for bags that don't really look like they're holding camera gear—that might make them less of a target by thieves.

 Choose a Digital Camera

When you're shopping for a digital camera, make a checklist of features and capabilities you want based on these criteria:

■ **Resolution**   Decide how large your finished images need to be, and look for cameras that can take pictures in the appropriate "megapixel" range.

■ **Optics**   Consider the lens quality, optical zoom range, and the possibility of adding lenses or filters for more capabilities.

■ **Flash**   Consider the flash range and special features like red-eye reduction. For serious flash photography, look for cameras that accept external flash units.

■ **Special effects**   If you want goodies such as movie modes or panoramic capture, worry about that after the essentials are out of the way.

■ **Transfer mechanism**   One last issue to consider is how the camera transfers images to the PC—this is a convenience issue.

Chapter 2

Understanding Exposure

How to...

■ Tell the difference between analog and digital camera operation

■ Distinguish between slide and negative photography

■ Select ISO settings for digital and film cameras

■ Match aperture and shutter speed settings for correct exposure

■ Use the Sunny 16 Rule

■ Modify the Sunny 16 Rule based on ISO and lighting conditions

■ Adjust exposure manually

■ Tweak exposure with your camera's EV settings

■ Choose metering modes for better pictures

■ Use exposure lock to optimize exposure

■ Tell when to ignore the camera and make your own exposure decisions

Some people think that photography is akin to magic. They turn on the camera, snap a picture, and a day or two later they've got a mystical re-creation of the scene they saw in the viewfinder. With a digital camera, or *digicam* for short, it's even more magical—the pictures are available instantly! How does it work? Who knows?

The problem with the Abe Simpson approach to photography (which I've so named based on an episode of *The Simpsons,* in which someone took a picture of old Abe and he shouted feebly, "You stole my soul!") is that you can never really improve if you don't know what your camera does or why, nor how you can influence the camera yourself to improve your shots. This chapter, consequently, walks you through the exposure process. Here you'll learn what constitutes a proper exposure and how to get one yourself—even on cameras that are mostly automatic.

How Cameras Take Pictures

The best place to start is often right at the beginning—how on earth does a camera take a picture, anyway?

All cameras, regardless of type, work more or less the same way—as depicted in the following illustration. They open their shutter for a brief time, allowing light to enter. That light then interacts with a sensitive photo-receptor (such as film or a computer chip), and an image is recorded. Let's start by looking at a traditional 35mm camera to give us a little perspective.

Inside a 35mm Camera

Traditional cameras rely on good old-fashioned film. But what is film, really? It's just a strip of plastic that has been coated with a light-sensitive chemical. The chemical soup on the film is loaded with grains of silver halide. When exposed to light, the silver halide reacts, and that is the essence of photography. The longer the film is exposed to light, the more the silver is affected.

There are two kinds of film in common use today: negative film and slide film. They work a little differently, but the end result is similar. When you use color negative film, also referred to as reversal film, the film itself becomes a

The Moment of Exposure

Depending on the kind of camera, the events that take place at the moment of exposure can be quite complicated. In a modern 35mm SLR, for instance, microprocessor-controlled sensors determine the exact amount of light needed to expose a picture at the moment you press the shutter release. The lens automatically adjusts the size of its opening to admit the correct amount of light, and the mirror mechanism that usually lets you look through the viewfinder flips up and out of the way, allowing light to reach the film. Finally, the aperture opens, and the shutter slides open for the programmed amount of time. Point-and-shoot cameras, in contrast, don't use mirror mechanisms to let you see through the lens before the shot, so there are fewer moving parts at the moment of exposure—but the trade-off is that you don't see the picture you're about to take as accurately with a point-and-shoot.

"negative" image of the scene you photographed. After processing—which includes letting the film sit in a chemical bath that coaxes the grains of silver to visually materialize on the film—the negative is used to create positive prints of the scene. It's a two-step process, and one that is highly subjective. When creating prints from negatives, photo-finishers often tweak the picture to improve its appearance. Of course, what the corner shop considers an "improvement" may not be what you were trying to achieve, and that explains why your pictures never seem to benefit from filters, exposure changes, or any of the other corrections you try to make when taking pictures.

But I digress. The other kind of film, simple slide (or reversal) film, uses a color positive development process: after fixing the slide film in its chemical bath, the film becomes slides that can be held up to the light to display images. Because of their far simpler development process, slides can't be tweaked by the processor. What you and your camera do determines how they turn out—and in that way, slide photography is much more like digital photography in a sense.

No matter what kind of film you have, it eventually needs to be exposed to light. When you take a picture, you obviously press the shutter release. The shutter release instructs the camera to open the shutter blades for a brief period of time and then close them again. If all goes well, that is just long enough to properly expose the film.

> **TIP** *If you want to shoot with 35mm film, scan the results, and then edit and print the results on your PC, you might want to work with slide film. Slides are more exacting—they require you to nail the exposure fairly precisely, as I explain in Chapter 11, but they'll better represent what you actually photographed than will the local photo shop's vision of what you photographed.*

How and Why Film Varies

As you no doubt know by shopping for film, not all canisters of 35mm film are alike. Film is differentiated principally by its speed, or ISO number.

A film's ISO number refers to how sensitive it is to light. The lower the number is, the less sensitive it is—requiring long exposures or very bright scenes.

A fairly typical ISO number for ordinary daylight photography is ISO 100. Increasing the ISO to 200 doubles the sensitivity of the film, meaning it would only take an exposure half as long to capture the same picture; dropping back to an ISO of 50 halves the sensitivity of the film, requiring an exposure twice as long as an ISO of 100.

The ISO number has a tangible effect on the mechanics of photography. To see why, look at Figure 2-1. This diagram shows a typical camera body as a picture is taken. The lens is equipped with a diaphragm—called an *aperture*—that has a certain diameter and consequently is designed to allow a specific amount of light through to

Did you know?

What ISO Means

ISO stands for International Organization for Standardization, and that's the group that helped establish how the film numbering scheme works. Film around the world uses ISO numbers, so you can buy it anywhere, and it'll all work the same. In the United States, photographers used to call this system ASA, which stood for the American Standards Association. That term was essentially abandoned about 20 years ago, so if you want to be considered a gristled old geezer, you can refer to ISO numbers as "ASA."

the film. With ISO 100 film in specific lighting conditions (say, at midday) the shutter might need to open for a 250th of a second (1/250) to adequately expose the picture.

But what happens if we instead try to take the same picture with ISO 200 film? The film is exactly twice as sensitive to light as the previous roll of film. And that means, all other things being equal, that we only need to leave the shutter open for half as long (a 500th of a second, or 1/500) to take the same picture.

That's not all. Suppose you're trying to take a picture in late afternoon, when there isn't as much light available? You might need to leave the shutter open for 1/30 in that situation to gather enough light with ISO 100 film. That shutter speed is a bit on the slow side, though. Not only might you jiggle the camera as you're taking the picture (it's hard to hold a camera steady for 1/30), but your subject might move as well, causing a blurry picture. You can probably guess what the solution is—stepping up to ISO 200 film will enable you to grab that picture at a much more reasonable 1/60, and ISO 400 would halve the shutter speed yet again, to a crisp 1/125.

FIGURE 2-1   Every camera—no matter what it uses for film—controls the exposure with some sort of aperture and shutter settings.

The F/Stop Ballet

So far so good—but there's one other aspect to consider, and that's the fact that camera lenses can change the diameter of their aperture, thus letting in more or less light as needed.

The size of a camera's aperture at any given moment is called the *f/stop,* also sometimes referred to as the *f/number* of the lens. F/stops are represented by numbers that start with "f/"—such as f/2, f/5.6, and f/11. The larger the number, the smaller the opening, so an f/22 is very, very small (not much light gets through to the film), while a lens set to f/1.2 is a huge opening that floods the film with light. Changing the camera setting by a "whole" f/stop, such as from f/5.6 to f/8 or f/11 to f/16, doubles or halves the available light, depending upon which way you're going. If you adjust a lens from f/8 to f/11, for instance, you've reduced the light by half.

We'll talk about this in more detail in Chapter 3 (it's really important, yet really simple), but for the moment take a look at Figure 2-2. This diagram shows the relationship between the f/stop and the shutter speed. As you reduce the shutter speed, you need to increase the diameter of the aperture in order to have enough light to take a properly exposed picture.

Of course, there's a relationship between aperture, shutter speed, and your film's ISO rating. Look at Figure 2-3. At a given film speed, you can take a picture with a specific aperture/shutter combination. If you double the film speed without changing the lighting conditions, though, you have to adjust the aperture and the shutter speed so that you still get a properly exposed picture. And perhaps most importantly for us, suppose you are in the situation I describe next.

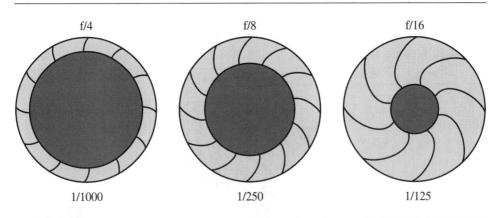

FIGURE 2-2   Each of these combinations results in the same amount of light reaching the film.

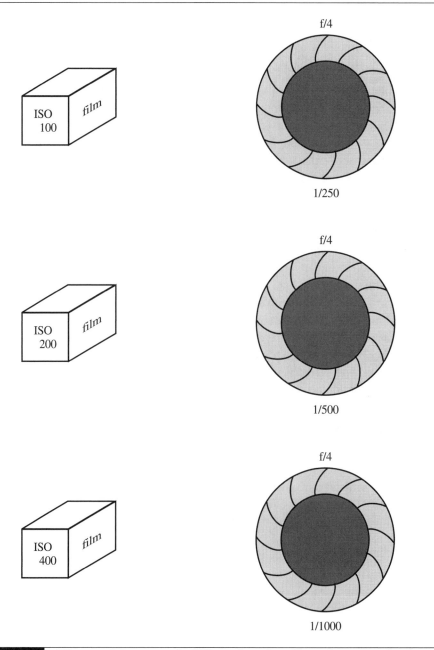

FIGURE 2-3   Film speed, known as the ISO number, also affects shutter speed and aperture.

F/Stops

You probably don't need to know this, but it might come in handy during a trivia game some day. Mathematically, f/stops are the ratio of the focal length of the lens divided by the diameter of the opening of the diaphragm. Thus, when you divide the focal length of the lens by a very small opening, you get a large number, while dividing the focal length by a comparatively large diameter gives you a smaller number.

You want to take a picture of frolicking lions at the zoo near dusk. The aperture is wide open at f/2—it won't open any farther. Nonetheless, your camera needs to use the relatively slow shutter speed of 1/15 second to take the shot. You know the image would be a blurry mess at that sluggish shutter speed, so what is there to do? Take a look at your film speed. It's ISO 100. Well, you might be in luck. If you're willing to pop the film out of your camera and put in film that's two f/stops (often, just called "stops") faster, you can keep the aperture at f/2 and change the shutter speed to 1/60. That's probably good enough to get the shot. Just do it quickly—it isn't getting any brighter out, and if you dally, you might find you need to increase the speed by three stops by the time you get the film loaded and ready to go.

How Digicams Are Different

All that talk about f/stops, shutter speed, and ISO settings may seem irrelevant to your digital camera, but it's not—all cameras use these concepts, even though they're sometimes disguised fairly well. The main difference between a digital camera and a film camera, of course, is the fact that digicams don't use film. That means you never load anything that has a specific ISO value into the camera. So how does the camera actually work?

Simple. When light enters the camera at the moment of exposure, it doesn't hit light-sensitive silver halides that are fixed in a chemical broth. Instead, the light hits a computer chip that acts as a sensor and is usually called a CCD (though some cameras use a CMOS sensor instead, both of which I talked about in Chapter 1). The sensor is light sensitive, and each of its many pixels register changes in light just like the film's many grains of silver react individually to light (see Figure 2-4). In other words, the silver grains in film and the pixels in a

190	200	210	210	200
180	160	100	120	190
160	150	100	153	160
170	160	90	110	110
130	125	90	120	110
125	100	88	120	110
	100	90	92	

FIGURE 2-4   A digital camera uses a dense grid of pixels on the sensor in place of chemically reactive grains of silver.

CCD or CMOS sensor are essentially the same thing. They contribute to your picture in the same way, and both are the smallest components that make up your picture.

The sensor makes a picture by noting the variation in light rays that travel through the camera lens. The CCD or CMOS passes this information on to the camera's microprocessor in the form of varying electrical charges. The image is transformed into digital bits and stored on a memory card.

Your camera's image sensor functions like the film in a 35mm camera, except that it differs in one important way—you can't swap the CCD out of your camera and insert one with more light sensitivity for low-light photography. The sensor is a permanent part of the camera. Camera makers understand that you might need to change the camera's light sensitivity on occasion, though, and that's why many cameras can have their ISO rating "adjusted" on the fly, whenever you want. In essence, what this does is allow you to "turn up" or "turn down" your camera's sensitivity to light by adjusting the gain of the circuit reading the sensor voltage.

Use ISO for Exposure Control

You can use the ISO control built into your digital camera to vary its sensitivity to light and thus mimic the effect of using different grades of 35mm film. This can come in handy in a number of situations, such as when you're shooting in particularly high- or low-light situations. Remember a few key facts about your digital camera's ISO ratings, though:

- It's not a real ISO adjustment, in the sense that your camera doesn't have real film. Each camera maker has a somewhat different way of implementing this feature, but they all use ISO numbers since that's comparable to 35mm film, which most people are at least a little familiar with.

- Don't leave your camera set at the highest ISO all the time. Some folks think that by setting their cameras to the highest sensitivity, they'll be prepared for anything and won't have to muck with the camera menu when they're on the go, trying to take pictures. In reality, boosting your camera's sensitivity to light also increases the amount of digital noise you're capturing. More ISO means more fringing, artifacts, and digital detritus, as in the image shown in the following illustration. Sometimes that's unavoidable, but stick with the lowest ISO value you can get away with most of the time. To do that, set your camera's ISO control to its lowest setting or to Auto, which usually accomplishes the same thing.

Change the ISO Setting

If you find yourself in a situation in which the lighting isn't quite right for your picture, it's time to bump up the camera's ISO value. Remember that most, but not all, cameras come with ISO adjustments, so review your user manual to see if this applies to your particular model. Figure 2-5 shows a typical ISO adjustment; you'll

FIGURE 2-5   A typical ISO adjustment on a digital camera

probably find it in the onscreen menu system, displayed in the liquid crystal display (LCD) screen on the back of your camera.

Here are some situations in which you might need to increase the ISO:

■ You're shooting in a low-light situation, such as early evening or indoors. Natural-light photos have a certain appeal, and by increasing the light sensitivity of your camera you may be able shoot a picture without using the flash at all. Using natural light can eliminate harsh shadows and produce more natural colors.

■ Your subject is too far away for the flash to have any effect. During the day you might be outdoors and want to take a picture of something, but there's not quite enough light—such as in winter or during very overcast conditions. Your camera wants to use a flash, but your subject is just too far away. As you'll see in Chapter 4, the flash on your digital camera has a very limited range; so to properly expose your picture, you need to use "faster film"— that is, increase the camera's ISO setting.

■ You're shooting at night. Most digital cameras have limited ability to take pictures at night or in near total darkness. As a result, if you want to capture anything at all with a night shot, you may need to increase the camera's light sensitivity to the maximum.

If night photography interests you, investigate what I refer to as "performance" digital cameras—cameras that include manually adjustable shutter speeds and apertures. Cameras like the Nikon CoolPix 5700, the Olympus C-5050, and the Canon PowerShot G4 are the sorts of models that are better equipped to deal with very low light such as you'll encounter at night. Using more full-featured cameras lets you perform long exposures for light trails, glowing illuminated signage, and other special effects.

Perfecting Shots with Aperture and Shutter

Let's return to the idea of aperture and shutter speed again for a moment. As we observed earlier in this chapter, they're essential ingredients to creating good pictures. Of course, with most digital cameras, you rarely have to worry about setting shutter speed and aperture size at all for typical photography.

How Cameras Choose Aperture and Shutter Speed

Here's what usually happens: when you apply pressure to the camera's shutter release, the camera's microcomputer samples the scene in front of the lens and determines how much light is needed to adequately expose the scene. With most digicams, the camera selects a shutter speed and aperture combination that is sufficient to get the job done. But, you might be wondering, how does it choose? After all, there are a lot of shutter speed/aperture pairs that will work. To take the same properly exposed picture at ISO 100, any of the combinations, shown in Figure 2-6, should produce exactly the same result.

Usually, the camera uses the following logic:

The photographer wants to take a picture using the fastest available shutter speed to minimize camera shake and motion blur from objects moving inside the picture.

Though there are some exceptions, most cameras tend to choose the combination that allows for the highest available shutter speed, limited only by how small they can make the aperture given the current lighting conditions and ISO setting.

This isn't always what you want your camera to do, though, and in fact you might sometimes want to choose a slower shutter speed, overexpose the image, underexpose it, or perhaps base the exposure on a completely different part of the picture. That's why you might want to investigate your camera and look for controls that let you tweak the shutter speed and aperture.

FIGURE 2-6   All three of these shutter speed/aperture combinations result in admitting the same amount of light into the camera.

The Truth About Shutters

Though I talk quite a lot about shutter speed in this book, the reality is that few digital cameras have a real shutter in the sense that 35mm cameras have shutters. The 35mm cameras usually have a physical barrier that blocks light from entering the chamber where the film is stored. This mechanism—the shutter blade—moves lightning fast, able to deliver shutter speeds as fast as 1/8000 of a second. That's fast.

Digital cameras, in comparison, often don't have real, physical shutters. You can verify this yourself with a simple experiment: When you press the shutter release on a 35mm camera, you can hear the quick, metallic click of the shutter blade opening and closing. A digital camera may not make any noise at all. Or it might make an obviously fake "click" sound through the camera's speaker. When I got my first digital camera, I actually had to look at the LCD display on the back of the camera to see if the picture was captured or if, for some mysterious reason, the camera was still waiting to grab the shot.

So if there's no shutter blade, how is the picture actually taken? Often, the CCD is simply turned on long enough to expose the picture. Since the CCD is an electronic component that acts as the camera's film, it can be actuated electronically for whatever exposure time is needed. In addition, the camera's aperture may close completely to keep light from reaching the CCD—prolonged exposure to sunlight can damage this sensitive part of the camera; but the aperture needn't spring open and closed as quickly as the shutter blade in a 35mm camera, so the sound it makes isn't as dramatic. You'll hardly notice it at all.

Adjust Exposure Manually

The most basic manual exposure control you can exert over your camera involves setting both the aperture and shutter speed. Some digital cameras allow you to set these controls as if you had a fully automatic 35mm SLR. There are two kinds of cameras you may run into with this capability:

- **Point-and-shoot**   Most point-and-shoot digicams that include manual settings for aperture and shutter speed require you to use the LCD display to make onscreen menu changes. The model shown in the following illustration, for instance, uses a pair of buttons on the right side of the LCD display to adjust shutter speed, and another set of buttons on the bottom of the screen to change the aperture settings. It isn't hard to do, but you need to remember

2

first to set the camera to its Manual Exposure mode, and then remember which buttons do what for fine-tuning the exposure.

■ **SLR**   A few digital cameras—pro-style SLRs, for the most part—use traditional SLR controls for making manual adjustments to exposure. Specifically, you can turn the aperture ring on the lens to change the f/stop or use a control on the camera to accomplish the same thing, as shown in the following illustration. Shutter speed is likewise affected with a dial on the camera body, and you can look through the viewfinder to keep tabs on the setting.

To set exposure manually, you must choose a shutter speed and aperture combination that will properly expose your scene at a given ISO. This is a great exercise for new photographers who are serious about learning photography theory.

Use the Sunny 16 Rule

At an ISO of 100, which many digital cameras use for general-purpose photography, you might want to rely on the traditional "Sunny 16 Rule" for a starting point. The Sunny 16 Rule is very old—it dates back to the earliest days of analog photography—and it suggests that when shooting outdoors in bright sunlight you should choose an aperture of f/16 and a shutter speed that's equivalent to your film speed. Since few cameras offer the ability to choose 1/100, most photographers that rely on this rule use 1/60 or 1/125 when shooting with ISO 100 film. Here is a chart that identifies other acceptable combinations. (All of these add up to the same overall exposure.)

Shutter Speed	Aperture
1/1000	f/4
1/500	f/5.6
1/250	f/8
1/125	f/11
1/60	f/16
1/30	f/22

Keep in mind that these recommendations are just a starting point. Here are some tips that can help you zero in on your ideal exposure:

■ Your camera will often recommend an ideal exposure, which you can accept or reject. If the camera considers your setting out of bounds, it may flash a warning in your viewfinder.

■ Adjust your exposure based on the ISO setting. If your camera is set to an equivalent of ISO 200, for instance, the Sunny 16 Rule would call for a shutter speed of f/16 and a shutter speed of 1/250.

■ Make adjustments for brighter or darker scenes. If you're shooting in a dark room, for instance, the Sunny 16 Rule doesn't really apply—but it's a good starting point. Open the aperture or lengthen the shutter speed to account for reduced light; close the aperture or shorten the shutter speed to account for increased light.

Use Shutter or Aperture Priority Adjustments

Instead of relying on an all-automatic or all-manual exposure system, you can compromise and use your camera's shutter or aperture bias, if it has one. The idea with these controls is that you select either an aperture or a shutter speed, and the camera automatically selects the other half of the exposure for you.

Aperture and shutter priority modes are discussed in more detail in Chapter 3. These settings are usually used to find the right balance between freezing (or blurring) motion in a picture and focusing attention on the subject by sharpening (or blurring) the background of an image.

Tricky Lighting Situations

Not all lighting situations are easy to shoot; that's why photography is both an art and a science. Specifically, it's fairly easy for real-life scenes to trick your camera's exposure sensor and consequently under- or overexpose a picture. You can fix that tendency to some degree on the PC afterwards (and we'll talk about how to do that in Chapter 12), but it's much better to expose the picture correctly to begin with. That's because an over- or underexposed image is missing information about colors, texture, and detail that can never be restored afterwards; only at the moment of exposure can you ensure that all the information will be in your image.

What are some examples of tricky photos? There are many, but just a few problems tend to surface most frequently. Take a look at the pair of images in Color Figure 1 (the first illustration in the color insert at the center of this book) to see what happens if you base your exposure on the wrong part of the picture. If you point the camera at the dark penguin, the rest of the picture is grossly overexposed. Pointing the camera at the light tiger, on the other hand, can result in overall underexposure. Only by adjusting the exposure manually was I able to get the third image, which is just about right.

There are several solutions to these kinds of problems, and you can experiment to see which works best for you in various situations. Here are some ways you can correct your exposures when you see a problem in the viewfinder:

- *Use exposure compensation.* Use the EV control on your camera to intentionally under- or overexpose your pictures beyond what the camera's exposure sensor recommends.

- *Switch metering modes.* Use a different kind of exposure meter to account for high-contrast images.

- *Use exposure lock.* Lock your exposure on a different part of the image, and then recompose the picture and shoot.

To see how to use each of these exposure techniques, keep reading.

Living with Dynamic Range

While digital cameras are just about the equal of film cameras in most respects these days, one area in which they lag behind is dynamic range. Simply put, a digital camera doesn't have the same ability as a film camera to capture the broad range of light and dark elements in a picture.

Most of the time, that's not a problem, nor would you ever notice it. But in particularly challenging photographic situations, you'll find that your digital camera lacks detail in extremely dark or bright parts of a scene. A common situation is taking pictures in snow—in your final pics, you may find that the snow is a uniform white, with no subtle color variations. In photographic terms, it is said to be "blown out." Likewise, digital cameras are far more likely to "blow out" a photo when overexposed than a film camera would, so you need to be careful not to overexpose your photographs.

There are a few techniques for dealing with dynamic range issues. You can bracket your photos (something I talk about later in this chapter) or capture multiple versions of the same image, then combine them afterwards on the PC. This is a cool technique in which gives you the ability to display a dynamic range that's even beyond the range of what film cameras can do. It only works for static scenes, but here's what you do

1. Set the camera on a tripod so you can capture two pictures with identical composition.

2. Take one picture with the camera set to expose for the darkest parts of the image. Don't worry of the brighter parts blow out.

3. Take another picture with the camera set to expose for the brightest parts of the scene. The dark regions will be badly underexposed, but that's okay.

4. Use an image editing program to combine the two photos using layers, bringing the best-exposed parts of both images to the top for a uniformly well-exposed photo.

Camera technology continues to improve, but the dynamic range limitation will be around for quite some time to come. Personally, I'm curious to see how new sensor technology like the Foveon X3 chip (which is a three-layered sensor that captures red, green, and blue information at each and every pixel point) deal with dynamic range compared to traditional CCD and CMOS sensors. But right now, it's too soon to tell.

FIGURE 2-7   The EV control lets you use your own judgment about exposure values instead of relying exclusively on the camera's meter.

Use Exposure Compensation

Most digital cameras come equipped with an exposure compensation control, usually referred to as the Exposure Value (EV) adjustment. The EV control allows you to lock in and use the camera's recommended automatic exposure setting but then adjust that value up or down based on factors that you're aware of but that the camera may not be smart enough to see. Each Exposure Value corresponds to changing the exposure by one stop, such as going from 1/60 to 1/30 (this is a change of +1 EV since it doubles the exposure) or 1/15 to 1/30 (this is −1 EV since it reduces the exposure by half).

Take Figure 2-7, for example. In the original picture (on the left), the dark stuffed penguin has confused the camera, making it think the scene was properly exposed when, in fact, it is horribly overexposed. The background and the other animal are nearly invisible as a result. When the camera is set to underexpose the scene by one EV (one stop), however, the scene is much better exposed. The image was saved, as you can see on the right side of Figure 2-7.

To use the EV control on your camera, do this:

1. Size up the scene you want to shoot. Decide if it calls for over- or underexposure.

2. If you need to add light to a scene to properly expose it, add exposure by setting the EV control to +1. If instead you need to underexpose

the scene, set the EV control to –1. Here's a typical digicam display set to EV +2:

3. Take the picture and review the picture in the LCD display. If you don't like the result, adjust the EV and shoot it again.

Most cameras allow you to adjust exposure by up to three EVs, either positive (overexposed) or negative (underexposed), and some models also allow you to set the EV in increments of one half or one third of an EV at a time for more fine control over your scene.

 You have a digital camera at your disposal, so frame your picture and take the shot. If you don't like the results, you can take it again with different settings!

Switch Metering Modes

As I mentioned earlier, it's really the camera's exposure sensor—known as an *exposure meter*—that does the majority of the work when figuring out how to shoot your picture. It decides how much light is needed to adequately expose your picture. So it should come as no surprise to learn that cameras distinguish themselves by the kind of meter they use. Some meters are better than others at metering a scene and applying the right exposure.

Center-Weighted Meters

In the old days, most cameras came with a simple center-weighted light meter. This meter measures the light throughout the image but applies more weight, or importance, to the central part of the scene in the viewfinder. The assumption—usually a good one—is that you are most interested in the stuff in the front of the picture, so the

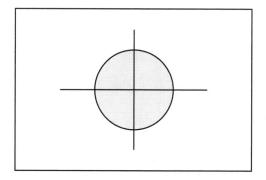

FIGURE 2-8   Many digital cameras use a center-weighted meter like this one.

camera tries to get that part of the scene exposed properly. You can see a center-weighted light meter in Figure 2-8. Many digital cameras rely on this kind of meter for ordinary picture taking.

Matrix Meters

A new innovation in digital photography is a kind of sensor that has been around in 35mm SLR photography for a decade or more. Often called matrix or multi-segment metering, this system is most prevalent in Nikon models, all the way from the CoolPix 3500 and CoolPix 995 to the high-end D100, but other camera makers use this system as well. The matrix meter, shown in Figure 2-9, is famous for its ability to properly

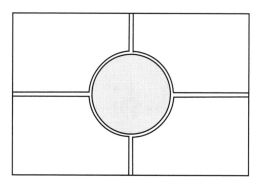

FIGURE 2-9   Cameras with a matrix meter are usually more accurate because they accumulate exposure information from several distinct regions of the frame (like the five regions shown here) and then use a sophisticated algorithm to decide the final exposure for the picture.

expose tricky scenes by balancing the lighting needs of several discrete regions within a picture. Instead of concentrating primarily on the middle, matrix meters gauge the light in many parts of the scene at once. If your camera has a matrix meter mode, you should use it most of the time, since it generally delivers outstanding results under a broad range of conditions.

Spot Meters

The last major kind of light meter is called a spot. The spot meter is never the only kind of meter in a camera; instead, it's an option that you can switch to if the center-weighted or matrix meter fails you. As you can see in Figure 2-10, the spot meter measures light exclusively in the center one percent of the screen, ignoring the rest of the frame completely. That can come in handy on occasion, but a meter that only measures the light in the central one percent of the frame will typically take very poor pictures—either highly under- or overexposed, depending on the situation.

So when should you use the spot meter? Any time you are trying to photograph a scene in which a small subject must be exposed properly for the picture to work and its lighting is different enough from the rest of the scene that you're worried it won't come out right otherwise. Imagine, for instance, that you are trying to photograph someone who is standing in front of a brightly-lit window. If you let the camera decide the exposure, the bright light from the window will radically underexpose the subject. So switch on the spot meter and expose the picture based on the subject. Yes, the window light will be overexposed, but that's okay—the important part of the picture is the person.

Varying the metering mode—especially the spot meter—is best used in conjunction with the third technique, exposure lock.

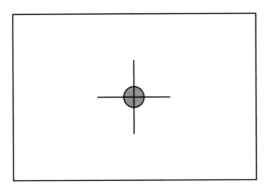

FIGURE 2-10   The spot meter is a great tool for reading the proper exposure in one precise point of the image.

Use Exposure Lock

The exposure lock feature in most digital cameras is borrowed from 35mm camera technology, and it is one of the handiest tricks you can master. Exposure lock is usually achieved by applying slight pressure to the shutter release—not enough to activate the shutter and take the picture, but enough that you feel the button move and the camera itself respond. Here's what happens when you take a picture:

1. Apply slight pressure to the shutter release button.

2. As you feel it depress slightly, the camera's autofocus lens locks the current subject into sharp focus.

3. At the same time, the camera's exposure meter measures the light and locks in an exposure.

4. Apply more pressure to the shutter release to press it in all the way. The camera then takes the picture and saves it to memory.

NOTE   *Very inexpensive cameras that use a fixed focus lens often do not include an exposure lock feature, or they use a separate button to lock the exposure. Inexpensive "budget" cameras may fall into this category. Refer to your camera's manual to see if it has exposure lock, and how to use it.*

The magic of exposure lock is that as long as you continue applying light pressure to the shutter release, the camera will use that "locked-in" exposure information regardless of where you later point the camera. You can lock in exposure information for the sky and then point the camera at your feet and snap the shutter release all the way. You'll take a picture of your feet using the sky's exposure data. You probably wouldn't want to do that since the result will be totally underexposed, but it gives you an idea of the potential.

Some digital cameras have a separate focus lock and exposure lock control; you should check your camera's manual for details. In such cameras, there's a separate button somewhere on the camera (usually where your thumb would fall on the right side of the camera body), often labeled AEL (short for auto-exposure lock). To use it, point the camera where you want to lock exposure settings and press firmly down on the AEL button. Continue to hold the button down while you re-compose the photo, and then take the picture by pressing the shutter release.

Exposure lock is a great tool for telling the camera that you'd like to take a picture with the exposure data from one specific part of the scene. Imagine, for instance, a scene like the one in Color Figure 2. Here we have a boy at the beach, standing in the water at sunset. The image can be dramatic, but only if exposed properly. We'd like to capture the overall dark tones inherent in a sunset scene, with exciting splashes of color to light up the subject in a subtle way. Just pointing the camera at the scene might result in the camera averaging the bright and dark bits of the picture, generating an image that might as well have been captured at midday. That would be quite ordinary and not at all what we want.

Instead of taking the average picture, here's what you should do, step by step:

1. Frame the scene in your viewfinder so you know what you want to photograph.

2. Before actually taking the picture, point the camera up into the sky. Include the brightest part of the sky that doesn't also include the sun—that might be overkill. Sounds like guesswork? It is, a little. This is art, not science. You can take the picture, see if you like the result, and reshoot as necessary.

3. Press the shutter release partway to lock in the exposure information. You should sense that the camera has also locked the focus at the same time.

4. Recompose your picture. When you're happy with the scene in the viewfinder, press the shutter release all the way to take the picture.

Obviously, you could also choose the spot meter (if your camera has one) and lock the exposure with that instead of the default center-weighted or matrix meter in that you used in Steps 2 and 3. It's up to you. Take a look at Figure 2-11. This is a real

FIGURE 2-11   This wolf is lit very differently than the rest of the scene, so a spot meter is the easiest way to accurately expose the wolf's fur.

Bracketing for Success

A common photographic technique, and one that you might occasionally want to try, is called bracketing. *Bracketing* your photos is simply the process of taking several pictures, each with a slightly different exposure, so at least one of them will look the way you want. When you're done, review all the bracketed pictures on your PC and discard the ones you don't like.

Suppose you're trying to take a silhouette, for instance (something we talk about in more detail in Chapter 4). You need to make sure the subject is sufficiently underexposed that it appears totally dark, with no detail. How can you do that? There are two common methods for bracketing:

- ■ *Use your camera's auto-bracketing feature.* Many digital cameras have something called auto-bracketing—turn it on, and it'll take three pictures in quick succession when you press the shutter release. One will be the "proper" exposure, but it'll also capture slightly over- and underexposed images as well for insurance.

- ■ *Use exposure compensation.* Take one picture normally, and then take additional photos after changing the EV dial to under- and overexpose. You should start with exposure variations of a half-stop or full-stop (1/2 or 1 on the display), since more than a full stop of exposure compensation can be dramatic.

challenge for most cameras, since the subject is a wolf sunning itself in an isolated patch of light. A center-weighted camera would probably average the light in the darker surrounding areas and determine that it needed to select a fairly wide-open aperture to add light to the scene. But that would wash out the poor little wolf. Instead, the best solution is to select the spot meter, frame the wolf carefully, and press the shutter release partially to lock in exposure on the bright subject. Then reframe the picture and shoot.

As you become more confident with your ability to visualize compositions and exposures, you can try different things to get the desired effect.

When to Take Control

As I mentioned at the outset, you may often be perfectly satisfied with the results you can get from the automatic exposure controls in your camera. But there will be times when you can do better on your own. Keep your eyes peeled for situations like those described next.

Very Bright Sunlight

Very bright sun can overwhelm your camera, especially if the scene is filled with brightly colored clothing, reflective surfaces, or other tricky subjects. You can reduce the exposure for better exposure. Underexpose the scene by EV –1 for starters, and see if that helps.

Backlit Subjects

If you are taking a picture of someone or something and the sun is behind the subject, you're usually in trouble—the bright background will cause the camera to underexpose the scene. That means the subject itself will look like it's in shadow. You'll get this if you follow the old (and very wrong) rule to put the sun behind the person you're photographing. The best way to shoot an outdoor portrait is to put the sun over your shoulder. Nonetheless, if you find the sun behind your subject, overexpose the scene, such as with an EV +1. Of course, this may overexpose the background, but that's probably okay—your priority is properly exposing the subject in the foreground.

Try wearing white clothing—it'll essentially turn your entire body into a giant reflector, sometimes allowing you to put the subject between yourself and the sun.

Low Light

In low light, such as at night, indoors, or under thick cloud cover, you can often get better results by overexposing the scene slightly, such as with an EV +1. Vary the EV level depending on how dark the scene actually is.

How to ... Consider Exposure When Taking a Picture

Most of the time, you can just compose your shot and press the shutter release. But don't forget to adjust the exposure when necessary. Use this decision process:

1. Do I need to adjust the depth of field—that is, make the background more or less sharp compared to the foreground? If yes, then adjust the aperture/shutter or use the aperture priority mode, discussed in detail in Chapter 3.

2

2. Do I need to change the shutter speed to depict motion in the picture? If yes, then again try to adjust the aperture/shutter, or instead use the shutter priority mode, discussed in detail in Chapter 3.

3. Is the scene significantly brighter or darker than the camera is designed for? If it is, under- or overexpose the scene.

4. Is the subject backlit, such as with the sun behind? If so, overexpose the scene.

5. Is the subject especially bright, such as on fresh, bright snow? Try underexposing.

6. Do I want to expose the scene based on the lighting in a specific part of the scene? If so, use a spot meter or just lock in the exposure for that part of the picture and recompose the scene.

Chapter 3

Composition Essentials

How to...

- Use the rules of composition to take compelling photos
- Take less cluttered snapshots by emphasizing a focal point
- Take interesting photos with the rule of thirds
- Avoid cropping out important pixels by filling the frame
- Use lines and symmetry for artistic images
- Break the rules for more engaging photos
- Understand the relationships among shutter, aperture, and depth of field
- Employ depth of field for pictures that emphasize the subject
- Zoom a lens to achieve the right field of view
- Apply rules of composition to common photographic situations

What does it take to take a good picture? Certainly, it requires more than a mastery of your camera's various controls. If that were all you needed, anyone who knew how to read a camera manual could be Ansel Adams. No, taking good pictures demands a little creativity and a touch of artistry. Perhaps more importantly, though, it takes a solid understanding of the rules of photographic composition and some knowledge—which you can acquire as you get better at photography—of when it's OK to break those rules.

Composition is all about how you arrange the subjects in a picture and how you translate what is in your mind's eye—or even right in front of you—into a photograph. After all, the camera sees things very differently than you do, and in order to take great photographs you have to understand that and learn how to see the world the way your camera sees it.

Taking a picture with a digital camera is really no different than taking a picture with a 35mm camera. That's why in this chapter we will be talking about the rules of composition: what they are, how to use them, and how to break them. If you are already an accomplished photographer and you're reading this book to make the transition to digital photography, you may not need most of what I offer in this chapter. But if you're not an expert, I encourage you to study this chapter. It is only through an understanding of composition that your images will go from snapshots—the ones that bring comments like "What a nice picture of a cat!"—to potential works of art that you'll be proud to frame in your dining room.

Why Composition Is Important

Have you ever been on vacation, pulled out your camera upon seeing a picturesque view, but later been somewhat underwhelmed with the final results? If so, you just learned the first rule of photography: reality, as seen by your camera, is quite different from what you see with your own eyes. If you frame all of your pictures without taking that into account, you will always be disappointed.

There are a few reasons why what your cameras sees is different from what you see. First of all, your eyes aren't little optical machines that function in a vacuum. Instead, all that you see is supplemented, enhanced, and interpreted by your brain. In a sense, when you see a majestic landscape while hiking through the backwoods of Kauai, some of the splendor of the scene is actually being added by your mind. Lift the camera to that same view, and you get a totally objective representation of the scene, without any intelligent enhancements. That's because the camera actually is a little optical machine. And it does not have a brain.

And then there's the fact that a camera has a much more limited range of focus, exposure, and composition than you do. When you look at a scene like the Hawaiian landscape I just mentioned, you might think you're seeing a fairly static scene with your eyes. But that's not really the case. In fact, as your eyes dart around, you are constantly recomposing the scene, since you can dynamically change the visual "frame" in which you are viewing the scene. To make matters worse, the aperture of your eyes, called the pupil, changes size constantly in response to changing lighting conditions and where you're looking. The result? You don't realize it, but your eyes, working in conjunction with your brain, are creating a visual feast that is difficult, if not impossible, to reproduce on paper.

In comparison, it's amazing that we can get good pictures at all with a camera. Film—and by film I mean both 35mm and digital—has a much narrower exposure range than your eyes because the aperture freezes a single instant in time with a fixed set of lighting conditions. And unlike the magical pictures in the *Harry Potter* series of books, real photographs cannot change their composition or framing on the fly. What you see in the viewfinder is, unfortunately, what you are stuck with forever.

What We See

Look around. What do you see? If you look carefully, you'll notice that your field of vision is a rectangle with rounded corners—almost a wide ellipse. In other words, we see the world panoramically. While there are techniques for creating panoramic photographs (which I'll cover in Chapter 12), most of the time this is not the kind of shot we take.

FIGURE 3-1   Changing the composition of a picture by turning the camera by 90 degrees can completely change the effect a photograph has on its viewer.

Nope—our job as photographers is to take the panorama that we see with our own eyes and translate it into an attractive photograph using the laws of photographic composition. As you can see in Figure 3-1, there's often more than one way to frame a picture; it's really your job to decide which works best for the kind of photograph you are trying to achieve. In this situation I had an extremely rare opportunity to photograph endangered monk seals, so I shot many different compositions.

Rules of Composition

For a few pages now I have been alluding to the rules of composition. I hope that you're curious what they might be. In truth, the rules of composition are no more rigid than rules of etiquette or the rules of Web page design. Certainly, those rules can be important, but they're simply guidelines to help us get the job done. If you violate any of these rules, nothing awful happens (unless you're still living at home when you break the rules of etiquette). And that's why we'll be able to break these rules later on. To begin with however, we need to learn the rules and apply them.

Isolate the Focal Point

I know what you're wondering: what is the focal point? The *focal point* is the main subject of your picture, such as a building or perhaps a person. In other words, the focal point is the main point of interest that the viewer's eye is drawn to when looking at your picture.

3

You should always strive to consider what the focal point of your picture actually is and then plan your photos accordingly. In my experience, the single biggest problem with photographs taken by new photographers is that they fail to consider what their subject actually is. When you don't know what you're taking a picture of, it's hard to emphasize that element in the final composition. That leads to muddy, confused arrangements in which there is nothing specific for the viewer to look at. Take a look at Figure 3-2, for instance. In this image, there is no real focal point, and thus there is nothing for the viewer to concentrate on. The photographer should have decided what the subject was and then rearranged the image to emphasize that. Indeed, all I would ask of this picture is, "why did the photographer take it?"

When your subject is simply too expansive to be considered a focal point in and of itself, try to contrive a focal point that adds some relief for your viewer. You might try such an approach when you are photographing a mountainous

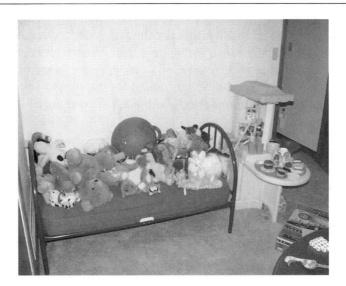

FIGURE 3-2   Without a focal point, your eyes wander the picture aimlessly, looking for something of interest.

FIGURE 3-3   Secondary focal points add interest to landscapes (and many other sorts of pictures).

landscape, for instance. In fact, landscapes really benefit from this approach. A tractor, a mountain cabin, or a gaggle of hikers near the horizon allow the viewer's eyes to rest on something familiar, even though the real subject fills up most of the frame. Technically, this is called a secondary focal point. You can see how I used this technique in Figure 3-3 to give the viewer a visual resting spot when looking at the backdrop of mountains. Remember: photography is subjective, and I did not intend for the cabin to be the photo's subject. Instead, the mountains were the subject, but by themselves they would make a terrible photograph.

> **TIP** *As a general rule, you only want a single focal point in your photograph. More than one main subject is distracting, and viewers won't really know where to look. If I show you a photograph in which several objects have equal visual weight, you probably won't like it, even though you may not be sure why. It is certainly possible to include multiple focal points in an image, but you should do it with care, and only after you have mastered the basics.*

Use the Rule of Thirds

Many snapshot photographers don't really think much about the organization of what they see through the viewfinder, so the *Rule of Thirds* helps restore some

3

FIGURE 3-4   Every picture has four "sweet spots" to which the eye is naturally drawn.

balance to their photographs. And though this is the second rule I'm going to talk about, in many ways I think the Rule of Thirds is the single most important rule of photography that you can learn and apply.

Here's what you should do: in your mind, draw two horizontal and two vertical lines through your viewfinder so that you have divided it into thirds. In other words, your image should be broken into nine zones with four interior corners where the lines intersect. (See Figure 3-4 for an example of this technique.) It is these corners that constitute the "sweet spots" in your picture. If you place something—typically the focal point—in any of these intersections, you'll typically end up with an interesting composition.

This really, really is the golden rule of photography. Thumb through a magazine. Open a photography book. Watch a movie. No matter where you look, you will find that professional photographers follow the Rule of Thirds about 75 percent of the time. And while the Rule of Thirds is very easy to follow, you may find it somewhat counterintuitive. Many people try to put the focal point of their picture dead smack in the middle of the frame. And trust me—there are few things in life more boring than looking at a picture in which the subject is always right in the middle. Compare the two images in Figure 3-5. I think you'll agree that the one on the right, in which the subject is not in the center, is the better photograph.

FIGURE 3-5   As a general rule, avoid putting your focal point in the dead center of the photograph. Shifting the subject ever-so-slightly to the left makes the picture on the right more interesting.

TIP   *If you position the subject off-center, the camera may have trouble locking the exposure. This is a perfect opportunity to use the exposure lock/focus lock button on your digital camera, as I mentioned in Chapter 2. Point the camera at the subject and press the shutter release halfway down to lock the exposure on your subject; then reposition the camera to compose the picture just the way you like.*

Fill the Frame

Don't forget to get the most mileage you can out of the frame in which you're working. What the heck does that mean? Essentially, all I am saying is that you should minimize the amount of dead space in a photograph. Once you decide what the focal point of your image is (remember the golden rule of photography!), there's no reason to relegate it to a small portion of the picture. Get close. Zoom in. Walk over to it. Whatever you need to do, do it in order to keep your focal point from being a small part of the overall image. Take a look at Figure 3-6, for instance. When I visited London and took pictures of the changing of the guard, I found that the common wide-angle shots of the event resulted in rather unimpressive photographs. I decided that the real star of the show was the guard's face, so I zoomed in for a very tight shot.

FIGURE 3-6   This shot is almost uncomfortably close, and that's why it is so captivating.

Certainly, all of your photographs don't need to be this close. Getting a tight shot of your subject is not always a natural or intuitive thing to do; so you should go out of your way to try this technique whenever you think of it.

The "fill the frame" rule certainly applies in the world of 35mm photography, but it is absolutely essential in digital photography. That's because in 35mm photography, it's not difficult to crop and enlarge an image and still retain a reasonable amount of image quality, as long as you do not overly enlarge the final image. In digital photography, however, we're dealing with pixels, not grains of silver halide. And it seems like there are rarely enough pixels to go around.

If you are using a 3-megapixel digital camera, for instance, the best you can hope to do is print your photograph at 8×10 or perhaps, if you're lucky, at 11×17 inches before the pixels start to become obvious. (See Chapter 15 for details on printing.) That's probably enough resolution for most practical applications, but consider what happens if you need to crop your image because the subject was just too small the way the photograph was originally taken. If you crop out half of the pixels in the photo, you'll have a really hard time getting a good-looking 8×10-inch photograph with the resulting crop. If your digital camera captures smaller images—for example, 2-megapixel—then you can imagine how critical it is to compose the picture properly the first time. There really aren't any pixels to spare.

Move the Horizon

This rule is closely related to the Rule of Thirds. If you follow the Rule of Thirds to the letter, you probably won't make this mistake anyway, but it is important enough to mention explicitly.

No doubt you have seen photographs in which the photographer chose to place the horizon right in the middle of the photograph. Actually, the photographer probably did not make a conscious decision to do this—if he or she had, then the horizon probably would have ended up somewhere else.

Running the horizon right through the middle of a photograph is akin to putting the subject smack dab in the middle. It's boring because it violates the rule of thirds. Instead, try putting the horizon along a Rule of Thirds line. As you can well imagine, that actually gives you two choices for where to put the horizon in any given picture. You can put the horizon in the top third or the bottom third of your composition. How do you decide which? It's easy: if you want to emphasize the distant landscape and sky, put the horizon on the bottom third line. If you are taking a seascape where you want to emphasize the foreground, such as in Figure 3-7, the horizon belongs in the upper third of the picture. Of course, these are guidelines. Digital film is cheap—it's basically free. Experiment.

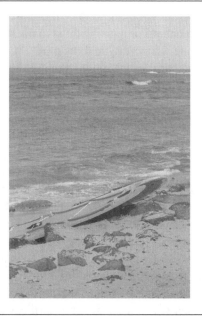

FIGURE 3-7   The horizon usually works best well above or below the center of the picture.

Use Lines, Symmetry, and Patterns

Photographs are two-dimensional representations of three-dimensional scenes. The question, then, is how best to lead viewers through a picture so they get a sense of the real depth that the image is trying to depict.

The answer to that question is simpler than you might think. When you compose an image in the viewfinder, look for natural or artificial lines that might lead the viewer's eyes through the photo. These lines can create a sense of depth and perspective that is often lost in the two-dimensional photograph. Lines can be formed in almost any situation: you might see a row of trees, the shape of a skyscraper from the ground, or the route of the backyard fence. Personally, I enjoy using the natural flow of a stream or road to lead the eye from one end of the picture to the other. Figure 3-8 is one example of this technique.

While lines like these can fit in with any kind of lens or composition, you may find that this works best when seen through wide-angle lenses. That's because telephoto lenses compress your scene and make it harder to see long, sweeping lines.

Another trick of the trade is to look for repetition and patterns, and incorporate those into your image. Patterns, like those that you see in nature or manmade objects, can create interesting effects. Like lines, they can add a sense of depth to your images. Try combining these patterns with a sense of symmetry. When you employ symmetry, you are balancing both sides of the photograph. That can also help lead the eye through your image.

FIGURE 3-8   A long, straight road is a powerful tool for creating a sense of implied motion in a photograph.

Keep the Horizon Straight

This may seem obvious, but how many times have you seen a photo in which the horizon was a little cockeyed? Vertically oriented pictures can get by with a slightly off-kilter horizon, but if you take a horizontally oriented image and the horizon is not straight, it affects the feel of the photograph. Try to be as careful as possible while photographing an expansive horizon. But if you goof, remember that it's a digital photo. You can always correct for an angled horizon on the computer (see Chapter 12). Any time you rotate or otherwise perform a "correction" on a photograph on your PC, though, you degrade the image ever so slightly. That's something to keep in mind of you want to preserve very high quality.

Use Foreground to Balance the Background

If you're trying to photograph a distant subject—a landscape or cityscape, for example—a common trick is to place something of interest in the foreground to provide a sense of balance. When done well, the viewer's eyes are drawn immediately to the foreground object, and then they'll wander to the background. This is a very effective technique for adding a sense of depth and perspective to a photograph, as well as giving the foreground a sense of scale. Figure 3-9, for instance, demonstrates this technique.

FIGURE 3-9   The barge in the foreground is the anchor that gives the New York skyline a sense of perspective.

Every Picture Tells a Story

Throughout this chapter, and in fact throughout the book, you'll notice references to "leading the viewer through a picture." What do I mean by that? Well, when you've done your job as a photographer, you've created an image with depth, motion, and some sort of story. When you look at a good photograph or painting, your eyes naturally start in one place and move to another. That's in sharp contrast to a typical snapshot that has no particular story to tell; the focal point is haphazardly placed, and it's cluttered enough that there's no obvious path for the eye to take. Good artists can use techniques like lines, symmetry, patterns, and multiple focal points to lead the viewer in a specific way through an image. If you can create an image like that, consider it a success.

Know When to Break the Rules

Now that I've spent the last few pages telling you what the rules of composition actually are, we can talk a little about how to ignore them.

Don't get me wrong—I love the rules of composition, and I think you should follow them. After you become comfortable with concepts like the Rule of Thirds and filling the frame with the focal point, however, you'll find that you can take even better pictures by bending or breaking those same rules. This is an area of photography that is best experimented with and learned on your own, but here are a few pointers to help you get started:

■ *Change your perspective.* Technically, we're not breaking any rules of composition here, but this is something that few people think about, yet it can have a profound impact on the quality of your photos. Simply put, experiment with different ways to view the same scene. Try taking your picture by holding the camera horizontally, and then see how you might frame the picture by turning the camera vertically. Take a look at the picture in Figure 3-10. I originally took this picture as you see it on the left. Afterwards, I found that I liked the picture better when I cropped it for a horizontal orientation. As it turns out, most people prefer the original framing, but that's okay: experiment and don't be afraid to try something even if no one else thinks it's a good idea. Get low to the ground or stand up on a chair or table to get a higher perspective on the same scene. You have a lot of options: try them.

FIGURE 3-10   Experiment with taking your pictures from many different angles, orientations, and perspectives. After all, you're not paying for the film anymore!

■ *Ignore symmetry.* Sure, symmetry is great. But just as often as symmetry works well in a photograph, I have found you can get an even better image if you intentionally skew the photo to strip out the symmetry. When the viewer expects symmetry and doesn't get it, you have introduced tension and drama into an image. And that's not bad, especially if all you've done is photograph some road, train track, or river.

■ *Surprise the viewer.* If you've seen one landscape or sunset, you've seen them all. That's not really true, but it can sometimes seem that way. Go for the unusual by framing your picture in a totally unexpected way. One of my favorite tricks is shooting landscapes through the side view mirror of a car—you can see it in Figure 3-11.

■ *Use several focal points.* While most pictures rely on just one or two focal points, sometimes you need even more, especially when you're shooting a picture like a family portrait. If you're taking a picture with several people in it, you can often overcome a cluttered look by arranging the subjects into a geometric pattern. If the subjects' heads form a triangle shape, for instance, you have introduced order into the photo despite the fact that there are a lot of people in it.

FIGURE 3-11   Successful pictures are often a matter of surprising the viewer.

Using Depth of Field

The last important frontier that you need to understand for proper composition is called *depth of field*. Depth of field refers to the region of proper focus that is available to you in any photographic image. When you focus your camera, you don't get a paper-thin region of proper focus in an image; instead, there's some distance in front and behind your subject that will also be in focus. This entire region of sharp focus is called the depth of field, or sometimes the depth of focus.

What determines depth of field? There are actually three factors that contribute to the depth of field that is available to you for any picture you plan to take. Let's look at these factors one at a time and then combine them.

- **Aperture**   The aperture of your lens is the first major factor that influences depth of field. We talked about aperture back in Chapter 2—it's the size of the lens opening that determines how much light reaches your camera's imaging sensor. Aperture is measured in f/stops, where lower f/numbers represent bigger openings and higher f/numbers represent smaller openings. In addition, the smaller the aperture's actual opening (or, in other words, the higher the f/number), the greater the depth of field will be. As you can see here, the aperture of your lens directly influences how deep the depth of field is in any given picture:

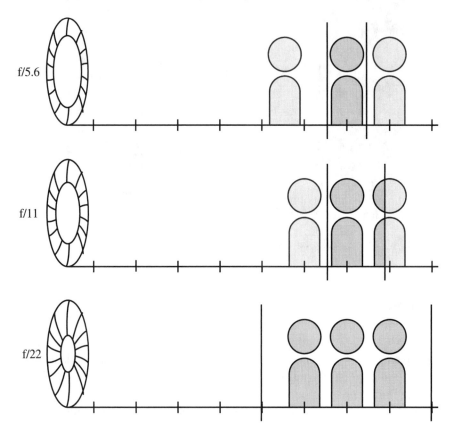

- **Focal length** As we will discuss in the upcoming section "Getting the Most Out of Your Zoom Lens," focal length is just a measure of your lens's ability to magnify a scene. And while most people focus on a lens's magnification, depth of field plays an important role here as well. In simple terms, the more you magnify your subject, the less depth of field you have available. When shooting with a normal or wide-angle lens, you have a lot of depth of field. If you zoom in to a telephoto magnification, your depth of field drops dramatically. Likewise, macro photography (also known as close-up photography) has very little depth of field as well, since you are greatly magnifying a small object. See Chapter 5 for details on macro photography. This illustration graphically demonstrates the effect of focal length on depth of field:

■ **Subject distance**   Last but not least, your distance from the subject determines how much depth of field you can get in your scene. If you photograph a subject that is far away, the depth of field will be much greater than it is for a subject that is close to the camera. In practical terms, that means the region of sharp focus for a macro shot—where the subject is only a few inches from the camera—is extremely narrow, and you need to focus very, very precisely. If you're photographing something very far away—like a distant horizon—a vast region in front of and behind the image will be in sharp focus. Here is what this looks like graphically:

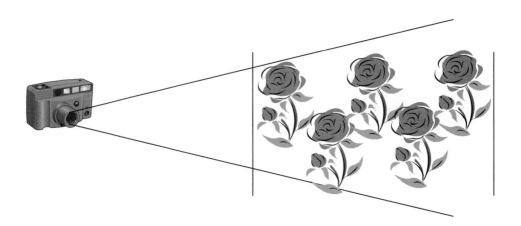

Applying Depth of Field to Your Pictures

As you can imagine, these three factors—aperture, depth of field, and subject distance—work together in any shooting situation.

Specifically, suppose you try to take a picture with an aperture of f/5.6. At a given distance from your subject, and at a given focal length, that f/stop will yield a certain depth of field. But what happens if you change the other two factors? If you get closer to the subject, such as if you walk toward it, or if you increase the focal length by zooming in, the depth of field decreases.

3

FIGURE 3-12   Varying the aperture changes the depth of field.

So what is the point of all this? Why do you care about depth of field at all? The answer is that depth of field is an extremely important element in the overall composition of your photographs. Using depth of field, you can isolate your subject by making sure it is the only sharply focused person or object in the frame. Alternately, you can increase the depth of field to make the entire image—from foreground to background—as sharp as possible. Figure 3-12 shows the effect of depth of field on a simple portrait; on the left, the child in the background is in sharp focus thanks to a deep depth of field. On the right, nothing has changed except the f/stop. By decreasing the f/number (and thus increasing the size of the lens opening), the background child is now blurry and indistinct. I think either of these two pictures would make a great album cover for some psychedelic band. But I digress.

Getting the Most Out of Your Zoom Lens

As I mentioned in Chapters 1 and 2, your digital camera probably comes with a zoom lens that allows you to vary the focal length from a wide-angle or normal perspective all the way through some moderate telephoto length.

FIGURE 3-13 These three views, all taken from the same position, show the effect of a zoom lens on the magnification of the subject.

As you probably recall, focal length is just a measure of the magnification the lens provides. A larger focal length produces greater magnification; hence long focal length lenses are great for capturing fast action or enlarging objects that are moderately far away. You can see the effect of a zoom lens on magnification in Figure 3-13.

A key fact to remember, however, is that the focal length of the given lens also affects the camera's angle of view. Because a telephoto lens magnifies distant objects, it has a very narrow angle of view. As you reduce the magnification and zoom out toward smaller focal lengths, the angle of view likewise increases. You can see this graphically in Figure 3-14.

At the extreme end of the scale—specifically, wide-angle lenses—the image is actually shrunk with respect to what the human eye can see. The angle of view becomes extreme, sometimes even greater than 180 degrees. This kind of wide-angle lens is known as a *fish-eye lens* due to the peculiar effect of the angle of view.

The focal length of your lens has one other important characteristic. Depending on whether you have your lens set to wide angle, normal, or telephoto, you'll get a very different depth of field. As you saw previously in this chapter, a telephoto setting yields minimal depth of field, while a wide-angle setting generates a lot of focusing depth.

TIP *The telephoto end of your zoom lens is great for capturing distant subjects, but the additional magnification can create blurry pictures. Especially if you are photographing in low light, where your camera might choose a slow shutter speed, I highly recommend that you take telephoto images with a tripod.*

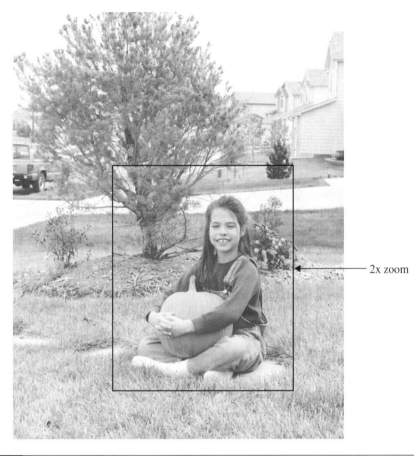
2x zoom

FIGURE 3-14   The longer the focal length, the narrower the region that a lens can see.

Taking a Zoomed Picture

Not all special effects need to be done inside a computer. The *zoomed* picture, like the one shown next, is a good example of a special effect that you can do "in the lens" of your camera without doing any processing on the computer whatsoever. Unfortunately, there are very few digital cameras that will let you achieve this effect. To take a zoomed picture, you need a digital camera that allows you to change the zoom setting during the exposure; generally, only professional SLR-style digital cameras are capable of this feat.

If you do have a camera like the Olympus e20n or the Nikon D100, however, here's how to do it. Start by choosing a scene that you want to zoom through. You'll get the best results with a brightly colored subject and a simple background that won't be too busy. Mount your camera on a tripod to minimize camera shake. If you have very steady hands, you might want to try holding the camera yourself.

Set your shutter speed for about 1/4 second. You'll need that much time to slide the zoom lens during exposure. Then, just as you press the shutter release, start zooming with a firm, steady, and consistent motion. Just as in golf, be sure that you follow through the zoom motion even after the shutter releases. That way, you won't stop moving the zoom in the middle of the exposure. You may need to practice this a few times to get the shot right; remember, electronic film is free.

Using Your Camera's Exposure Modes

Almost every digital camera on the market makes it easy to take quick-and-dirty snapshots using an automatic exposure mode. Automatic exposure is great much of the time, but I hope that you will sometimes want to get a little more creative. And when that happens, you may need to adjust the exposure of your photographs as we talked about both in this chapter and in Chapter 2.

3

Maximizing Depth of Field

There are three ways to maximize the depth of field in your image:

- Use a lens with a short focal length, such as the normal or wide-angle setting on your camera's zoom.

- Focus on a distant subject. If you're trying to get both a nearby tree and a more distant house in focus simultaneously, for instance, focusing on the house, rather than the tree, is more likely to deliver both subjects in focus.

- Use the smallest aperture you can, such as f/11or f/16. This is often the easiest element of your picture to control and the reason that many digital cameras have an *aperture priority* mode for dialing in an aperture setting for your photos.

Not surprisingly, you can minimize the depth of field in a picture by doing exactly the opposite of these things.

Not all cameras provide manual exposure settings; if yours does not, then you might want to think about upgrading at some point in the future to a more full-featured camera. In my experience, most cameras that cost about $500 have at least some manual exposure adjustments. And by the time you reach $1,000 price tags, these cameras are about as full featured as they come, with all of the amenities you'd expect from a 35mm SLR camera. Here's what each of these settings does, and when you would want to use them:

- **Automatic**   In this mode, both shutter speed and aperture settings are selected by the camera to match the current lighting. Some digital camera automatic modes try to select the fastest shutter speed possible in order to minimize camera shake when you take a picture, while most choose something in the middle, a compromise between speed and depth of field. There's generally nothing you can do to change the settings that the camera chooses when set to fully automatic, except for adjusting the exposure compensation (the Exposure Value, or EV) dial to over- or underexpose the scene.

- **Program**   The program mode (usually indicated by the letter *P* on your camera's dial or LCD display) is similar to an automatic mode. Although the camera selects both the aperture and shutter speed, you can generally modify the camera's selection by turning a dial or pressing a button. The effect: you can increase or decrease the shutter speed, and the camera will adjust the aperture to match. This is a good compromise between fully automatic operation and manual selection. Use this mode if you don't want to worry about devising your own exposure values but still want some say over the shutter speed or aperture.

TIP *The program exposure mode is often the best all-around setting for your camera. In this mode, the camera chooses a good exposure setting, but you can turn a dial to tweak the shutter speed. The camera will instantly compensate by changing the aperture setting, keeping the overall exposure the same.*

■ **Scene**   Many digital cameras come with a handful of scene modes with names like Night, Portrait, Sand & Snow, Sports, and Landscape. Select the scene name that best represents the kind of picture you're trying to take, and the camera will automatically set the depth of field, exposure, and other factors to give you a good picture. Sports mode sets the shutter speed very high, for instance, while Sand & Snow compensates for the very bright background, which would otherwise underexpose your photo. When used appropriately, these scene modes work great and let you properly expose a wide variety of settings with little effort. Cameras with just a few scene selections may place the icons on the body (such as on a control dial, see the following illustration), while cameras with many scene selections tend to place them in the onscreen menu.

■ **Shutter priority**   This setting is usually indicated by the letter *S* on your camera's mode dial or LCD display. Using this mode, you can dial in whatever shutter speed you like, and the camera accommodates by setting the appropriate aperture to match. This mode is ideal for locking in a speed fast enough to freeze action scenes or slow enough to intentionally blur motion.

3

- **Aperture priority**   This setting is usually indicated by the letter *A* on your mode dial or LCD display. Using this mode, you can dial in the aperture setting you like, and the camera accommodates by setting the appropriate shutter speed. Use this mode if you are trying to achieve a particular depth of field and you don't care about the shutter speed.

- **Manual**   The manual mode (typically indicated with an *M*) is like an old-style noncomputerized camera. In manual mode, you select the aperture and shutter speed on your own, sometimes with the help of the camera's recommendation. This mode is best used for long exposures or other special situations when the camera's meter is not reliable.

Choosing Exposure Modes and Lenses in Special Situations

Now that you know what your camera's various exposure modes are for, you can think about using them when you encounter unique photographic situations. Every situation is a little bit different, but here are a few general guidelines that can get you started.

Portrait Photography

Taking pictures of people can be fun but intimidating. It's hard to get a natural pose from people when they know they are being photographed. The best way to capture good portraits is to work with your subjects so they are a little more at ease. If you're trying to capture spontaneous, candid moments, then back off and try to blend in with

Shift Program Mode

Some cameras have a "shift program" (also called a *flexible program*) mode. Your camera has this if you set it to program and then see an asterisk appear next to the *P* in the LCD display when you turn the camera's settings dial.

Shift program mode lets you shift the shutter speed up or down while in program mode. The camera automatically adjusts the aperture setting, so you can do things like change the shutter speed or vary the depth of field while knowing that the camera will continue to properly expose the picture using your program mode settings.

the background. If you're trying to capture a fairly formal-looking portrait, you have a little more work cut out for you. It's up to you as the photographer to put your subjects at ease. Talk to your subjects and get them to respond. If you can get them to loosen up, they'll exhibit more natural responses and look better on film. Take pictures periodically as you pose your subjects to get them used to the shutter going off, even if it isn't a picture you intend to keep.

I should mention that digital cameras have a cool advantage for portraiture that SLRs don't: the LCD display lets you put your subject more at ease. Try framing your picture using the LCD display, keeping the camera some distance away from your face. That leaves you free to interact with your subject without having an intimidating camera obscuring your head.

The best way to capture portraits is typically with the medium telephoto lens: in the 35mm world, that would be about 100mm. For a typical digital camera, that's near the maximum magnification for your zoom lens. I also suggest that you work in aperture priority mode if that is possible for your camera. Aperture priority will allow you to change the depth of field quickly and easily as you frame your images. Specifically, good portraits have very shallow depth of field. You want to draw attention to the subject of your picture and leave the background an indistinct blur. Figure 3-15, for instance, demonstrates shallow depth of field in a fairly candid portrait.

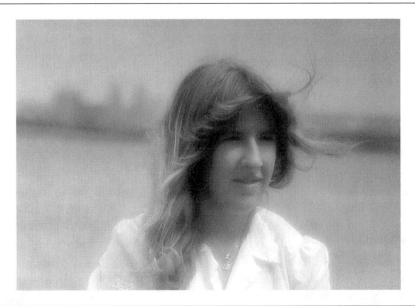

FIGURE 3-15   Portraits tend to work best with a moderate telephoto magnification and low f/numbers.

> **TIP**   *You can't see the effect of aperture on depth of field in the optical viewfinder, but the LCD display can show you the depth of field. To see, press the shutter release halfway down. That locks in the focus and triggers the aperture to close to the proper position for the impending picture. It's now—with the shutter halfway depressed—that you can see the depth of field in your picture. Even so, depth of field can be a hard thing to see—especially on an LCD display in bright daylight.*

Action Photography

Action photography is often considered the most exciting kind of photography, but it's also the most demanding for both your technique and your equipment. As in all kinds of photography, you can no doubt take some great pictures with anything from a wide-angle lens all the way up to the photographic equivalent of the Hubble telescope. And wide-angle lenses do, in fact, have a role in action photography. But the essence of many action shots is a highly magnified immediacy—something you can only get with the telephoto lens.

The shutter priority setting on your digital camera was born for action photography. To freeze action, you'll need to use a fairly fast shutter speed. Luckily, this higher shutter speed works to your advantage by opening up the aperture and diminishing the depth of field; this focuses the viewer's attention specifically on your subject. On the downside, of course, focusing is more critical since the depth of field is more shallow.

In general, I recommend that you use the fastest shutter speed available to capture action. On the other hand, you can use a technique called *panning* to capture the subject in good, sharp focus and keep the background as a motion blur. See Figure 3-16 for an example of panning that I used to freeze a child's wild ride at a Renaissance festival. This is convenient both when you want to make a somewhat artistic statement about the subject's motion and when you know the camera can't muster up a fast enough shutter speed to freeze the motion the ordinary way.

Panning involves some effort on your part. To create a good pan, you need to twist your body in synch with the motion of the subject as you press the shutter release. Here's how:

1. Position yourself where you can twist your body to follow the motion of the moving subject without having the camera's line of sight blocked by something else.

2. Set the camera's shutter speed for about 1/60. Feel free to experiment with this, but if you set the shutter speed too slow, you can't capture the subject

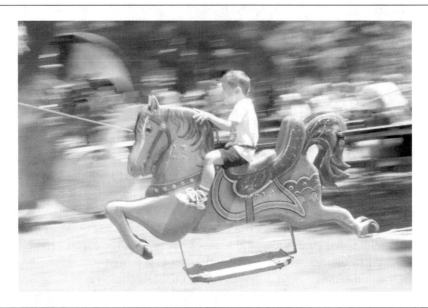

FIGURE 3-16   Panning freezes the subject while it blurs the background.

effectively—it blurs. And if the shutter is too fast, you won't get the pretty blur in the background.

3. Twist your body with the motion of the subject and track it through the camera's viewfinder or on the LCD display. Press the shutter release and continue tracking the subject until after you hear the shutter close again. Just like in baseball or golf, ensure that you follow through the motion even after the shutter releases. That way, you don't stop panning in the middle of the exposure. You may need to practice this a few times to get the shot right, but electronic film is free.

TIP   *The farther away the background is, the less motion blur effect you'll get. For best results, get close to the object and its background. If the background is too far away, the blur will be minimal and it'll just look out of focus.*

There's another way to show action—hold the camera rigidly in place and let the action scream through the viewfinder as you take the picture, capturing *its* motion, not the background's. If you're shooting in broad daylight with a reasonably fast shutter speed, you can hand-hold the camera for this kind of shot. If you're shooting with a slow shutter speed in a dark location, though, I recommend mounting the camera on a tripod. Here's an example of capturing motion in a New York subway station at about 1/15 second:

Dealing with Shutter Lag

The most common complaint I hear about digital cameras is this: "There's a long pause between when I press the shutter release and when the picture is actually taken." The result: when trying to take an action shot, the subject sometimes moves before you can take the picture.

Indeed, that pause is responsible for more frustration than all of the world's child-safe medicine bottles combined. Older digital cameras had a "shutter lag" that lasted a second or more, but even many of the newest digital cameras have some lag—and that's a real problem for action photos.

Shutter lag happens because digital cameras have a veritable checklist of tasks to perform when you press the shutter release. Not only does the camera need to measure the distance to the subject and lock in the proper focus, but it has to measure the ambient light, calculate the best exposure, and lock in an aperture setting and shutter speed. It also has computer-like "housekeeping" chores to perform, like initializing the sensor chip, flushing buffers, and reading white level.

If your camera's lag doesn't bother you, fine. But if you want to minimize the lag, there are a few things you can do. The biggest time-saver is auto focus. If you prefocus your picture, you can save valuable milliseconds of lag (see the discussion of the two-step shutter in the upcoming section "How To... Capture the Moment.") If you're more adventurous, you can also try presetting the camera's white balance (see Chapter 4 for details). If the white balance is set on auto, it'll have to adjust the colors in the image each and every time you take a picture. Instead, you can use the camera's menu to set the white balance for whatever lighting conditions you're actually shooting in, such as daylight, nighttime, florescent, or incandescent lighting. Just remember to change the white balance for every new lighting situation you find yourself in.

If you try all those things and still find lag a problem, you need to shoot predicatively. By that I mean press the shutter release a heartbeat before you want to capture the photo. Also, try panning at the same time to better freeze your subject.

Some digital cameras try to get around the lag problem by offering a continuous fire mode. When set to that position, you'll capture a series of pictures in quick succession, usually about 1/3 second apart. The presumption is that one of them will look good. Experiment with that mode and see if it helps you get better action shots.

Nature and Landscapes

Unlike action photography and portraiture that rely on telephoto lenses to compress the action into an intimate experience, landscapes typically work best with wide-angle lenses that allow you to include huge, expansive swaths of land, air, and sea in a single frame. Zoom out for best results most of the time, and adjust the camera's exposure in aperture priority mode (if possible) to get deep or shallow depth of field, depending on what works best for the picture in question.

There are a few special kinds of nature shots that warrant special mention.

Photographing a Waterfall or Running Stream   There are two ways to capture running water in a photograph: with a fast, freeze-framing shot or with a longer exposure that blurs the water into a continuous stream effect. Both effects can look good, but I have a fondness for the latter. The effect looks great, and it's very easy to do: you simply need to take a long exposure of the water. Here's how:

1. You need to ensure that your camera will give you a long exposure, on the order of a half second. You can get this by shooting in automatic mode in the early morning or late afternoon, or using a manual mode if your camera allows.

2. Set your camera on a tripod (the long exposure requires a steady support).

3. Compose the image and take the shot.

TIP *If you can't get your camera to use a setting that's slow enough to blur the shot, try adding a neutral density (ND) filter to the front of your lens. ND filters reduce the light entering the lens without affecting the color; they're handy for creative photography when you can't wait for the sun to go down. Read more about ND filters in Chapter 6.*

Shooting Wildlife   Wildlife photography is like action photography; it typically requires a telephoto lens, fast shutter speed, and a tripod. Try to fill the frame as much as possible. Figure 3-17, for instance, shows a pair of wolves frolicking that would have been impossible to shoot without a fast shutter and a lens with a long reach.

FIGURE 3-17   Wildlife photography requires many of the same shooting skills as action photography.

Capture the Moment

Most digital cameras have a two-step shutter release; only very inexpensive fixed-focus cameras do not. Knowing how to use this feature is key to taking great pictures.

When you put a little pressure on the shutter release button, the camera springs into action: it locks in both the focus and the exposure setting. If you continue to hold down the shutter button, the focus and exposure won't change; you can then recompose the picture and, when it meets your approval, press the shutter release all the way to actually take the picture.

There are a lot of reasons why you might want to use the focus/exposure lock step without pressing the button all the way down:

■ Focus lock takes a fraction of a second. If you're taking an action shot or some other photo in which you want to precisely control the instant of exposure, lock the exposure and focus first; then wait with your finger on the shutter until you are absolutely ready to take the picture. Then, all it takes is a hair more pressure to capture the scene more or less instantly.

■ If you want to use the camera's spot meter, it's usually found in the dead center of the frame. To lock in an exposure value based on some other part of the image, point your camera accordingly and press the shutter release halfway down. Then recompose the picture and snap the shutter. This is a handy technique, even with other exposure modes. To get a rich, blue sky, for instance, it might help to tip the camera up and lock the exposure in based on what's above the horizon. Then tip the camera back down and take the picture.

If you want something that's off to the side of your picture to be in sharp focus—and this commonly is the case if you follow the Rule of Thirds—then point the camera at your off-center subject and lock the focus. Then recompose the shot to put the subject off to the side, and snap the picture.

Chapter 4   Flash and Lighting

How to...

- Use your flash for primary lighting

- Fill in shadows with your flash

- Keep from underexposing close-ups

- Use the various flash settings on your camera

- Optimize lighting outdoors

- Optimize lighting indoors

- Avoid red eye in low-light photos

- Balance your scenes based on the kind of lighting around you

- Use a reflector to fill in shadows

- Take interesting photos at night

Photography is all about light. In previous chapters, I have talked about how to work with the existing light in a scene to control aspects of your photograph such as depth of field. Sometimes, using the light that you already have isn't quite enough, however. That's why photographers spend so much time with flash units, strobes, reflector units, and other gadgets that help enhance or supplement natural light.

In this chapter, we'll talk a fair bit about using the electronic flash. Almost every digital camera made today—with the exception of very inexpensive models—comes with a built-in flash unit. The flash is a way to bring extra light with you and brighten many kinds of pictures. On the other hand, I have found that most people don't really know how to take advantage of the flash built into their camera, so in this chapter I discuss techniques such as fill flash, red eye reduction, and bounce flash.

Lighting isn't just about using the built-in flash, either. You can use a reflector to spread light around for a more pleasing effect. For better lighting control, you can also play with the white balance built into your camera. And let's not forget about night photography. It's one of my favorite subjects, and in the next few pages I will explain how you can try your hand at this as well. Taking pictures at night can yield some of the most artistic and beautiful images you'll ever see.

The Basics of Flash Photography

These days, most digital cameras have an electronic flash unit built right into the camera body. The flash is designed to fire for a very short period of time and illuminate your scene in one of two ways:

- As the main source of light indoors or in the dark

- As a secondary source of light to fill in shadows when you're shooting in bright light, such as outdoors

In general, your flash will probably know when to fire and can illuminate most pictures without your direct intervention. When your camera is set to the fully automatic exposure mode, the flash will probably come on as needed and not fire when it is not needed. On the other hand, you can probably figure out when you need a flash more effectively than your camera can. For example, there will be situations when you may want your flash to fire when it would probably stay off, and vice versa. That's why your camera has several flash modes to choose from. We'll talk about those a little later, in the section "Master Your Flash Modes".

Stay Within the Range of Your Flash

How far will the light from your flash travel? That's something you need to know if you expect to get the most out of your flash. The flash built into most digital cameras is not extremely powerful; at best, you can expect to get a range of about 20 feet. To find the range of your camera's flash, refer to the owner's manual that came with your camera. You can almost always find the flash range listed in the specifications section of the manual. If you cannot find the range of your flash listed there, assume it is no more than about 15 feet.

The range of your flash also depends on two other factors: the current ISO (light sensitivity) setting on your camera and the focal length setting of the zoom lens. The first factor—ISO—is pretty obvious. The more sensitive the CCD is made to light, the more effective the flash will be. To understand the relationship between focal length and flash range, though, take a look at Figure 4-1. It is an unfortunate side effect of zoom lens technology that when you increase the focal length to telephoto, you typically let less light through the lens than when you are using a wide angle lens or normal focal lengths. Since there's less light getting through the lens barrel to the CCD at telephoto magnifications, the flash has less effective range.

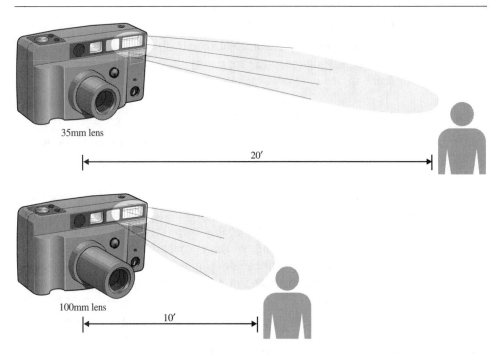

35mm lens

20'

100mm lens

10'

FIGURE 4-1   Because it processes less light, a telephoto lens reduces the effective range of your flash.

If you're used to the great range you would get from an external flash unit mounted on top of a 35mm SLR camera, you might be disappointed by the range from a digital camera flash. It stands to reason, though, that the small flash built into a digital camera could not have the same power as the large flash head, powered by lots of AA batteries, mounted on an SLR.

That means you'll have to be aware of how far you're trying to get the flash to throw light, especially at night or in very dark conditions. If your subject is very far away, such as 25 feet or more, it is unlikely that the built-in flash will have any effect at all on your photograph. In Figure 4-2, you can see that the flash is less effective at increased distances from the subject. In fact, some digital cameras disable the flash automatically when they sense that the lens is focused on infinity or when it is set to a "landscape" scene mode, which focuses on infinity anyway. You might want to check your camera manual or experiment to see if that applies to you.

Getting Too Close

Believe it or not, it's possible to get too close to your subject as well. Some digital camera flash units overexpose the subject when you are within a foot or two of the

4

FIGURE 4-2   These snapshots demonstrate the falloff in light intensity as you back away from your subject at night.

subject. Since you know about the light-reducing properties of a telephoto lens, you might expect that you can get closer when you zoom in than if you are zoomed out. And you'd be right; with a typical camera, you cannot shoot any closer than about three feet when set on normal zoom, but you can shoot to within a single foot if you are zoomed in to telephoto.

As you can see from Figure 4-3, close-up photos are easy to overexpose if you leave the flash turned on. There are a few ways to work around this problem, depending on what your flash unit is capable of doing:

- Turn the flash off completely and shoot with natural light.

- Bounce the flash off a plain white reflector, such as the ceiling or a reflector card. You'll probably need an external flash unit to bounce, though.

- Reduce the flash's power setting to 50 or 25 percent—most cameras have a setting in the menu that lets you do this.

- Cover the flash with a tissue or gel (available at any camera shop) to reduce its intensity.

FIGURE 4-3   Your flash may overexpose close-ups if you get too close; natural light was used for the image on the left, but the flash was enabled for the image on the right.

TIP   *For many digital cameras, there's an optimum range for your flash photographs. Try to stay between about 5 and 14 feet from your subject. Avoid using the flash in situations where the subject is more than about 15 feet away or closer than 3 feet.*

Master Your Flash Modes

In this digital age, choosing between "on" and "off" is just too easy. Instead, your camera's flash has three or more modes, each intended for a specific photographic situation. Here's the rundown of your options. Your camera may not include all of these features, so you might want to check out your camera manual before you get your heart set on trying all of them out. Your camera should have some, if not all, of these modes:

 Off   This one is easy. When you set your camera to this mode, no matter how strongly your camera believes that you need extra light, the flash will not fire. This is handy for situations where you are not allowed to fire a flash, such as in a church or a museum, or when you're too close to the subject and think you might overexpose it. You may also want to turn off the flash in many night photography situations. I'll talk about that later in the chapter.

Auto **Auto**   This is the standard mode that you'll probably want to leave your flash set to most of the time. When set to auto, the flash determines whether it needs to fire based on the amount of light in the scene. This is a good mode to use when you don't want to think about whether the flash needs to fire. For typical snapshot photography, just set your flash to auto.

Forced   This mode goes by many different names depending upon the camera you are using. Sometimes called "forced flash," "fill flash," or just "on," forced flash is probably the most appropriate name. When you set your camera's flash to this mode, it will fire regardless of how much light is available. Why would you want to use this mode? It's most useful as a fill flash: when you're shooting outdoors in natural light, the fill flash can erase shadows that would appear based on the way the sun hits your subject. Fill flash, or forced flash, is great for portraits

4

Red eye   Red eye reduction mode has become extremely popular in all sorts of cameras, both digital and analog. By preflashing the camera flash several times quickly right before the picture is taken, the red eye reduction mode forces your subject's pupils to close down to a smaller size, thus decreasing the chances that the retinas will reflect the light of the flash. When you use this mode, remember that it will take a fraction of a second longer for the picture to be taken; don't pull the camera away as soon as you press the shutter release, or you'll blur the picture. If you're photographing people in a dark room, it is probably worth the extra time it takes using red eye mode. You do not need to use red eye reduction outdoors or in bright light. If the red eye mode isn't completely effective, or if you forget to turn it on, you can eliminate red eye on the PC in an image-editing program—see Chapter 12.

TIP   *Taking pictures at the tavern? The red eye mode can also help reduce the red eye effect in people who have been drinking.*

Low   **Low power**   Some digital cameras let you control the power output of the flash. You might be able to reduce the intensity of the flash by 50 percent or more. You can use this mode when you are using the flash to fill in shadows or when you are taking a close-up and a full flash burst would overexpose your subject.

Slow   **Slow**   In the world of 35mm photography, this slow setting is sometimes referred to as a *rear curtain flash*. Most digital cameras refer to this feature as *Slow Sync*. Of course, that name may not help you understand what the slow setting does. When you set the camera to slow flash, it fires the flash at the tail end of the exposure. This setting is used most often at night, when the exposure is long (such as a second or more). What does it do? Suppose you were trying to take a picture of a car driving down the street. With an ordinary flash exposure, the flash fires right away, thus freezing the car at the start of the frame. In a long exposure, you will then see headlights cut through the car and out of the frame. The slow mode, however, saves the flash for the end. In a picture taken with this mode, you will see headlights that travel through the frame and then meet up with the rear of a flash-frozen car. The car is leaving the picture at the end of the exposure, just like it should. As you can see, you won't use this mode all the time, but it is indispensable when you need to get a certain kind of long-exposure photograph.

Add an External Flash

Many digital cameras are compatible with external flash units. Your camera can accept a flash if it has a flash shoe on the top of the camera body, which looks like this:

If your camera does have such a mount, check out the camera manufacturer's Web site or your local camera store for information on compatible flash units you can attach to your camera. External flashes have these major advantages:

- Greater range for better flash photography in a wider range of environments.

- The ability, with some flash units, to pivot, swivel, and tilt the flash head. By angling the flash, for instance, you can use it to bounce light off of walls and ceilings, which adds up to softer lighting effects.

- Getting the flash off the lens axis. Many flash units, with the right bracket adapter, can be held away from the camera. In addition to giving you more creative control over the direction the light is coming from, these lens brackets let you eliminate red eye effects because the flash isn't right in line with the lens.

■ Better battery life. Since an external flash has its own batteries, it can last longer and not wear down the camera's own batteries at the same time.

Be aware, though, that all flash units are not the same, nor are they all compatible with all cameras. In theory, pretty much any digital camera should be able to fire pretty much any flash designed for a 35mm film camera, but the advanced, automatic exposure features probably won't work—you'll have to shoot in manual mode, which isn't much fun. It's also possible that an incompatible flash can damage your camera. That's why you should check to see what flash unit is made for your model by your camera's manufacturer.

Improve Your Outdoor Photographs

In my experience, people are more disappointed with their outdoor photographs than any other kinds of images. They complain about the washed-out sky—it was very blue when they took the picture—as well as ugly shadows on people's faces, bad exposure, highly contrasting, and harsh shadows that go through their pictures.

Why do all these problems occur? At the most basic level, it's because your digital camera works very differently from the way your eyes do. When you look around outside, your pupils—the apertures of your eyes—change diameter constantly to adjust to varying light conditions throughout the scene. When you look toward the sky, your pupils close so you see rich, blue colors. Look under a tree, and your pupils immediately open to help you see in the deep shadows that are down there. And then there's the fact that your eyes have a much wider range of exposure values than a camera does. When you press the shutter release on your camera, it has to choose a single exposure level and try to depict the entire scene with that one reading—regardless of how dramatically the light changes throughout the picture. As I mentioned in Chapter 3, it is a miracle that we can get good pictures at all. That said, there are many strategies we can employ to get great pictures outdoors.

Beware the Sun

When you take pictures outdoors, always check your watch. By that I mean that there are better and worse times during the day to take pictures. Perhaps the worst time of all is midday, when the sun is directly overhead. The noon sun creates extremely harsh shadows and casts unflattering light for almost any kind of photographic project. People look their worst when you photograph them between about 10:00 in the morning and 2:00 in the afternoon, when the extremely bright, overhead light (particularly in the summertime) can tend to overwhelm a digital camera. If you're shooting on a cloudy or overcast day, though, even midday is fair game since there's no direct sunlight to interfere with your photos.

The alternative? Shoot early or late in the day. Photographers traditionally like the warm colors created by the sun in the late afternoon, but the morning is almost as good. If you are traveling on vacation, for instance, and want to get really great pictures, plan your photo exploits for the early morning hours and then again for late in the day. Heck, it's too hot in the middle of the day to pay too much attention to photography anyway.

If you make a conscious effort to take your best pictures before or after the high noon sun, you're halfway there. You also need to think about the position of the sun in the sky.

In the old days, new photographers were taught to take pictures with the sun to their back. The reason was simple: the sun would best illuminate the subject. Unfortunately, if you were photographing people, the sun would blast that light in their faces, causing them to squint. That made for some mighty ugly pictures. A much better solution is to position the sun over your left or right shoulder. But no matter where you put the sun, don't shoot into it unless you are intentionally trying to photograph a sunset or a silhouette.

 Some digital camera experts warn that shooting directly into the sun can damage the camera's sensor, much the way looking directly at the sun can hurt your eyes. The jury is actually out on this topic, but it's better to be safe than sorry—so don't make a habit of exposing pictures with the camera pointed directly at the sun.

Add Fill Flash

While most people think of their camera's flash as something to use at night or in the dark, it's also a great way to improve the look of your photographs in the daytime. Set your camera's flash to its forced flash mode, and use it to shoot portraits and other outdoor photographs. You'll find that the flash fills in shadows nicely, dramatically improving the quality of your images. You'll be surprised, in fact, at how much fill flash can do to improve photos that you thought were

4

FIGURE 4-4   A little fill flash can go a long way.

pretty good to begin with. Check out Figure 4-4, for instance. Here you can see two portraits—one with a fill flash, and one without. Remember, you'll need to be fairly close for this to work. Stay within 10 to 15 feet of your subject.

Shooting Silhouettes

It's easy to photograph a silhouette—in fact, new photographers do it all the time. They just don't always do it on purpose.

The easiest way to photograph a silhouette is simply to position yourself so that the subject you would like to silhouette is arranged against a bright background, such as the sky. Point the camera directly into the sky and slightly depress your camera's shutter release—that locks in the exposure based on the bright sky. Then recompose your picture and shoot. What you'll probably get is a grossly underexposed subject, since the exposure was based on the brighter sky, as in the image below. If your subject isn't quite silhouetted, you can underexpose the image even more using the Exposure Value (EV) controls on your camera. You might also want to use your camera's spot meter (discussed in Chapter 5) to lock the exposure on a bright piece of sky.

You may find that the subject is out of focus because the camera locked its focus on infinity when you pointed it at the sky. If that's the case, check to see if your camera has a separate exposure lock button, and use it. If not, you may need to set the exposure manually (or use the EV control) or focus the camera manually instead. One way or the other, if your subject is too close to focus at infinity, you need to find a way to separate the exposure and focusing aspects of your camera.

Reflect Some Light

A second source of light is just the ticket to eliminate shadows, reduce contrast, and even out the lighting in your pictures. Sometimes you can do that with fill flash, and sometimes a small reflector will do the job.

A reflector is often better than a flash because the light from a reflector is softer, and that typically makes better pictures. In other words, it's always better to use natural light, which includes reflecting it, than to use an electronic flash.

There are two ways to get into reflectors: the cheap way and the expensive way. Believe it or not, you don't need an expensive reflector from your local photo shop in order to move light around—you can have a lot of success using a glossy white sheet of poster board. Purchase a sheet of poster board from your local art supply store for a dollar or two to try it out. The problem with poster board, of course, is that it is often difficult to carry around. For a more compact reflector solution, pick up a photo reflector at your local camera store. Personally, I really like PhotoFlex Litediscs. These clever little reflectors fold up so small that you can almost put them in your pocket. Take them out of the bag, however, and they pop open to a variety of handy sizes. I use a Litedisc that measures about 24 inches in diameter (see it in Figure 4-5), and I find that's a great size for most of the things that I want to photograph.

When you're ready to take a picture with your reflector, you'll probably need some help. It's fiendishly difficult to hold a reflector and take a picture at the same time. So instead of trying some feat of photographic gymnastics, ask an assistant to hold the reflector such that light reflects from the sky onto your subject. Try to hold the reflector to minimize shadows or illuminate the dark side of your subject.

Reflectors serve a second important purpose as well. When you're out in the field trying to take a picture, the wind can sometimes get in the way. You'll notice this most often when you're trying to take a close-up of a light, bendable subject

FIGURE 4-5   Instead of using a flash, ask someone to hold a reflector near your subject. By holding it level with the ground, you can reflect light up into the subject's face.

FIGURE 4-6   Reflectors can block the wind as well as reflect light.

like a flower. As I talk about in Chapter 5, just a little breeze can create an out-of-focus and blurry macro photo. The solution? Compose your picture so that you can use the reflector not only to add light to the scene, but also to serve as a wind break. That's right, reflectors can block the breeze and give you a more stable picture. See Figure 4-6 for a look at how you can use a reflector this way.

A common way to use a reflector is to hold it roughly parallel to the ground, just under a person's face. That throws light upward, into the shadowy areas of the face, giving you softer, more even illumination.

Improve Your Indoor Photographs

Indoors, we are often much less concerned about harsh sunlight than we are about having enough light and light of the proper color. The evil red eye is also the nemesis of many indoor photographs. For common snapshots, there's probably nothing wrong with simply using your flash and leaving the camera in its fully automatic mode. But if you want to get really good at indoor photos, there are a few things you can do to shift the odds in your favor.

4

Bounce Your Light

If your digital camera has a hot shoe (a rectangular connection on the top of your camera for attaching a flash unit) or an input for a flash synch cable, you can attach external flash units for additional light and control over your images. I love using external flash units because the flash head tilts. That means you can tilt the flash so that it reflects light off the ceiling or a wall, thus diffusing the light and creating a softer effect. Be sure that you're not reflecting light off of colored walls, though, or the reflected light might paint your subject some horrible shade of yellow. You may also want to disable the built-in flash in your camera if you use an external flash. Check the camera's menu system for flash controls. Try it both ways, though, since some pictures can benefit from dual flash units, arriving on the scene from different directions.

Use Window Light

The best light is natural light. Whenever possible, position your subject near a window so that you can take advantage of the natural light pouring into your house. If you want to try the window technique, here are a few tips:

- Avoid using windows where the light streams in directly and thus creates harsh shadows. Instead, pick a window in which you get more diffused, indirect light.

- Position yourself with your back to the window and turn your subject to face mostly head-on into the window, with some light spilling over to the side of the subject's face.

- If necessary, fill in the side of the subject's face with a reflector to eliminate shadows. You can also use your camera's flash as a fill flash.

Avoid Red Eye

As I mentioned earlier in the chapter, the dreaded red eye is the effect that happens when the flash reflects off your subject's pupils. You can get this effect with any living subject—although, if you've all seen the *Omen* movies, it looks particularly creepy on dogs. Red eye happens most frequently indoors and outdoors at night because everyone's pupils are wide open to see better in dim indoor light.

Once you understand what causes red eye, it's easy to prevent. Here are the most common ways to avoid red eye:

- *Use the red eye reduction mode on your digital camera.* This is the easiest solution most of the time. When you turn on the red eye reduction mode, your camera triggers the flash several times rapidly right before the picture is taken. When you use this mode, remember the delay between when you press the shutter release and when the picture is actually taken—often, about a second. That doesn't sound like much, but it's enough to make you move the camera and ruin the picture if you're not paying attention.

- *Use an external flash off-camera.* If you have a digital camera with a hot shoe for an external flash, or one that includes a flash synch cable port, you can connect external flash units. The Nikon CoolPix 995, for instance, lets you connect as many as five separate flash units to the camera. The cool thing about using a separate flash is that you can hold it away from the camera. The farther you get the flash away from the camera lens (to the left or right of the camera), the less susceptible your picture will be to red eye, since the light won't reflect directly back to the camera.

- *Photograph people outdoors, or near windows.* If you can arrange your subjects near a bright source of natural light, you can avoid the red eye problem entirely because their pupils will already be closed due to the strong light source.

Correct the Color Balance

The color of artificial light is dramatically different from natural outdoor light. In fact, every kind of artificial light has its own unique properties. And that means that different kinds of artificial light have subtly different colors.

It is because of these variations in color that many indoor photographs simply don't look natural. Your camera has a way to adjust for these different light sources. Called *white balance,* it will help you to make sure that you get natural colors in your pictures regardless of what kind of artificial light you use. If you find that the automatic white balance setting in your camera gives you unpredictable results, then be sure to read the next section, and manually adjust your camera's white balance before every indoor photographic session.

Correcting Images with White Balance

As I mentioned above, many digital cameras come with a control for something called white balance. White balance is important because different light sources

4

have different *color temperatures,* meaning that a scene will appear to have a slightly different color tone depending on how it is illuminated.

You have probably noticed this yourself without really even paying attention. You may have seen, for instance, that ordinary light bulbs appear more yellow than the light that streams in from outdoors. And other sources—like candlelight and fluorescent lighting—are certainly a very different color than sunlight.

Photographers and scientists have gone to the trouble of cataloging the different color temperatures exhibited by various light sources. Lower temperatures appear warm, or slightly reddish, while warmer light sources tend to add a blue tone to your pictures. It's not at all unlike the way a flame has different colors at its outside and center. Why? Because those different parts of the flame are different temperatures.

As a point of comparison, this chart shows the approximate color temperatures of several common light sources:

Source	Color Temperature (Degrees Kelvin)
Candlelight	2,000
Sunset	2,000–3,000
Tungsten light	3,200
Fluorescent light	5,000
Daylight	5,500
Camera flash	5,600–6,000
Overcast sky	6,000–7,000

If your camera is balanced for one kind of light source (daylight, for instance) and you photograph a scene that has been illuminated by a very different temperature of light (such as tungsten), the resulting image won't reflect the true colors in the scene. What should be white will turn out looking somewhat reddish. Ordinarily, we don't notice this ourselves because, as I've said before, the human brain is very good at interpreting what the eyes see. Our brain adjusts for different color temperatures so that white almost always looks white, no matter what color light we're seeing it in. Of course, cameras aren't quite that smart. And that's why we need a white balance adjustment.

The white balance setting on your camera allows you to specify exactly what the color temperature of the scene is. In many cases, your camera can automatically adjust to conditions—but your camera often guesses wrong and gets the improper white balance fairly often. If need be, you can do it yourself. You'll know that you need to adjust the white balance if your pictures routinely come out shifted to the blue or red end of the spectrum. If your whites are not white—in other words, your camera doesn't do a good job of correcting the white balance—then you need to do it yourself.

TIP   *If you get in the habit of manually adjusting the white balance, remember to reset the white balance to auto when you are done with each shoot. Otherwise, you might forget that your camera is balanced for fluorescent light when you shoot outdoors, and you'll get very funky results.*

Adjusting White Balance Presets

Most digital cameras let you choose from a small collection of white balance presets. In addition to automatic white balance selection, your camera probably includes white balance settings for conditions such as incandescent lights, fluorescent lights, an external flash unit, and cloudy or overcast days.

Choosing a White Balance Preset

Changing your white balance setting varies from camera to camera, but the process is typically fairly simple. For the specifics on your camera model, check your camera's user guide. In general though, this is the process:

1. Turn your camera on and set it to its normal record mode. If your camera has a separate record mode specifically for manual photography, you'll probably need this one instead.

2. Press the menu button on your camera so that you see a set of menus in the LCD display.

3. Find the option for white balance.

4. Scroll through the white balance options until you find the lighting conditions that best represent your scene.

5. Press the menu button again to turn off the menus. You can now take your picture.

Measuring White Balance Yourself

Sometimes these white balance presets just don't get the job done. If you are in a tricky lighting situation, such as a room that has both incandescent light and candlelight, you may need to set the white balance manually based on the actual lighting conditions in the room.

4

One of the hardest lighting situations on planet earth is a school gymnasium. Because of the way gyms are lit, no white balance preset ever seems to work properly. For best results—and to avoid the inevitable yellow cast in your photos—try to arrive early and manually set the white balance with the help of a white or gray card.

This may sound complicated, but it's really not that hard. Before you start, you'll simply need one additional item: a white surface that the camera can use to set the white balance. Typically, you can get by with a small square of white poster board or typing paper. For better and more consistent results, though, I recommend that you purchase an 18-percent gray card from your local photo shop. Professional photographers use these small gray cards to judge exposure all the time, since the exposure meters in most cameras assume that images average out to about 18 percent gray overall. You can get a gray card for just a few dollars, and you'll be surprised at how handy it is for setting white balance.

So, here is how to set the white balance yourself:

1. Ask your subject or an assistant to hold the gray card with the gray side facing you. Make sure the card is where you're actually going to take the picture, so you are measuring the actual light as it will be in your scene.

2. Turn on your camera and set it to the record mode.

3. Activate the menu system on your LCD display.

4. Find the white balance controls in the menu system.

5. Scroll through the white balance until you find the option to record it yourself. Select this option.

6. You should now see something on the LCD display directing you to photograph a white object. Compose your scene so that the gray card— or whatever you are using to set the white balance—fills the frame.

7. Take the picture and exit the menu system.

The camera will now expose any pictures you take using this new white balance value. Be sure to reset the white balance back to automatic when you're done taking these pictures; otherwise, you may try taking pictures a day or two later in very different lighting conditions and get bizarre results because the white balance is completely askew.

NOTE   *Many cameras set white balance in the way described above, but your camera may do it slightly differently. Refer to your camera's user manual for exact details.*

Trying Your Hand at Night Photography

Taking pictures at night is a rewarding, exciting activity; unfortunately, digital cameras don't always make it easy to do. On the plus side, taking pictures with a digital camera is essentially free, since you're not buying film. So you can experiment to your heart's content without wasting any film.

Experiment with White Balance

Don't think that white balance is only used to get perfectly white whites in your pictures. Certainly, that is the reason most people use this mode. On the other hand, photography is an art, not a science. By changing the white balance values of your camera, you can get some creative results that you might like better than if the white balance were set properly. As one example, I sometimes like the warmer colors I can get by misadjusting the white balance when shooting portraits. By making my subject's face a bit redder, I think the photo looks richer and more lifelike. Try it yourself and remember that photography is all about trying new things. Check out Color Figure 3 to see how the same picture can look quite different depending on the white balance settings.

Not every camera is cut out for night photography. Low-light photography requires long exposure times; if your digital camera is not capable of shutter speeds of one second or more, you will probably have some trouble getting decent night shots. In fact, your camera should have a manual exposure mode so you can dial in the shutter speed by hand. Automatic exposure settings may not give you anything even remotely interesting. If you're shopping for a camera and are specifically interested in night shots, try to get a camera with a bulb setting—that's photography lingo for a shutter that stays open for as long as you hold the shutter release down—or at least a maximum shutter speed of eight seconds. Not all night exposures are measured in seconds, though. I captured this image with a tripod and only about a one-second exposure, something virtually any digital camera should be able to do:

TIP   *A camera with a wireless remote control can also be handy for night photography because you can activate the shutter without shaking the camera. If you don't have a remote, then you might want to trigger the camera with the self-timer feature.*

TIP   *If your camera does not let you manually choose the shutter speed and aperture, try using its EV adjustment to overexpose your picture by one, two, or even three stops. For example, set your camera to EV –3, focus the camera on the darkest part of the scene, and then shoot.*

Take Your First Night Shots

So, you're ready to take your first pictures at night. I recommend that you choose an interesting locale to begin with. Go downtown, where there are lots of neon store lights and cars with headlights on. Alternatively, try a local carnival or fairground. The idea is to find a location that has lots of interesting lights and motion.

To take your first night pictures, do this:

1. Mount your camera on a tripod. Your exposure times will be a half second or longer; there is absolutely no way you can hold the camera for that amount of time without introducing an incredible amount of blur.

2. Switch your camera to its manual exposure mode, if it has one. Set the aperture to a medium setting, such as f/5.6. Set the shutter speed to 1/2.

3. Point the camera at something interesting. If this is the first time you are trying night photography, I suggest you go to a fairly busy intersection downtown and frame the street and a store or two in your viewfinder.

4. When a car is about to enter your viewfinder, take the picture. You should be able to get fairly instant feedback on how your picture came out by looking at it in the camera's LCD display. No matter how good or bad the picture came out, do not delete it.

5. Now double the shutter speed. Try an exposure of one second, and shoot the same scene again.

6. Take more pictures, varying the shutter speed so you can get a feel for what kind of results your camera gives at night at various shutter speeds. You will very likely find that your camera won't expose a picture for more than a few seconds; many cameras limit the shutter speed to five or ten seconds. That's OK—just work your way up until you hit your camera's maximum shutter speed.

7. If your camera automatically records exposure information for each picture, great. If not, write down all of your exposure information so you'll remember what you did later and learn from your efforts.

FIGURE 4-7   Longer exposure times lead to longer light trails and brighter points of light.

After you've taken a batch of night shots, you can compare your pictures side by side and see the effect of increasing exposure time. As you can see from Figure 4-7, there is no such thing as the "one perfect exposure" in a night photograph. Increasing the exposure means longer light trails and brighter points of light. Eventually, too much exposure time will lead to obviously overexposed images and perhaps digital noise (which I discuss in the next section). But for the most part, the exposure you choose is a matter of personal taste.

CCDs and Noise

Night photography is a little trickier with a digital camera than with a 35mm SLR. Don't get me wrong—film has its own problems. *Reciprocity failure,* for instance, is a phenomenon that affects 35mm film. What it means is that film reacts somewhat unpredictably during very long exposures, such as at night. Film is designed to be exposed to light for a fraction of a second; so if you leave the shutter open for ten seconds, the reliable relationship between the aperture size and shutter speed begins to fail. That makes night photography for 35mm photographers something of a guessing game.

Don't trust your camera's exposure meter at night. You might want to start with whatever your camera's meter suggests, but you can almost always get more interesting pictures by doubling or tripling the shutter speed that's suggested by the camera.

For digital photography, we have a completely different problem to contend with. When you expose a CCD to light, it gets hot. This heat manifests itself in the form of

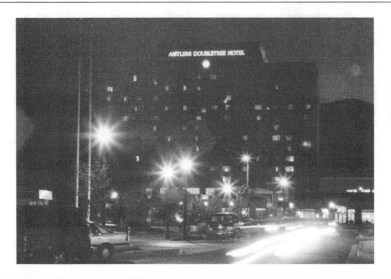

FIGURE 4-8   CCDs are not always optimized to take long exposures at night.

noise in your final picture. After all, light and heat are forms of energy, and the heat energy collecting on the CCD has a negative effect on the picture. For short exposures, this is rarely, if ever, an issue. You might see some noise in your picture if you set the camera's ISO value to a very high number when you're shooting in bright light, but usually the shutter speed is so short that there is little time for the CCD to generate noise in the final image. When you are measuring the exposure in seconds, however, noise can build up quickly. Take a look at Figure 4-8. Here you can see how digital noise affects a picture when the shutter speed is more than a few seconds long.

Some cameras are designed to minimize this noise that occurs with long exposures. The CCD is built directly onto a heat sink to carry excess energy away during long exposures. Other digital cameras don't have such a feature, however. Instead, there are three ways to minimize this effect:

- Keep the shutter speed as short as possible.

- If it has one, turn on your camera's noise reduction feature—it often does wonders for minimizing digital noise.

- As a last resort, run a noise reduction or despeckle filter on your picture in an image editor after you transfer it to the computer.

Cool Things to Photograph at Night

There are all kinds of things to photograph when the sun goes down, and each one requires a somewhat different technique. Here are some suggestions to get you started:

- **The moon**   When shooting the moon, remember that it is a very bright object. The Sunny 16 Rule (discussed in Chapter 2) may work for you in this situation, but I've found that many cameras get confused by the dramatic variation in brightness with shots like this, so you may need to experiment a bit. If you can get enough magnification out of your lens so that the moon fills up at least half of the frame, you'll need to shoot at fairly fast shutter speed or even set the EV to underexpose the frame. And be sure to use a tripod.

- **Sunset**   The sky is full of rich, gorgeous colors around sunset. Base your exposure on the sky itself, not on your subject or anything on the ground. And take a few extra pictures, bracketing your exposure (see Chapter 2 for details) to make sure you get the shot.

- **Dusk**   I have found that photographing lighted buildings and headlight trails works particularly well when you can get the rich blue colors of dusk in the sky at the same time.

4

Chapter 5

Taking Close-Ups

How to...

- Set your camera to its close-focus mode

- Close-focus a manual-focus camera

- Ensure proper focus when shooting very close-up

- Use the correction marks in the optical viewfinder

- Use optional close-focus lenses

- Interpret diopter numbers

- Configure a tripod for semi-steady macro shots

- Blur the background

- Maximize your depth of field for sharper pictures

- Eliminate reflections from glass display cases

Close-up photography, also known as *macro photography,* is one of the most exciting ways to experiment with your digital camera. It's a whole different world down there when you get within a few inches of your subject; we're used to seeing things from five or six feet off the ground. But when you're within an inch or so of your subject and it's magnified to several times its normal size, photography suddenly seems like magic.

You might think I'm exaggerating, but macro photography really is a lot of fun. And just because you have a digital camera—not a multithousand-dollar large-format camera—don't think that you can't play along. Certainly, having a digital camera means that you may have to shoot your close-ups in a different way than traditional photographers do. But that is true of any kind of camera when shooting close-ups. Each format has its own unique characteristics, and here in the land of digital photography we will talk about how to get the most out of your digital camera when you are taking pictures in the Lilliputian world.

Capturing the Microscopic World

First of all, let's talk about some terminology. When we discuss close-up photography, what we really mean is macro photography. We're not talking about close-ups in the portraiture sense—there are no "I'm ready for my close-up, Mr. DeMille" situations in this chapter. I hope I didn't disappoint you.

Instead, close-up photography is all about photographing the world around us to capture small objects, highly magnified. That usually means getting pretty close to the subject—like within a few inches, as in this shot:

Using 35mm SLR equipment or even larger gear, such as medium- and large-format cameras, you can get incredibly magnified views of small subjects. You could magnify the eyes of a fly to fill up an 8×10-inch print. In digital photography, we typically can't get quite as close as that, though we can take impressive close-ups nonetheless. If you would be happy with getting the fly itself blown up to 8×10 inches, then keep reading.

Coaxing a Digital Camera to Take Close-Ups

Virtually every digital camera on the market has a close-focus mode. Such a mode exists because the camera lens typically can't focus properly when you get very close—within inches—of a subject. The optics must be rearranged to accommodate such close focusing. How that mode works, though, depends on whether your camera has a fixed-focus or autofocus lens.

Autofocus Cameras

In cameras with autofocus lenses (and that represents about 98 percent of the cameras on the market today), you usually enter close-focus mode (also called *macro* mode) by pressing a button on the camera body and sometimes spinning a dial or turning a navigation wheel at the same time to make the appropriate selection. A tulip shape typically represents close-focus; you should see a button somewhere on your camera with such a symbol. Can't find it? On a few cameras, the macro mode is buried in the onscreen menu on the LCD.

You can see a typical close-focus button control in Figure 5-1. Often, camera buttons perform more than one function. You might need to press the button several times to cycle through the various modes before the macro mode is actually enabled, or you might need to hold the button down while turning a selector dial. When you're in macro mode, it's usually indicated by a tulip somewhere on the camera's LCD display. That tulip is a reminder that you are in close-focus mode, and you will get sharp focus when shooting very close to the subject. (Often, the effective macro range is in the neighborhood of 8 to 30 inches, though some cameras can focus to within an inch or so of the subject.) In addition, some digital cameras require your zoom lens to be within a certain macro range—zoom in too far, and the camera won't be able to focus properly. If in doubt, check your camera's manual.

Fixed-Focus Cameras

Though they are increasingly rare, fixed-focus cameras still exist. If you have one of these relics, I suggest you upgrade to an autofocus camera as soon as possible. Nonetheless, even these models usually include a close-focus mode, though it's harder to use. You might need to slide a manual-focusing dial or lever to get your picture in the proper focus (as in the ancient Canon PowerShot pictured in Figure 5-2), or you might need to position your camera a specific distance from the subject. Some fixed-focus cameras require you to be at a specific distance when shooting macros—around eight inches. As you might surmise, it's not easy to capture good, sharp photos when you have such a rigid focusing distance.

Tulip ——

FIGURE 5-1   Follow the tulip on your camera to find the close-focus or "macro" mode.

FIGURE 5-2   If your camera has a fixed-focus lens, for the love of God, throw it away! It may focus only at a precise distance or have a manual focus control for close-ups.

 Ensure Good Focus in Close-Up Mode

Close-focus photography is a bit temperamental. For starters, the acceptable focusing distance for macro lenses is much shorter than in the normal photo world. You should check your camera manual to discover what the minimum and maximum focus distances are for your camera's lens. Typically, you might be able to get as close as five inches or as far away as three feet. These numbers vary, though.

Here's what you should do when you're trying to take a close-up photo:

1. Verify the close-focusing range of your camera.

2. Press the macro button on your camera to enter the close-focus mode.

3. Position your camera in front of the subject somewhere inside the range.

4. Press the shutter release down half-way to lock in exposure and focus. Look for the camera's visual focus indicator. (Most cameras use a light near the viewfinder to indicate that the image is in focus.)

5. If you're having trouble getting the image in focus, point the camera at an edge or some sharply-defined region of the subject (without changing the distance to the subject). This may help the camera lock onto the subject. Or you can carry a small card with sharply defined black-and-white stripes on it (a business card and a magic marker is all you need). If you're having trouble getting good focus, hold the card right next to the subject and get the camera to focus-lock on that instead. Also, some digital cameras have trouble focusing in low light; you might want to carry an inexpensive light that you can use to illuminate the subject when focusing.

6. When you're ready, take the picture by pressing the rest of the way down on the shutter release.

That's it in a nutshell—the point is that you need to be very sensitive to focus when shooting close-ups, and you may need to reorient the camera slightly to get a good, solid-focus lock. Also, when you do get a lock, make sure that you're actually focused on the right subject. The depth of field is quite shallow at this close distance to your subject, and it's easy to get an out-of-focus image.

 When you're done shooting in macro mode, be certain to return the camera to its ordinary focusing mode or you'll end up with a memory card full of out-of-focus images!

Close-Up Enemy No. 1: Parallax

Most digital cameras are of the point-and-shoot variety, as I mentioned back in Chapter 1. Point-and-shoot cameras are models that don't show you an accurate representation of the actual scene in the optical viewfinder. Instead, using the viewfinder is like looking through one window in your house, while someone else looks through a nearby window. You both see essentially the same scene, though they are not identical. If the two if you look to the horizon, for instance, the two scenes are virtually indistinguishable. If you're both looking at a person walking toward the house, though, as the person gets closer and closer, your two views become increasingly different.

And that is what it is like when you look through the optical viewfinder and the camera uses the nearby lens to take the photograph. SLR-style cameras don't have this problem, because the optical viewfinder actually looks through the lens right up until the moment of exposure.

The problem, as you have probably guessed, manifests itself when you try to take a close-up with a point-and-shoot digital camera. Since your subject is only a few inches away, the difference in view between the viewfinder and the lens means that you're not even looking at what the lens is about to take a picture of. That's why most digital cameras have indicators in the optical viewfinder. Called *close-focus marks, parallax marks,* or *correction marks,* these lines show you how to line up the photograph when you are shooting a close-up. See Figure 5-3, for instance. Here, you can see the effect of parallax on a photo. The image on the left represents what I saw in the viewfinder; the image on the right represents what the lens actually photographed.

Framing a Close-Up

So, now you understand the principle behind parallax and close-up photography. Let's apply this so you can see how to take a close-up photo.

Look through your camera's optical viewfinder. Hopefully, you can see some correction marks. If the lens is located to the right of the optical viewfinder (as it is in most cameras), you should see correction marks on the left side of the

FIGURE 5-3   You can't trust your window-style viewfinder when taking close-ups because it sees a slightly different scene than your lens does.

viewfinder. Why is that? Well, these marks represent the left edge of the photo when shooting at close distances. Since the lens is off to the right of the viewfinder, you will need to point the camera slightly to the left in order to take the picture you desire. In actual operation, just recompose the scene so the correction marks help frame the left edge of your picture.

You might have correction marks at the top or bottom of the viewfinder as well. If the lens is below the optical viewfinder (as it often is), correction marks at the top of the frame show you how to reorient the camera slightly higher than you would otherwise.

If all this is just a little confusing, take a look at Figure 5-4. Here, you can see how I have oriented my camera to use the correction marks at close distance.

Correction marks are a guide to help you frame macro photographs. But there are some very important things to remember about correction marks:

- *Correction marks are only approximate.* They help you adjust for parallax error, but they are not perfect. This should be obvious when you realize that parallax varies depending on your distance from the subject.

- *Correction marks work only at close range.* Parallax, by definition, diminishes with distance from the subject. At ordinary distances, you don't need to worry about the marks at all. In fact, if you use them when shooting a subject that is ten feet away, they will simply introduce

Correction marks indicate left edge of photo when close

FIGURE 5-4   The correction marks help you overcome composition errors caused by parallax.

composition error in exactly the opposite direction. Remember though, that they are important when using your macro mode.

■ *You can avoid using correction marks entirely.* Instead of relying on the optical viewfinder when shooting close-ups, try to use the camera's LCD display instead. The LCD display shows you almost exactly what the lens sees, and therefore there's no parallax at all when using it.

TIP *Whenever possible, frame your macro shots with the LCD viewfinder. The only time that may not work is in very bright sunlight, when the LCD is too difficult to see.*

Using Add-On Lenses

The macro mode built into your digital camera is certainly a nice start for taking close-up pictures, and you can get some pretty good results with it. But if you yearn for greater magnification than your camera is capable of providing, there is an answer: add-on lenses.

Many cameras are designed to accommodate additional lenses and filters. Of course, SLR-style digital cameras with interchangeable lenses spring directly to mind. Cameras such as the Nikon D100 accept all of the traditional 35mm lenses in the Nikon family, and the Canon D60 works with a whole slew of Canon lenses. Many of these lenses have macro modes that allow you to get excellent magnification.

But what if you're not using a camera like that?

Actually, many digital cameras accept add-on lenses as well. These are lenses that snap or screw on to the front of your camera's built-in lens. Sometimes, the manufacturer sells add-on lenses for its own models, such as the Kodak DC 4800 in Figure 5-5. In other cases, your camera may have standard threads on the front of the lens, in which case you can visit your local camera shop or search online for filters and lenses that fit.

TIP *You can look online for data on lenses for your camera. First, check out the camera manufacturer's Web site for compatible accessories, including lenses. Also visit Tiffen (www.tiffen.com) and Raynox (www.digitaletc.com). Tiffen is the largest manufacturer of add-on lenses for digital cameras, and it's likely to have something for your camera; while Raynox has a variety of macro lenses as well. Last, but not least, camera-depot.com has a great selection of common lenses and filters in stock, and they ship promptly.*

FIGURE 5-5   Many cameras are compatible with snap-on or screw-on lenses that provide telephoto, wide-angle, and macro capabilities.

The most common close-up lenses for digital cameras look like the ones shown in Figure 5-6. The macro filters in Figure 5-6 have 62mm threads, making them ideal for cameras such as the Olympus e10 and e20n. This set of four, in fact, sells for about $40. Such filters are usually made from a single element of glass and are threaded to screw onto the front of the camera lens, an adapter, or even each other. Of course, the specific close-up filters you get will depend on the size of the lens on your digital camera.

That's right—you can actually combine close-up lenses by threading them together. Adding a +1 lens to a +2 lens, for instance, yields an impressive +3 magnification. For that reason, I suggest getting close-up lenses as a set instead of one at a time. That way, you can combine them however you see fit to get the magnification you need for a given picture. Check out Figure 5-7. This picture shows the effect of four different magnifications: the camera's built-in macro capability, in addition to various combinations of +1, +2, and +4 filters.

NOTE   *If you add too many close-up lenses, you can start to get a vignette effect—that's when the lens and filters get in the way and cut off the corners of your picture. You can see an example of vignetting in Chapter 6.*

FIGURE 5-6   A typical set of close-up lenses

TIP

When combining close-up lenses, put the highest magnification on first, closest to the camera lens. That way, you can remove the lenses in smaller increments to achieve just the right magnification. Also, you may find that some lens combinations cause your images to curve unnaturally, thanks to something called "barrel distortion," discussed in Chapter 6.

Understanding Macro Lens Lingo

With rare exception, close-up lenses are not described in terms of focal length, as are other lenses. That's because they're essentially just magnifying glasses that go in front of the camera's normal lens. Instead, close-focus lenses are described using the term *diopter.*

A diopter is an indirect measure of focal length. It tells you both how close you can get to the subject and what relative magnification the lens provides. Specifically, the diopter number indicates how close your camera lens can focus with the lens set to infinity and the close-up lens attached, in fractions of a meter. A +2 rating will let your camera focus 1/2 meter away, while a +3 rating focuses at 1/3 meter away, and so on. Believe it or not, these diopter numbers hold true no matter what the focal length of your camera lens. Close-up lenses typically come in a variety of strengths, from +1 to +10.

FIGURE 5-7   These images show the differing magnification effect of the Olympus e20n's standard macro mode, plus varying intensities of screw-on macro filters.

Close-Up Techniques

As I've already mentioned, taking close-up pictures is a very different experience from taking images at ordinary focal lengths. Though it's not particularly difficult to get really good macro photos, it does take a little more care and a slightly different approach.

First of all, you'll find that your subjects are slightly different in macro photography. Obviously, you won't be taking a lot of people pictures from two inches away. There are numerous choices, however. I suggest that you start by taking pictures of things that don't move, such as in the example shown here:

5

Once you have coins and stamps pretty well in hand, you can move on to photographing insects, flowers, and other mobile or semi-mobile subjects.

In fact, lots of subjects look radically different at close range and magnified than they appear from a human perspective. Some subjects can even take on an almost fractal appearance—that is, their underlying structure can seem to have a nearly infinite amount of complexity, as you can see from these ice crystals on a tree branch, captured on a chilly April morning:

That's why I think macro photos make for some very exciting images. Here are a few subjects you might want to consider trying your hand at:

- Hobby subjects such as stamps, coins, and models
- Wildlife such as plants, flowers, leaves, insects, and butterflies
- Found objects such as rubber bands, paperclips, and fabric
- Snow, ice, and water

A Steady Base

Without a doubt, you should invest in a tripod if you plan to take many close-up photographs. Although you can get away with holding the camera in your hands most of the time, the extreme magnification provided by close-up lenses tends to make even the most subtle shake ruin your picture. In close-up photography, I highly recommend planting your camera securely on the floor, or ground, with a tripod.

You do not need to purchase a large or particularly heavy tripod. Some of the very large tripods that feature separate, expensive head units are designed for the rigors of 35mm photography, where the camera itself can weigh over 10 pounds. Most digital cameras only weigh a pound or two, so, in many situations, a lightweight tripod is sufficient.

> TIP   *Even if you have a digital camera, the outdoors can be unkind to your photos. If you're shooting in the wind, the heavier your tripod is, the better—especially for a light digital camera. A light camera is more likely to be blown around than a heavy one. If you have a light tripod, you can hang something heavy from the center of the tripod to help stabilize it. Of course, in a strong wind, it'll also be hard to keep your subject still unless you have some means to block the wind.*

When you set your camera up on the tripod, you can leave the head unit somewhat loose. That helps you move the camera around and position it with minimal fuss. This is really up to you—try leaving the head a little loose, and if you can consistently get sharp images, work this way. If you find that your images are always a bit blurry and you think it's because you're leaving the head unit loose, then tighten everything up before you take your picture.

Here's a perfect example: In Figure 5-8, you see a bee that I photographed hovering around a columbine. If I had tightened down every knob and lever on my tripod, there's no way I could have caught the little guy as it flitted around somewhat randomly. Instead, the tripod gave me the support I needed, and I left the head unit loose so I could move the camera around to catch the bee at just the right moment.

FIGURE 5-8   A loose tripod head comes in handy when you're taking pictures of moving insects.

Bean Bag Camera Supports

I heartily recommend getting a tripod. The problem with tripods, though, is that they're bulky and are a pain to carry around, and heavier ones always tend to work better than lighter ones. What's one to do?

Well, you can carry a bean bag instead.

I'm not suggesting bean bags as the ultimate, full-time replacement for tripods, but I have run into situations when they can steady your camera in a pinch. If you have something you'd like to lean the camera on top of, such as a fence post, a boulder, or even the ground, try putting a bean bag under the camera. It'll conform to the shape of the camera as well as to the shape of whatever you're placing the camera on, and the dense clump of beans in the bag will help steady the camera as you press the shutter release.

And if you don't have a bean bag, improvise. As a scuba diver, for instance, I always have bags of soft weights when I go on dive trips. They're filled with small beads of lead shot, and aside from being a lot heavier, they act a lot like bean bags.

Finally, if you want a bean bag that has been designed especially for photographers, check out The Pod, a bean bag–style camera support with a tripod bolt sticking out of the top. It's available for about $15 from www.thepod.ca.

Keep the Subject Sharp

In Chapter 3, I spent a lot of time talking about depth of field. If there were ever a time when depth of field was important, this is it. The reason? At high magnification in very short focusing distances, depth of field becomes vanishingly small. In fact, it's not unusual to find that the total depth of field in a close-up photograph is only about half an inch. In Figure 5-9, for instance, you can see that only part of the flower is in sharp focus, while most of the image is blurred. Even parts of the flower are out of sharp focus. Or go back and check out the photo series in Figure 5-7. As you move from picture to picture, the magnification gets greater, and you can actually see the depth of field get smaller and smaller in each image.

FIGURE 5-9   It's easy to blur the background in a close-up; the hard part is getting everything you want to be in focus actually in focus.

That said, the focusing range of your camera is always at a premium in close-up photography. Even if you want your background to be out of focus, you often want the most depth of field you can possibly get your hands on, since the background will almost certainly be out of focus anyway.

Here are a few things you should keep in mind to help you control the depth of field in your photograph:

- **Distance**   Remember that the closer you get to your subject, the less depth of field you will have available. So to regain depth of field, back away from your subject. To do that, you may have to remove a close-up lens from the front of your camera if you're using one or more add-on lenses.

- **Aperture**   Another way to increase depth of field is to close the aperture as much as possible. You may need to enter your camera's aperture priority or manual exposure mode to control this.

- **Light**   The more light available, the more you can close the aperture. You can use the camera's built-in flash, an external flash if your camera allows it, or just shoot in situations where there is a lot of natural light.

CAUTION *Be careful when you compose your picture so that the subject is parallel to the lens, not perpendicular. If your subject has depth with respect to the axis of your lens, part of it will be in focus and part of it will not. When you can, turn the subject or the camera so that the entire length of the object is in sharp focus.*

Mind the Background

The background is an important part of your photograph. In general, you probably want your background to be fairly indistinct. As luck would have it, that is not too hard to do in a close-up photograph. After all, there's precious little depth of field to begin with, so the background will probably be blurry. Here are a few tips for tweaking the background of your photograph:

- *Turn it black.* If you use your flash, you'll throw so much light onto the primary subject that the background—especially if it is more than a few inches away from the subject—will be black. This is a good effect in certain situations, but it doesn't look particularly natural. That's why many professional macro photographers avoid using flash units when shooting flowers in the field.

- *Use a plain background.* You can insert a prepared background—a piece of poster board, for example—between the main subject and a distracting background. If the poster board is far enough away, it'll be out of focus and give you a plain, diffused look. I use big slabs of colored foam board from the local hobby and craft store for this purpose.

- *Blur it out of existence.* As I have already mentioned, depth of field is perhaps your most powerful tool when taking close-ups. You can check how much depth of field you currently have by half-depressing the shutter release. The camera's LCD display will show you the image with the aperture closed to the appropriate level, and that will give you your final depth of field. If you need more or less depth of field, let go of the shutter release and tweak the camera settings. Just check your depth of field over and over in the camera's display until you are happy with the result. I took the image shown in Figure 5-10 with a very wide aperture to blur the background while keeping the monk's head flower quite sharp.

Beware of the Flash

You might start to get the impression that I am not a big fan of the electronic flash unit built into many digital cameras. Flashes that have limited range can make your pictures look artificial and can sometimes create harsh shadows. Nonetheless, flash units are admittedly an essential tool, and I don't hesitate to use them when needed.

On the other hand, you should be aware of two key limitations that may be inherent in your camera's flash unit when used in close-up photography:

■ **Overexposure**   Unfortunately, some digital camera flash units are not designed for very close range. When you're taking a close-up (and you're within, say, a few inches of your subject), most camera flash units won't fire at all (they're disabled in macro mode) or they'll badly overexpose the subject. Most flash units expect the subject to be several feet away and don't react well when the subject is much closer. You can find out very easily if your camera suffers from this problem. Just take a test picture or two and evaluate the results. Of course, there are workarounds to this problem. You can try underexposing the picture using the EV controls on your camera, or try a low-tech solution: lay a piece of thin tissue or some photo gel (available at any camera shop) in front of the flash to diffuse the light.

■ **Blockage**   Some flash units are positioned so that the lens itself blocks some of the light when the subject is too close to the camera. In my book (and hey! This *is* my book!), this is a camera design deficiency, plain and

FIGURE 5-10   This image was taken with a very wide aperture and no flash.

simple. Nonetheless, if your camera is affected by this particular glitch, it's easy to see for yourself. As in Figure 5-11, there will be a huge shadow in part of the picture where the lens got in the way of the flash. Ordinarily, your camera may not suffer from this problem, but it may become prone to light blockage if you add snap-on lenses.

Shooting Through Glass

Sometimes you might want to take a close-up of something that is under a sheet of glass—jewelry in a display case, for example. There's a common problem with this kind of subject, though: light from the sun or overhead lamps can reflect off the glass and cause unwanted glare in your picture. Not only is glare like this ugly, it can actually make it difficult to see what it is you were trying to photograph under the glass. The solution? Use a polarizing filter. A polarizer does a few nifty things for your photograph, but the most important one is that it eliminates reflections caused by glass and water by blocking polarized light.

Polarizing filters are sold in many sizes and for many digital cameras. It's not a bad idea to carry one in your camera bag for those occasions when it might come in handy. Polarizers are usually two-piece devices that rotate on the end of your camera—you turn the outer layer until the reflections are minimized.

FIGURE 5-11   Some cameras block the flash when the subject is too close; if yours does this, use only natural light to illuminate your subject.

CAUTION *You want a circular polarizing filter. You probably won't have trouble on that count, since most photographers today buy circular polarizers. But a less-common linear polarizer simply won't work right for you because it confuses the camera's light sensors.*

That may sound complicated, but it's actually pretty easy. The LCD display on your camera gives you immediate feedback on the effect of the filter. If you can see a reflection in the display, continue turning the polarizer until the reflection is gone (or at least minimized). Keep in mind that a polarizer is most effective when you photograph at a 34-degree angle from the reflective surface, as demonstrated in this illustration:

Not sure what 34 degrees works out to be? Just experiment a bit and you'll quickly find the right position. If you use your polarizer properly, you can reduce glare significantly—sometimes completely. In Figure 5-12, for instance, you can see the effect of a polarizing filter. The image on the left is uncorrected; it's what you would get without a polarizer. The image on the right has had its reflections stripped away using a polarizing filter.

Your Own Macro Studio

It's not always easy to get perfect results from close-up photography. There are so many elements to worry about: wind, lighting, the narrow focusing range, and limited depth of field. Lighting is especially tricky, in fact, because certain subjects look pretty bad when you hit them with an electronic flash. Lots of people try to photograph reflective items such as coins and jewelry, for instance, to sell on ebay.com or post on a Web site, and they're disappointed with the reflections from the flash.

Polarized has no effect   Polarized has maximum effect

FIGURE 5-12   By turning a polarizing filter on the end of your lens, you can minimize
the reflections caused by light and glass.

If you are excited about macro photography and expect to do a lot of it, you
might want to invest in a product called the Cloud Dome (available from
www.clouddome.com). This clever little gadget is a plastic dome (it looks like an
upside-down salad bowl) that covers your subject and has a hole at the top for
mounting your camera. The dome itself diffuses light from the outside,
illuminating the macro subject evenly and professionally. I swear by this gadget.

When using the Cloud Dome, you're shooting in a controlled environment. The dome takes care of the lighting, and it even blocks wind if you use it outdoors. The dome securely holds the camera in place, acting like a tripod. All you need to worry about is framing your subject and getting the focus sharp. If you need more light than what is getting through the dome, just shine a table lamp or some other sort of light at the dome. You can see the Cloud Dome ready to shoot in Figure 5-13.

On the downside, the Cloud Dome is not inexpensive—in fact, at about $200, it costs an awful lot of money. I've experimented with household items like oversized plastic food containers and lamp shades, though, and haven't come up with anything that works nearly as well as the Cloud Dome. Perhaps the best inexpensive substitute you can find is a small white umbrella.

5

FIGURE 5-13   The Cloud Dome comes with a bracket that fits almost any size of digital camera and creates a virtual studio in which you can make the focus and lighting perfect with little effort.

Chapter 6

Pushing Your Camera to Its Limits

How to...

- Take pictures in special color modes like black and white or sepia
- Determine when to use special color modes on the camera or wait and process images on the PC
- Shoot a series of panoramic photos
- Add wide-angle and telephoto lenses to your camera
- Avoid vignetting when using add-on lenses
- Correct for distortion caused by wide-angle lenses
- Interpret lens magnification numbers
- Take a series of time-lapse photos
- Turn time-lapse photos into a movie
- Extend the life of your camera's batteries

These days, cameras are no longer just cameras. Take a look at the most common cameras in the local computer or camera shop, and you'll find that many models are designed to record movies, take panoramic photographs, record sound, and do a host of other things as well. It seems that camera manufacturers think that if you like a camera, you'll like a camera that washes your dishes and plays music even better.

Most of this book concentrates on how to use your camera to take good pictures. A lot of the extra features that you find on cameras are, in my opinion, usually just gimmicks. On the other hand, every once in a while you may find a useful, creative application for one of the gizmos built into your camera. And that's where this chapter comes in: look here for information about all those other things your camera can do.

And that's not all. This chapter is about pushing your camera to its limits. That means we'll talk about how to do unusual things with your camera, such as use it to perform time-lapse photography. Your camera is no good without batteries, so we'll talk about how to get the most battery life out of your camera as well.

Get Creative

Your camera may come with photo modes besides the ones that we have already discussed, especially if it's a high-end model. The most common features you'll encounter in digital cameras are additional color modes. By setting your camera to the appropriate mode, you might be able to take pictures in black and white or with a sepia tone.

> **TIP**   *If your camera does not come with one of these special effects modes, you can always convert your images to black and white or sepia on a computer after you've taken them. Refer to Chapter 13 for information on how to do that.*

6

Using the black-and-white or sepia mode on your camera allows you to capture images that have a somewhat old-fashioned look. Very old photographs, of course, have a brownish tint that is called sepia that comes from the dyes that were used to print them.

You might also want to use the black-and-white mode if your final output is going to be in print, like a newsletter. Black-and-white images take up less space on a memory card, so you can typically take more black-and-white images than color images. Black-and-white images also make a strong artistic statement, so people use this mode to be creative. So if your pictures will be black and white in the end anyway, you might consider taking them in black and white to begin with.

The downside? If you might want some of those images in color for a different application, it's simply not possible to put the color back in later. If you're not sure how your images might be used, I recommend that you start with ordinary color and save them to your computer's hard disk in that format. Later, you can convert the images to black and white in an image-processing program if necessary.

In summary, here are the pros and cons of using the special effect modes on your camera:

Pros	Cons
Images typically take up less space.	If you later need the original color image, you won't have it.
You get a specific effect immediately without the need to process it on a computer.	If you forget to switch out of the selected mode, you may find a whole memory card full of sepia-toned images.

The Old-Fashioned Look

If you want an authentic-looking old-time photograph, you can get a pretty authentic imitation with your camera's sepia mode. People instantly recognize the brownish hue of the sepia-toned image as something that is quite old—or at least something that's supposed to look that way. But in addition to just using a little sepia color, there are other things you can do to ensure that the image looks more authentic. Try these tips:

- Pay attention to costumes and props. If your goal is to take a picture that is set in a specific period, it will look more authentic with the right garb, regardless of whether it is colored sepia or not.

- Use natural light. Avoid using an electronic flash, which can get in the way of the picture's look.

- After you take the picture, fine-tune it with an image-processing program. In Chapter 13, you'll see how you can make the picture look more authentically aged.

Make a Panorama

Panoramic photographs have been around for a long time. Before digital photography came along, there were two ways to make a panorama. Special cameras—loaded with special, extra-wide film—were capable of taking photos that were much wider than they were tall. In fact, Advanced Photo System (APS) cameras still do this with contemporary film.

Unfortunately, APS cameras cannot make very wide panoramas; actually, all you get with a panoramic shot using APS film is a picture in which the image has been cropped to make the film seem wide. In other words, APS cameras simply throw away information to give you the impression that you have taken a panoramic photograph. Here's an illustration that demonstrates the various ways in which an APS negative can be printed:

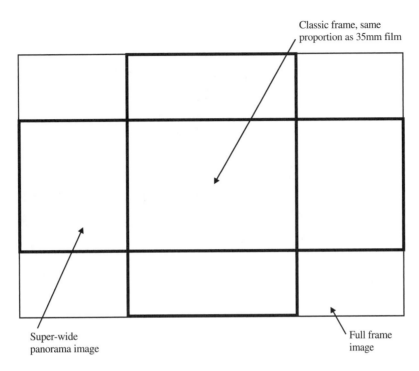

Classic frame, same
proportion as 35mm film

Super-wide
panorama image

Full frame
image

6

The other traditional way to make a panorama is to take a series of photographs and connect them, sort of like a collage. This collage technique allows you to make very, very wide panoramas. Unfortunately, you can often see the seams between each photograph, since each print is simply layered, one on top of the other.

Digital photography allows us to make panoramas in an entirely new way. Using a still camera, it is a piece of cake to take a high-resolution photograph that spans your entire field of view from left to right, including your peripheral vision—like the ones in Figure 6-1 that I took from a Circle Line tour boat in New York harbor. Heck, you can keep going around and take a 360-degree photograph. I can't easily show such a picture on the pages of this book, though, because to squeeze a very long image onto the page, it would become so narrow that you wouldn't be able to see what was in the picture. Nonetheless, you can read more about them in Chapter 12.

Some cameras boast right on the box that they have this capability. Some cameras don't. Either way, you can make a panorama; so don't despair if it appears that your camera does not have a panorama mode. Creating a panorama on the PC is actually pretty similar to making a collage of prints. The software simply takes a series of photographs and stitches them together digitally so that the seams are essentially invisible.

FIGURE 6-1   Panoramic images allow you to see a picture more or less the same way your eyes see the real world.

Before we get there, though, we need to take the initial batch of pictures. Believe it or not, you can get some very nice panoramic photographs even if you are a bit sloppy when you take the original images. For best results, however, you should be as careful as possible when you take your pictures. Just like the old computer axiom "garbage in, garbage out," the better your original images are, the better the final panorama will be.

Have the Right Hardware

You can take a series of panoramic photographs by just holding the camera up to your eye. I've done that myself. In England a few years ago, I made a panoramic photo in front of Abbey Road Studios, where the Beatles recorded virtually all of their music. This was something of a religious experience for me, and I was distressed that I didn't have a tripod with me to make the shot perfect. But I made do with what I had—essentially, my body and an Epson digital camera—and the results were fine.

For the best results, though, it pays to travel with the right gear. To take a good panoramic shot, each image should be taken level with the ground. Remember that there are two different axes to keep under control. The lens needs to be parallel to the ground, and the horizon needs to stay level in each picture. That's not easy to do when you're holding the camera in your hand.

Instead, mount the camera on a lightweight tripod. Some companies even sell special panorama heads for tripods for just this purpose, but I've never felt the need to use one. Instead, I just keep the camera loosened on top of the tripod so I can spin it slightly for each picture.

Getting the Right Overlap

Perhaps the single most important step in making a panorama is getting the correct overlap. The software on your PC will need to know how to combine each image in order to make the finished panorama. To do this, you should try to get about 30–50 percent of the scene to overlap between each pair of pictures. If you make sure that some of the scene that you photographed in the first image also appears in the second image, the stitching software on your PC will be able to match them and combine them into one wide picture—see Chapter 12 for details.

How do you ensure the right amount of overlap? That's where your camera comes in. Some digital cameras have a panorama mode built-in that helps you line up each picture using a series of guide marks.

Switch your camera to panorama mode and look in the LCD display. You should see a set of guide marks like the ones shown here. As you take each picture in your panorama, the guide marks help you keep part of the previous shot in the next picture you are about to take.

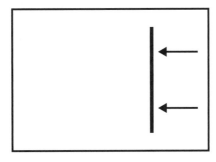

TIP *If your camera does not have a panorama mode, just be sure to include some overlap in each image, using your eyes to estimate distance.*

How to ... **Take a Panoramic Series**

Ready? It's time to actually take your panoramic series. Here's what you should do:

1. Set up your camera on a tripod in front of the scene that you want to photograph. Make sure that the camera is level with respect to the horizon.

2. Turn on your camera and set it to the panorama mode. Frame the rightmost edge of your panorama and take the picture.

3. Turn your camera on the tripod slightly to the left so that it is framing the next part of the scene. Make sure, however, that the leftmost 30–50 percent of the first image now also appears in the second image. It is this overlap that will allow your computer to line up the image into one seamless panorama.

4. Continue turning the camera and taking additional pictures until you reach the leftmost edge of your panorama. Or if you are taking a 360-degree panorama, continue taking pictures until you reach the first image with a suitable overlap.

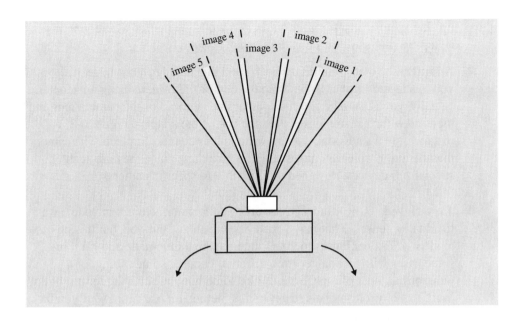

Adding Lenses for Different Perspectives

As you've already seen in Chapter 5, you can attach additional lenses to many digital cameras to enhance your photographic options. In Chapter 5, for instance, you saw how to add close-up lenses to shoot macro photographs.

Your options don't end there. There are add-on lenses that cover the spectrum of photographic possibilities. Even if your camera only comes with a 2X zoom, you can probably enhance that with a set of telephoto, wide-angle, and close-up lenses.

The first thing you'll need to know is how you will be attaching additional lenses to your camera. Typically, there are three ways of doing this:

■ **Threads**   Many digital camera lenses are threaded at the end. If your lens has screw threads, you can probably screw additional lenses directly onto the end. Even so, you may need something called a step-up ring. This is a device that screws onto the end of your lens and provides a different diameter for screwing on the additional lenses. Lens manufacturers typically only make lenses in a few sizes, such as 37mm and 43mm. If your camera has a different thread size, you will need the step-up ring. You can get such an animal at your local camera shop, from a filter company like Tiffen (www.tiffen.com), or a Web store like B&H (www.bhphotovideo.com). Your camera's manufacturer may sell a step-up ring specifically for your camera as well. No matter where you buy it, a step-up ring shouldn't cost more than about $10–15.

- **Adapters**   Some cameras do not have a threaded lens, but instead allow you to snap additional lenses onto the end of the camera using an adapter. Usually, you'll snap or clip the adapter onto the end of the camera lens and then screw the add-on lenses onto the end of the adapter. Figure 6-2, for instance, shows a Kodak camera with its lens adapter in place. The camera manufacturer typically makes adapters like these since they are such specialized devices, designed to affix only to specific cameras.

- **Jury-rigged**   Unfortunately, not all camera manufacturers include a way to add new lenses. That may sound like the end of the line, but it is possible to affix additional lenses to your camera using homemade adapters, in some cases with an adapter for a different camera, some tubing, or a judicious amount of tape. Sounds like something a fourth grader might do? Well, lots of professionals resort to this method on occasion, so if you try it, you are in good company. Personally, I've taken pictures just by holding a filter in front of a digital camera lens, and I'm sure many other experimenters have done so as well.

FIGURE 6-2   Lens adapters are a common way to add wide-angle and telephoto lenses to your camera.

Choosing Lenses

Be sure to visit your camera manufacturer's Web site or your local camera shop to see what kinds of lenses are available for your camera. Even if your camera manufacturer does not sell lenses for your specific model, you can probably get a suitable substitute from a company like Tiffen (www.tiffen.com), which sells a wide variety of lenses and probably has something that would work for you.

Lenses are typically identified by their X power. In other words, the lens will be marked as something like .5X, 2X, or 3X. This designation tells you what the new focal length will be once the lens is attached to your camera. If it is a 2X lens, for instance, the lens will double the focal length of your camera. Obviously, a 2X lens is a telephoto, and attaching it to a typical digital camera should yield a focal length in the vicinity of 200mm.

If you are looking for a wide-angle lens, shoot for one that has an X power of less than 1. Suppose you purchase a .6X lens. When you attach it to your digital camera, it will reduce the focal length by 40 percent. Zoomed out at a focal length of 40mm, your camera will actually provide a focal length of 24mm, which is quite wide. If you zoom in to your camera's telephoto position, the add-on lens will still work. Now, your usual 100mm will only be 60mm.

You can sometimes purchase add-on lenses in a complete set, such as the one in Figure 6-3.

FIGURE 6-3   A collection of add-on lenses that all fit common digital cameras

Add-On Lens Precautions

While add-on lenses are a powerful tool for expanding your photographic options, you need to take some care to avoid an effect known as vignetting. *Vignetting* is what happens when the lens barrel itself gets into the picture, causing the frame to lose its square shape. Subtle vignetting might simply cause the corners of your pictures to be dark, blurry, or rounded off. Extreme vignetting (like the example in Figure 6-4) can feature a perfectly round vignette; in this case the edge of the lens itself is included in the photo.

You can avoid unwanted vignetting by keeping an eye on the camera's LCD display. If your add-on lens is prone to vignetting effects, zooming farther into the telephoto range will usually eliminate the problem. You can also crop the darkened corners out of your picture or paint over the edges with nearby bits of the picture. See Chapter 12 for tips on how to do that with the Clone brush.

FIGURE 6-4   This image suffers from a particularly serious case of vignetting, thanks to an add-on telephoto lens. Reducing the zoom setting will reduce the vignetting effect.

Distortion is another potential effect of adding lenses to your camera. All lenses have some small amount of distortion; after all, no piece of glass or group of optical elements is perfect. But you'll rarely notice any distortion from your camera's principal lens by itself. When you add the equivalent of a big magnifying glass on the front, though, you can start to see some effects. Most of the time, it'll be either pincushion or barrel distortion—vertical lines will bend in or out of the frame instead of being perfectly straight.

Eliminating Lens Distortion on the PC

Obviously, if you can clearly detect distortion in your photos when using an add-on lens, you may want to avoid using that lens. On the other hand, it's possible to remove this sort of distortion from your pictures once they're on the PC. There are utilities available that are designed to straighten such images.

If you're using Paint Shop Pro 8, there's a tool built-in that corrects barrel distortion. Simply open the image with the distortion and choose Adjust | Lens Correction | Barrel Distortion Correction from the menu. From there, you can just experiment with the tool strength until your distortion goes away.

What if you are using a different image editor? As long as it can use standard Photoshop-style plug-ins, I suggest that you try LensDoc, sold by Andromeda Software (www.andromeda.com). *Plug-ins* are small programs that extend and enhance Photoshop and other image editors with additional capabilities.

If you have a picture with obvious lens distortion, here's how to use LensDoc to fix the problem:

1. Load the distorted picture into a graphics program.

2. Start LensDoc by choosing it from the Filter menu. In Paint Shop Pro, choose Image | Plug-In Filters | Andromeda | LensDoc. The LensDoc program should start.

3. Turn off the three green squares by clicking the second button in step 2 (the button with three connected green circles).

4. One at a time, grab the three yellow squares in the image and position them along a line that should be straight but isn't. Avoid positioning the squares too close to each other.

5. When you're ready, click the Correct button. Your image should be straightened. See the next two images for a before-and-after look at lens distortion. A wide-angle lens created this highly distorted view on the left, but LensDoc straightened the image quickly and easily.

You can increase the accuracy of LensDoc by using the green squares to mark a second line.

Infrared Photography

Just for fun, you might want to try shooting some pictures in a completely different part of the color spectrum: infrared.

Infrared light is off at the south end of the spectrum, just below the "red" in the ROY G BIV, color spread that you no doubt learned in high school. Humans can't see infrared, but photographs exposed to infrared light can look dramatically different, as if you're seeing the world through the eyes of a bat or one of those aliens from the movie "Predator." Trees and plants can glow a bright, luminous white, while the sky is often much more visually turbulent. Indeed, different plants and trees respond differently to infrared, so you can get a spread of infrared effects shooting flora outdoors. Indeed, infrared photography is often like peeking into another world. Best of all, for our purposes, you never really know what you're going to get before you press the shutter release. It's like a photographic grab bag.

Getting the Gear

Before you can try your hand with infrared, you need to learn if your digital camera is capable of seeing in infrared. Not all cameras can; some include something called a "hot mirror," which is explicitly designed to block infrared light.

Go grab an infrared remote control, like the one that operates your television or stereo. Point it toward your camera's lens, turn on your camera, and look at the camera's LCD display. When you press a button on the remote, can you see a red light at the end of the remote? If you can, the camera is sensitive to infrared and you're ready to go. If you don't see the remote light up, then your camera has a hot mirror and you can't shoot infrared, sorry.

As you have probably guessed, you need some way to prevent visible light from entering the camera lens when you shoot in infrared. What you need is a filter. Infrared filters are designed to block most or all of the visible light in a scene. All that reaches your camera's CCD is infrared light, which is what your camera will use to take the picture.

Here's the bad news: infrared filters are a specialty photographic items and typically aren't available at your local photo store. You may be able to special-order an infrared filter, but it's probably cheaper from an online photo store like Adorama (www.adorama.com) or B&H (www.bhphotovideo.com). Either way, an infrared filter will set you back around $50–75. They come in a variety of strengths, but I've found any one will do. Just be sure to order one that will fit the

6

thread size on the front of your digital camera; if you camera doesn't have screw threads, you may be able to order an adapter.

Taking the Shot

When is the best time to shoot infrared photos? In the early morning or late afternoon hours. You can't shoot at night, of course, because there's little or no infrared light available to expose your picture. You'll find out very quickly that infrared photography is dramatically different than visible light photography. The most important difference, of course, is that an infrared filter blocks nearly all of the visible light coming into the camera.

The lack of visible light means that exposure times are much longer than usual. You might find your camera exposing picture for a quarter-second or half-second in broad daylight—which means that a tripod is essential.

There's so little light that you may run into another problem: it's hard to see through the lens. As a result, the camera's LCD display is very nearly useless for framing your shot. The LCD will be very dark, and you'll have to concentrate quite hard while blocking glare on the LCD to see anything at all. If your digital camera has a window-style optical viewfinder that doesn't get its information from the lens, you can use it to frame the scene instead. Alternatively, you can line up your scene with no filter in place and then screw the filter onto the lens and take the picture. Obviously, you'll need to use a tripod.

Editing Your Pictures

When you get the images back to the computer, you may find that the infrared shots have a relatively narrow dynamic range. Load your images into an image editor such as Paint Shop Pro and use the Histogram Adjustment tool (which I explain how to use in Chapter 12) to fix the image. After you tweak the image, you can leave the red tint or convert it to a grayscale image.

Connecting Your Camera to a Telescope

Folks with 35mm SLR cameras can easily connect their camera to a telescope to take extreme-telephoto pictures or even photograph the heavens. If you want to try that with a digital camera, you're in luck—companies such as LensPlus (www.lensadapter.com) sell just the sort of adapter you need. LensPlus, for instance, sells a gadget called the LE-Adapter, which acts as a docking port between your digital camera or digital camcorder and other optical gadgets such as telescopes, binoculars, spotting scopes, and microscopes. It works with a wide

Essential Add-On Lenses

Granted, this is a matter of opinion, but there are a few add-ons that I highly recommend keeping in your camera bag. I suggest that you carry these lenses if you like to experiment with different perspectives and focal lengths:

- UV filter. If your camera has screw threads on the front of the lens, add a UV filter to protect the lens from bumps, bangs, dust, dirt, and over-aggressive cleaning. A $15 filter can protect your expensive camera investment for quite a long time, making it one of your smartest investments.

- A 2X telephoto.

- A .5 or .6 wide angle.

- A set of close-focus (macro) lenses.

- A circular polarizer. Discussed in Chapter 5, this add-on filter lets you cut reflections from glass and water.

- A neutral density filter. This is a translucent piece of glass that fits over the lens. It's designed to reduce the light entering the camera by one or two stops, thus letting you slow the shutter to add more "blur" in action shots (such as the one shown here) or increase the depth of field on a bright day.

6

variety of digital cameras—all you need is a set of threads on the front of your camera's lens to screw on the LE-Adapter.

The adapter comes ready to screw onto cameras with either 37mm- or 52mm-diameter threads. If your camera has a different diameter lens, you can buy a step ring that goes from your camera's threads (the size is usually inscribed right on the front of the lens) to either 37mm or 52mm.

If you go shopping for a step ring, be sure to get the right size. If your camera's lens is larger than 52mm, you'll want a step-down ring. A step-up ring will have threads that go the wrong way, so the distinction is important.

Once you screw the LE-Adapter onto your camera, you then bolt the other end of the adapter onto your telescope, binoculars, or other optical system, and start taking pictures. In most cases, your digital camera should be able to autofocus right through the new optics.

The LE-Adapter works pretty well, as long as you understand that the optics won't necessarily be as bright and as sharp as you're used to with your ordinary lens. A set of binoculars, for instance, may give you a lot of magnification, but the optics aren't designed to take professional-caliber photos. Personally, I've had a blast photographing the moon through my six-inch reflector telescope, though, and it's a way to capture photos that are otherwise absolutely impossible with your digital camera:

Your results will also vary depending on what camera you own. In testing, I have found that the Nikon CoolPix 4500 works just fine, though Sony DSC P5 suffers from terrible optical degradation. The preceding shot of the moon was taken with an Olympus e10, which you can see in position here:

Taking Time-Lapse Photos

If you've ever been impressed by a time-lapse movie of a flower opening or traffic moving on a busy highway, you might want to try it yourself. It's not hard to do, though it's certainly easier if your camera supports time-lapse operations to begin with.

First, a little theory: time-lapse photography is just the process of shooting the same subject over and over with a certain time interval between each shot, so that when you play the images back later in sequence, it's like a movie in which events happen faster than normal time.

If your camera has a time-lapse feature, this is a piece of cake. The control might be on the camera itself (in the menu system) or on your PC. If it's only on your PC, you may need to connect a laptop to the camera to control the time-lapse operation. If the control is on the camera, though, you don't need any special equipment. All you need to do is configure the camera's "interval time," which is the interval between photos.

If your camera doesn't have a time-lapse control, you can still take a series of photos, but you'll have to shoulder more of the work. Specifically, you'll have to turn the camera on, take a shot, and turn the camera off. Then you need to wait the appropriate time period and repeat the process. When you use automatic time-lapse photography, the camera does all that on its own.

The final results can be worth it, though. Figure 6-5 shows a series of photos that were captured with the time-lapse mode of an Olympus e-10 digital camera.

FIGURE 6-5   Time-lapse photography lets you see changes over a long or short period of time.

If you want to try your hand at time-lapse photography, here are a few pointers to keep in mind:

■ *Use a tripod.* This is probably obvious, but I once saw someone try to take a time-lapse series by hand. The effect is ruined if each and every image isn't composed exactly the same way.

■ *Choose a subject.* Most of the time, a time-lapse photo series works best— in other words, it looks its best—when you find a single subject that is going to change over time and make it the focal point of your photos. If too much changes in the frame, the image loses its impact. In simple terms, it looks like a mess.

■ *Find the right interval.* This may take some experimentation, but it can make or break your photos. Choose an interval between shots that best highlights the changes in your subject. If the interval is too long, the subject will change too much between shots, and it'll look disjointed and confusing. If the interval is too short, not enough will happen between frames to make a visual difference.

■ *Start fresh.* Make sure that you have plenty of room on your memory card to take your series. You might want to start with a blank card and reduce the resolution of each image to a manageable 640×480 pixels. If you plan to take a lot of pictures, be sure the camera batteries are fresh (so you don't run out of gas halfway through the series), and perhaps start with a large memory card.

■ *Use automatic exposure.* Most of the time, make sure the camera is set to automatic exposure. That way, it can react to changing light conditions throughout the day. The exception: if you're taking a series of night shots, configure the camera for the desired manual settings, such as f/5.6 for eight seconds each.

Making Movies

Once your time-lapse series is complete, you might want to turn it into a film. There are two ways to do this: by using video-editing or animation software.

■ **Video-editing software**   If you have a camcorder and you make your own home movies, this is a great solution. Just open your favorite video-editing program and import all the still time-lapse frames. Arrange them in the

Movies on Your Camera

These days, it seems that most digital cameras come with some sort of movie mode. Thus, instead of simply snapping stills, you can record a short video that can be played back on the camera or on a PC.

While the movie mode is easy to operate, not all cameras treat movies the same. Some digital cameras have no microphone, for instance, so they can't capture sound. Likewise, some camera set a fixed length for your movies—say, 15 or 60 seconds—while other cameras will record any length, right up till the point you run out of memory on your storage card. Depending on what kind of camera you have, the movie will either be recorded in MPG, AVI (also known as Video for Windows), or MOV (QuickTime) format. No matter which format your camera records, it should be playable on any PC with the appropriate viewer application.

Finally, when you make a movie, remember that you can often choose the video's resolution—but even the biggest movie will still be fairly small on the computer screen.

filmstrip or timeline so they each play for some small fraction of a second, and then render the movie. Using this technique, you can save your movie so it plays "full screen" on the PC or on a television, directly from the PC or from videotape.

■ **Animation software**   Using a program such as Jasc's GIF Animator (included with Paint Shop Pro), you can arrange the individual stills, configure them each to play for a fraction of a second, and save the finished result as an animated GIF or some other kind of animation file that plays in a small window on the computer screen. This technique is better if you want to upload it to a Web site, e-mail it, or just view it on the PC.

Taking Care of Batteries

Digital cameras are battery hogs, plain and simple. You shouldn't expect the batteries in a digital camera to last very long since they are responsible for running a number of key functions within the camera, including the following:

■ The imaging system, including the exposure system and the zoom

■ The LCD display

■ The flash

■ The image storage system

That's a lot to expect from a set of batteries, and, in fact, they don't last long—you should expect to get between 100 and 300 shots from a set of batteries, depending on how aggressively you use features like the zoom and LCD display.

Rechargeable Versus Alkaline

If your camera uses typical AA-style batteries, I recommend that you avoid alkaline batteries. Instead, invest in one or two sets of NiMH rechargeable batteries. Yes, they're initially more expensive. But they quickly pay for themselves, since you can use rechargeables over a hundred times on average. Do the math: Let's say that you use your camera every weekend for a year, and you have to replace the batteries about once a month. Here's how the cost stacks up over the course of a year:

6

AA Alkaline (Energizer "Titanium" High-Performance Batteries)	NiMH Rechargeables (Charger and One Set of Batteries)
12 × $8 = $96	$20

The more you use your camera, the more obvious the cost savings become. Once you've bought your first set of rechargeable batteries, additional sets are less expensive (usually under $10) because you don't have to buy another charger. So I think you can see how useful rechargeables actually are.

TIP *In general, I avoid compact digital cameras that use proprietary lithium ion batteries. Yes, I know that they're all the rage these days, but I like the security of knowing, in a pinch, I can simply pop in a pair of AA batteries and keep shooting. If I have a camera with a fancy lithium ion brick and no spare, I'm out of commission until the battery charges.*

Batteries Wear Out

Rechargeable batteries lose a teeny little bit of their life every time you charge them. Most rechargeables last for about 1,000 charges, after which they stop holding a meaningful charge and you need to throw them away. You can extend the life of these batteries by recharging only them when they're actually run down; "topping them off" is like a regular recharge in that it heats the chemicals in the battery casing, which slowly reduces the battery's life.

Get the Most Out of Your Batteries

With so many demands on your camera batteries, it's not all that surprising that they don't last very long. But there are certainly things you can do to extend the life of your batteries, making them last longer between charges or replacements. Just follow some of these commonsense tips:

- *Use the optical viewfinder.* If your camera lets you, turn off the LCD display and look through the optical finder instead. The LCD screen is one of the biggest energy hogs on your camera, and you can significantly extend the value of your batteries by not using it.

- *Don't review your pictures.* Likewise, avoid gawking at your pictures on the camera's LCD display. Review them briefly if you need to select images for deletion (to free some room on the camera's memory card) or to see if you need to reshoot a particular picture. But save the slow, careful replays for your computer screen.

- *Disable the flash when you don't need it.* Sure, there are excellent reasons to use it, even outdoors (we talked about fill flash to improve portraits in Chapter 4), but if you are shooting subjects that are 40 feet away and the flash can't possibly help, turn it off. Your batteries will thank you.

- *Leave the camera on.* If you're taking a lot of pictures in a brief time, don't turn the camera off after each and every picture. You might think that you're conserving battery life, but in fact you're burning energy every time the camera has to power on. That's especially true if your camera has to retract the zoom lens every time it powers down and extend the lens when you turn it on again.

■ *Use AC power when it's available.* When you're transferring images to the PC, don't rely on battery power. You should have an AC adapter to power the camera when you're working at your desk near electrical power. If your camera didn't come with an AC adapter, it's probably wise to invest in one for exactly this reason. The AC adapter might also come in handy if you're shooting a lot of pictures inside a house from a somewhat stationary position. You can save battery life for when you really need it by tethering yourself to an AC outlet.

6

TIP   *If your batteries die in the middle of a shoot and you don't have any spares, here's a trick you can try that might give you a few extra shots: turn the camera off, wait a minute, and then turn it back on. Often you can sneak in a few more pictures before the batteries are completely exhausted.*

Carry Spares

I never go anywhere without a spare set of batteries in my camera case. I don't need to tell you how frustrating it can be to run out of energy in the middle of Yellowstone National Park. If you can fit it, I also suggest bringing a charger with you so you can charge your batteries as needed. I am particularly fond of slim-line chargers like the one shown here, since it takes up so little space and can be used to hold a second set of batteries without consuming any more precious space in your camera bag:

In addition, you might want to invest in a set of Instant Power back-up batteries. Instant Power (www.instant-power.com) sells a great emergency-power solution for digital cameras, camcorders, PDAs, cell phones, and other devices. They're disposable fuel cells that provide hours of operation if your primary batteries die. The cells have a long shelf life when left sealed in their pouch, meaning you can put a set in your travel bag and leave them there for months at a time.

Also, it pays to spend a little more money on a smart charger, which can totally charge a set of batteries in 60–90 minutes, rather than the dozen hours it takes most run-of-the-mill chargers. Need to charge anywhere, anytime? Be sure to check out your local camera or computer shop for special-purpose chargers that can charge your batteries using the power adapter in your car or even solar power (like the iSun Solar Power Charger (www.isunpower.com), shown here, which can top off a dozen AA batteries at once via solar power, a wall outlet, or your car's power port:

Using Batteries in the Cold

You may want to run outside in the dead of winter to photograph snowmen, snowball fights, and freshly fallen snow clinging to the trees. But because they're electronic devices, digital cameras don't function as well in cold conditions as in the heat of summer.

You can prevent most problems, though, just by keeping your camera batteries warm. If the batteries get too cold, the chemical reactions that generate power are inhibited, and they'll simply stop working. Here's what I suggest: carry a spare set of batteries in your pocket, where your body heat can keep them warm. If the current in the first set of batteries drops off due to the cold, swap them out with the ones warmed by your body, and then continue shooting. Since the first set of batteries will recover some of their charge when you stick them in your warm pocket, you can swap back and forth a few times—unless you're shooting in the Arctic where the ambient temperature is 50 below zero.

Part II

Transferring Images

Chapter 7

Conquering File Formats

How to...

- Use image file formats

- Distinguish among formats such as JPG, TIF, GIF, and BMP

- Recognize file extensions on the PC

- View file extensions in Windows

- Understand the value of JPG compression settings on the camera

- Select the best image compression on a camera

- Determine when to use the TIF format to capture pictures on your camera

- Know when to save images in various file formats

- Batch-save a large number of images in a different format automatically

- Choose the best JPG compression level on the PC

Like it or not, working with a digital camera means that you are going to have to learn some of the nuances of your PC. That can be bad news. After all, computers can be a pain in the neck, and Windows, in particular, can be a nightmare.

Nonetheless, the pictures stored in your digital camera are not terribly useful to you unless you understand how to work with them. The images are stored in individual files not unlike the document files you'll find on the computer itself—such as word processing files, music files, or the saved game files created by a computer game. In this chapter, we will look in some detail at the image files created by your digital camera. We will talk about file formats, image quality, and what you need to know about all of this to get the best results with your camera. Don't worry, though: this is not a computer class, and we won't go into any more detail than you will actually need to manage your pictures.

What Are File Formats and Why Do I Care?

When you take a picture with your digital camera, the camera's imaging sensor interprets the scene and records a representation of it on the camera's memory card. The scene is essentially a grid, or matrix, of pixels.

How many pixels there are depends on the resolution of the camera.

If you were taking a 1-megapixel picture, for instance, the image's resolution might be 1280 pixels across (the X dimension) by 960 pixels down (the Y dimension). It would look something like Figure 7-1, in which you can see each individual pixel that makes up the image, assuming you can zoom in far enough. The picture is a sort of paint-by-numbers grid—just add the right color to each of the pixels in Figure 7-1, and you'll end up with a picture of something.

So far, so good. The problem comes in when you want to save all this data to the memory card. How do you do it? Essentially, you need to save the data in some standardized format so the information will be understandable to software and devices other than the digital camera itself. In the old days of computing, every word processing program stored its documents in a unique file format that was understandable only to that program—a real hassle if you needed to open a document on someone else's PC using a strange word processing program. Likewise, if your camera stored information about the color value of each one of those pixels however it felt like it, odds are good that only the camera would ever be able to understand that information again.

And that is a somewhat long-winded explanation of why we have file formats. By writing the color information about each of those pixels in a standard and predictable way, each picture that the digital camera saves can be read by your computer's software, even if the software didn't come from the same company that made the camera.

7

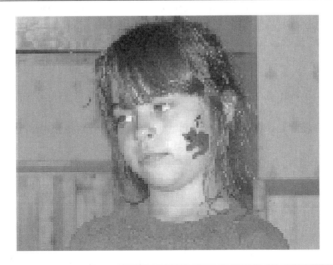

FIGURE 7-1   A digital image is little more than a grid of colored pixels.

Digital cameras and graphics programs use more than one file format—many more. In fact, there are well over a hundred file formats in use by image software on computers today. Only about a half dozen are particularly popular—most are really just historical curiosities used by very few programs—but even that small number can be confusing. Why are there so many file formats? Good question. It's not just to confuse everyone. Instead, different file formats exist because some are better at certain tasks than others. Some file formats compress well—in other words, a large picture will only take up a small amount of space on the memory card or hard disk. Other file formats more accurately represent the original image, are optimized for the Web, or are designed to work well on both Windows and Macintosh computers. And most importantly, they were all invented at different times, under unique circumstances, and they simply tend to hang on because some folks still use them.

The Most Common File Formats

As I said earlier, there are really just a few file formats that most people use most of the time. So while you may occasionally hear about file formats such as IFF, IMG, and KDC, you typically need to pay attention to just a very few.

By the same token, you really should get to know the most common file formats and use them when it's appropriate. Here is a quick overview of the most common formats and what they are used for:

- **JPG**   Short for Joint Photographic Experts Group (pronounced "jay peg"), this file format is considered *lossy*. That means that when you save an image in this format, some of the data is lost. That's because JPG files are compressed to save storage space. Why do people put up with a file format that sacrifices image quality? The answer is that the JPG format does an outstanding job of preserving all the visual information that the human eye can generally see in a picture. When you save a picture in the JPG format, you'll typically have to zoom in quite a bit to begin to see any artifacts or digital noise caused by the format.

- **JPEG2000**   A fairly new file format, called JPEG2000, uses the same basic compression technology as JPG, but it offers better image quality for roughly the same file size. JPEG2000 has a lot of fans, and it's supported by most image editors. On the other hand, digital cameras still use the JPG format—so to use JPEG2000, you'll have to convert the images from JPG to JPEG2000 format on the PC. I'm pretty ambivalent about JPEG2000. It's certainly an improvement over JPG, but unless or until digital cameras adopt this format, I'll stick with JPG.

■ **TIF**   Short for Tagged Image File format, this format is also very popular, but for exactly the opposite reason that JPG is popular. TIF files can be saved in two different ways: with a small amount of compression or without compression. Either way, TIF files are absolutely *lossless*—they preserve 100 percent of the information about every pixel in the original image. TIF files are also popular because they are used on both the Windows and Macintosh platforms; that makes TIF a good choice if you need to share files with someone who is using a different kind of computer than you.

■ **BMP**   This is the old standard bitmapped file format for Windows users. It can be used for general-purpose storage, for image editing, and as the wallpaper on your Windows desktop, but it isn't generally readable by Macintosh computers. In addition, BMP files are not used on the Internet. That makes this a relatively unpopular format. Another reason that BMP files aren't particularly popular is that they tend to be quite large because the BMP format makes no effort to compress the data at all. In general, the only reason you will tend to use this file format is if you want to display a digital image as the wallpaper on the Windows desktop. Even then, newer versions of Windows let you use JPG images for wallpaper—relegating the BMP format to the "where are they now" file for most savvy users.

7

■ **GIF**   Short for Graphics Interchange Format (pronounced either "giff" or "jiff," depending on who is doing the talking), this format was originally developed by CompuServe and is commonly used on the Web, along with the JPG format. GIF has a few advantages over JPG on the Web. For one, you can make the background of GIF images transparent, which comes in handy if you want the area surrounding an irregularly shaped image to be the same as the background of the Web page. You can also make GIF images display in *interlace* mode—that is, in chunks, which means that you can get an overall impression of the picture even before it has fully downloaded.
That is a valuable feature on the Internet, since many people still have slow modem connections. You can also save a GIF image with fewer than 16.7 million colors. If you save a GIF image with just 256 colors, for instance, the file will be dramatically smaller and may not look terribly different from the original full-color version. On the other hand, that's not a good practice for digital images—you're more likely to save GIF images at a lower color count if the image in question is a graphic such as a company logo or a hand-drawn picture.

Using File Formats

Now that you understand file formats, you are probably wondering which one you should use on your own system. As in all things, it depends on how you're going to use your images. Let's look at your choices, and I'll make a few recommendations about how you might want to work with and save your images.

On the Camera

Let's start with your camera. No doubt, you realize that your camera saves images in one of the file formats we've already discussed as soon as the images are taken—but which format?

Understanding File Extensions

The many file formats used on computers today are generally referred to by the letters that make up their three-letter extension. Computer files are generally named using a standardized system that looks like this:

```
filename.ext
```

The *filename* can generally be almost anything—a random collection of numbers and letters or a word or two that describe the contents of the file. Filenames also use a three-letter *extension* that tells the computer what kind of data is within the file. Here are a few common file extensions:

- **.doc**   Word processing document (usually created by Microsoft Word)

- **.xls**   Spreadsheet document (usually created by Microsoft Excel)

- **.mp3**   Digital music file, commonly downloaded from the Internet

- **.htm**   Web page document

In other words, you and I, as users, control the first half of the filename. The file extension, though—the part that comes after the period—depends on the program that made the file or the file format that the data corresponds to. If you open a folder on your computer and find a bunch of image files, you can immediately tell what format they are in by looking at their extension, as in the illustration below. For example, *mypicture.jpg* is saved in JPG format, while *pretty-flower.tif* is saved in the TIF format.

Windows may not be configured to show you the complete filename including the extension. To turn on the extension view in Windows XP, follow these steps:

1. Open a folder on the Windows desktop.

2. Choose View | Folder Options from the folder's menu.

3. Click the View tab so that you can see the Advanced settings in the bottom half of the window.

4. Find the entry Hide Extensions For Known File Types (it's about halfway down the list), and remove the check mark from this selection.

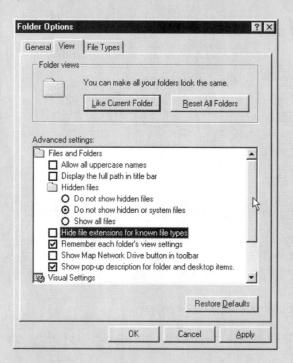

5. Click OK to save this change.

Actually, this is the easy part. Most digital cameras, by default, save their images in JPG format. JPG is a pretty good compromise between quality and file size for most users and in most photographic situations. But what you may not realize is that you have a fair degree of control over how aggressively your camera compresses the JPG images. Take a look at your camera, and you will no doubt find that somewhere—whether it is in a menu system or controlled via a button on the camera housing itself—there is a setting for image quality. Note that image quality is quite different from resolution. *Resolution* is a measure of how many pixels are in the image; *quality* determines how much each image will be compressed and, consequently, how much image quality will be sacrificed.

Most cameras tend to have several quality settings, such as high, medium, and low. I recommend that you stick with the highest setting for your JPG images—the lower-quality settings tend to make for some pretty unsatisfactory images. On the other hand, the highest image quality and resolution setting takes more space on your memory card, reducing the number of images you can keep on a card at once. Which is the bigger deal? Well, consider this: you can always buy another memory card to store extra images. But once saved at a lower resolution, you can never buy back the lost image quality. If you're only using your pictures for low-impact applications such as Web pages and e-mail, small differences in image quality may not mean a lot to you. But if you're planning to print your pictures, even a little color fringing or digital noise can make a difference.

Be sure to check your camera menu for details on setting image quality and resolution because every camera is a little bit different. Some cameras make it easy to distinguish between resolution and image quality because they are set with two different controls.

Other cameras offer these two controls in a single, somewhat confusing menu selection. You may be forced to work with a camera menu that gives you a choice of SHQ, HQ, and SQ, for instance, where both SHQ and HQ are the same high resolution, but with different amounts of JPG compression. In the following illustration, you can see how a FujiFilm camera on the left limits you to choosing only what resolution you can work with, while the Olympus camera on the right uses SQ and SHQ to distinguish between image quality. Inside each of those selections is the ability to choose a specific pixel resolution. The moral? Read your camera manual to see how to set the resolution and image quality.

7

Compression Versus Reduction

In this chapter, I use the term *image compression* a lot. The loss of quality in JPG images, I contend throughout this chapter, is the fault of the file format's efforts to compress the original image.

In reality, there are two techniques used to save disk space in many file formats: compression and reduction. *Compression,* by definition, is simply removing redundant data from a file in such a way that the file can be made smaller without losing any truly unique information. Consider the number 1,000,000,000, for instance. Using data compression, I can represent that value as 1E9. It's the exact same information, but I've managed to write it in far fewer digits on the page. WinZip and other compression utilities used to download programs from the Internet can compress programs without losing any information—otherwise, the original program would never work again after being compressed!

Reduction, on the other hand, is a programming term that refers to making a file smaller by actually sacrificing some data. Small changes in color between adjacent pixels might be approximated, for instance, or numbers might be rounded off with the philosophy of "good enough." With many lossy file formats—such as JPG, MPG, and MP3—a lot of effort goes into developing mathematical models that can sacrifice data the human brain won't notice much.

The distinction between compression and reduction is a subtle one, though, so I'll mainly use the term "compression" to refer to both techniques.

Lossless Image Files

Many digital cameras have a second file format option—TIF. Remember that the TIF format, unlike JPG, can be used to ensure that the image is absolutely pristine, without any data loss at all. Many cameras have a special setting that you can use to save your images in this lossless TIF format.

You might want to work in TIF if you are shooting a special photograph that you plan to crop, enlarge, and print. Truly professional work may call for TIF images—but even then, a high-res, high-quality JPG may be sufficient. Remember: the TIF format exacts a serious penalty—measured in megabytes, TIF files are so large that you may only be able to fit a very few on your memory card.

If you want to work in TIF format a lot, you should get the largest memory card you can afford. Consider a 256MB memory card in a typical 5-megapixel digital camera. Such a card might usually be able to store about 64 high-quality JPG images. When set to TIF format, though, the same card might only hold 16 images. That's a pretty radical difference, so it's worth asking how significant the difference between TIF and JPG really is. Here's my take: the differences are typically only apparent when enlarged, and even then it isn't always readily apparent. It's most noticeably important when trying to print an enlargement on a good color printer.

There's another issue with TIF: it takes a long time to save these images to memory. Since TIF files are the size of several JPG images, your camera has to spend the time to store the equivalent of several pictures each time you press the shutter release. I've found that it can take anywhere from 30 seconds to a full minute to write each TIF image. Worse, some cameras won't let you take another picture until that one is done getting stored on the memory card.

7

TIP

In general, I suggest that you forget about the TIF mode on your digital camera. It's not worth the sacrifice, since a high-res, high-quality JPG is more than adequate 99.9 percent of the time. Worse, it can take a long time to write a TIF file to memory.

RAW Files

There's one other file format you might encounter with certain digital cameras. The RAW format does TIF one better, storing not just totally uncompressed data, but also storing that data before the camera's processor has had a chance to do anything to it.

What am I talking about? Well, consider this: your digital camera's processor does a lot to each image you snap before it gets stored on the memory card. First and foremost, each pixel of the image sensor can only capture a single color, so the camera's processor combines adjacent pixel information to interpolate the colors you finally see in your finished image. RAW images store the unprocessed, uninterpolated data—and consequently, don't include the camera's white balance settings or any other tweaks, such as the sharpening filter that many cameras run on images right before they're saved.

In other words, the RAW file is like a digital negative—totally unprocessed, unfiltered, untouched. Some pro photographers use the RAW files because they allow greater creative control over the finished images. But not all digital cameras let you save RAW mode pictures. In my experience, very inexpensive digicams don't have this feature, while better, performance-oriented cameras usually do.

Even then, be aware that all RAW files are not the same. Nikon's NEF format is similar to—but incompatible with—Canon's RAW format, for instance. And some cameras disguise the RAW mode by simply calling it TIF, so it pays to read your camera's user guide to learn the details.

Most image-editing programs can't deal with RAW files. Instead, the only way to load RAW files from your digital camera is to use the file transfer and conversion software that comes with your digital camera or to invest in an image-editing program that has hooks for your camera's RAW files. Adobe Photoshop, for instance, offers a plug-in that works with many Canon, Fuji, Minolta, and Nikon camera RAW modes.

On the PC

When you transfer your images to the PC, you'll find them in the same file format that the camera used. There's no magical transformation as they go from camera to computer. But just because they arrive in JPG format doesn't mean they have to stay that way. You can save these images in any file format you like.

NOTE　*When you save a JPG picture in TIF format, you essentially "freeze" the image at its current level of detail and image quality. That way, when you edit and save it again later, you're not degrading its quality like you would by resaving it in JPG format. But remember—just saving an image in TIF cannot restore quality that wasn't there to begin with. Your image will never look any better than it did in JPG format.*

I highly recommend saving any files that you plan to edit or manipulate in a lossless file format such as TIF. I have nothing against JPG—it's a great format—but since it is lossy, every time you edit and resave the file, it degrades a bit more. This is very important! Many people assume that resaving a JPG image doesn't affect the image quality, but that's not the case. Think of it this way: a JPG is nothing more than an approximation of the original that conserves disk space by reducing the total image quality slightly. Every time you save a JPG file, the JPG compression algorithm runs, reducing the image again. Each time you click the Save button on a JPG image in an image-editing program, you're making an approximation of an approximation.

Figure 7-2 shows the effect of opening and saving the same image a dozen times in an image-editing program like Adobe Photoshop. Notice that the veins in the leaf are much less sharply defined in the image on the right after it has been resaved multiple times using the JPG format.

That said, don't be alarmed about JPGs that you don't edit. If you take a picture in JPG format, transfer it to the PC, and then only open it *to look at it,* you can leave it in JPG format because you're not saving it over and over.

Choosing a File Format

The TIF format is great if you plan to print enlargements of your images or if you want to preserve an image precisely, without any compression artifacts. Digital images have lots of uses, though, and that's why there are lots of file formats. Here are a few file format tips you might want to keep in the back of your mind:

- ■ **Web publishing**   If you're publishing pictures on the Web or in a page layout program such as Adobe PageMaker, JPG is often the best choice. But GIF files can have transparent backgrounds, so text can be made to flow professionally around an irregularly shaped image, as you can see in Figure 7-3. I'll show you how to do that in Chapter 16.

- ■ **Print publishing**   Creating a newsletter? If you're printing a black-and-white document, such as on a laser printer, it often pays to convert your image to grayscale before you insert it into the page layout or word processing program. There are two reasons for this. First, you can see exactly what you're going to

7

FIGURE 7-2   Every time you click the Save button in an image editor, your JPG file degrades a little bit more—the image on the right is a many-times-saved, degraded copy of the original on the left.

Change the File Format

When you open an image to crop it, brighten it, or perform some other minor (or major) editing job, you should save your changes as a new file with a .tif extension. Here's how to do that:

1. In an image editor, choose File | Save As from the menu.

2. In the Save As dialog box, click the list arrow in the Save As Type box, and choose the option for TIF. It is sometimes spelled out as Tagged Image File.

3. Change the filename if you desire, and then click Save.

If you no longer need the original JPG file, you can delete it from your hard disk to save space. You might want to keep it, though, in case you want to go back to the original image (prior to the edits you just made).

be printing, and viewing it in shades of gray lets you determine whether the image needs brightness adjustment or other edits. Second, you're sending less information to the printer, and the software should work somewhat faster.

- **Enlargement printing**   If you want to print digital images at large sizes, such as 5×7 inches or beyond, TIF or JPG is fine, but stick with TIF if you are editing and saving the file first.

- **Onscreen display**   The JPG format is perfectly adequate for most onscreen applications, including e-mail, slide shows, PowerPoint presentations, Web photo albums, Windows desktop wallpaper, and that sort of thing.

FIGURE 7-3   In an image editor, be sure to save your image with a transparent background. Then you can make text wrap around it in your Web design or publishing program.

Tweaking JPG

The JPG file format is very flexible. Just as on the digital camera, where you can usually select from several grades of JPG image quality, desktop-based image-editing software usually lets you specify an image quality level as well.

Remember the trade-off with JPG settings: the higher the image quality, the larger the file size. In a program such as Paint Shop Pro, for instance, you can find the JPG controls in the Save As dialog box:

With the JPG file format selected, click the Options button. You should see a slider control for increasing the compression level. Most people stick with a compression level in the range of 10 to 15. Beyond 15, the compression artifacts start to become quite noticeable, though the file size shrinks dramatically. Check out Figure 7-4, for instance. Here you can see a conservative compression of 10, on the left, and an aggressive compression of 50, on the right. The difference is dramatic, especially in the image's background.

FIGURE 7-4   When you save JPG images, use as little compression as possible to avoid this kind of degradation.

Batch Processing

Some people like to convert their images to TIF (or some other file format) as soon as the images make their way from the camera to the PC. It can be slow and boring to do that by hand—how would you like to access the File | Save As menu item 50 times in a row to save each of your images as TIFs?

Instead, there are various ways to automate the process. If you're using the excellent image management program called ACDSee (www.acdsee.com), you can "batch process" a slew of images at once. Just select all the pictures you want to convert to another format, such as TIF, and then choose Activities | Edit | Convert from the menu. Choose the file format, and you can even tell ACDSee to delete the original unneeded files when it's done. There's also a batch editor built into Paint Shop Pro 8 (www.jasc.com) and Adobe's Photoshop Elements. Using these programs to batch process is easy—just create a lit of operations to perform, and select the images you want to modify, as in this illustration:

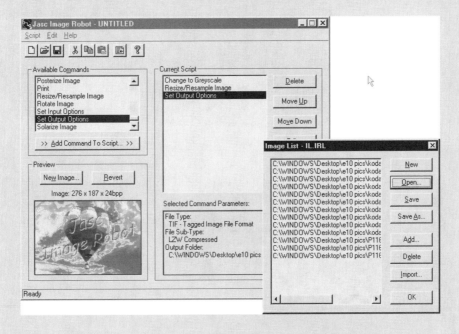

If you work with dozens or hundreds of images at once and frequently need to convert them to another format, investigate one of these programs.

Chapter 8

Working with Digital Film

How to...

- Choose a camera based on its memory card format
- Understand the advantages and disadvantages of various kinds of memory cards
- Use a serial connection cable to copy images from the camera to the PC
- Troubleshoot serial port problems
- Correlate serial ports and COM port numbers
- Use a USB cable to copy images from the camera to the PC
- Solve USB port problems
- Delete images from your memory card
- Care for memory cards

Often, you'll hear people describe a digital camera's image sensor—be it the Charge-Coupled Device (CCD) or Complementary Metal Oxide Semiconductor (CMOS) as the equivalent of a 35mm camera's film—heck, I use that comparison myself pretty often. That's because the sensor behaves like film. It's sensitive to light and is primarily responsible for sensing the scene in the same way that the silver halide solution on chemical film records a scene. But, in just the same way that about 50 different people each stake a claim to being the Fifth Beatle, another component in your camera is "like the film in a digital camera." This is your camera's removable memory and that's the subject of this chapter.

Removable memory cards like SD, SmartMedia, CompactFlash, Memory Stick, and even the new xD card are just like film in the sense that this is where your images are stored. If you remove the memory card from your camera and hold it in your hand, you're holding your pictures. If you insert that memory card in your PC, you can transfer those pictures to your computer for editing or printing. And, because memory cards can be erased and used again, digital imaging is much more flexible and, potentially, a heck of a lot cheaper in the long run than 35mm photography. To learn how to get the most out of your computer's digital film, read this chapter.

The ABCs of Digital Film

All digital cameras have to store their images somewhere—it's the *where* that's the big question. There's no single standard way of storing images in a digital camera; almost a half-dozen typical storage schemes are in use by cameras today, so what kind of storage system you want to use might be a consideration when choosing your camera. Almost all cameras use one of the following methods of storing images.

Internal Memory

Although a few low-priced digital cameras use a few megabytes of internal, nonremovable memory for storing images, this animal is a dying breed. In fact, it's almost extinct. Most cameras include the capability to insert some sort of removable memory. That way, you can insert a fresh memory card when your camera is full of pictures. With only internal memory at your disposal, you can easily run out of storage space and be unable to take more pictures unless you delete a few old images or you download your pictures to the PC—something that can be hard to do if you're shooting snapshots on vacation.

SmartMedia

SmartMedia—originally known by the somewhat cumbersome name of Solid State Floppy Disk Card (SSFDC)—is the oldest of all memory formats. It's also the thinnest, weighing in at a mere .75mm thick. Because it's so thin, SmartMedia has little on-board "intelligence" and it relies on its parent device (such as your digital camera) to understand how to read and write data on the card.

While this approach makes for a more streamlined memory card, it also poses a potential problem. Older devices, such as one-megapixel digital cameras, often can't accept larger-density SmartMedia cards. This is because the camera's firmware wasn't programmed to understand those higher capacity cards, which didn't yet exist when the camera was manufactured. Another problem: SmartMedia cards are wafer thin, somewhat flexible, and have unprotected electrical contacts on the outside of the card. That makes SmartMedia a more easily damaged than other kinds of memory. These cards also top out at a capacity of 128MB, so you'll never be able to store a genuinely large number of images on any one card, especially if your camera is a 3-megapixel model. To add insult to injury, SmartMedia writes data quite slowly and comes in two incompatible flavors (3.3- and 5.0-volt versions).

On the other hand, SmartMedia cards are small enough to fit in an adapter that slides into your PC's floppy disk drive, so you can copy images to your PC as if they were stored on a floppy disk. They're also plenty large for one- and two-megapixel cameras, especially if you carry a spare card when you go shooting.

Here's the bottom line on SmartMedia: I don't like them. Not one bit. Not a lot of digital cameras still use SmartMedia (though Olympus does, unfortunately), and this technology has reached its end of life. In its place, there's a new format, called xD. More about that one in the upcoming section "xD".

CompactFlash

I often call *CompactFlash* the most versatile memory card format on the market. They're quite small, come in a wide range of capacities, and are priced affordably to boot.

CompactFlash is the same age as SmartMedia—together, those two formats are the great-grandparents of today's mobile storage gadgets. I think CompactFlash is for a good bet for photographers who need to pack a large number of images onto each card. As you can see in the following, CompactFlash is reasonably small (it's about an eighth of an inch thick), yet it comes in capacities up to 4GB—as much storage space as a small hard disk. CompactFlash cards are ideal for high-megapixel cameras and situations in which you can't easily swap out memory cards when the first one is full (underwater photography is an excellent example). A variation on the CompactFlash format is a small device called the Microdrive. IBM's *Microdrive* is, a tiny hard disk packed into the CompactFlash format. Two Microdrives are available: a 340MB card and 1GB. Not all camera manufacturers certify their cameras to work reliably with the Microdrive, even if the camera accepts the slightly thicker "Type II" CompactFlash cards (like the Microdrive), so you should check before investing in one.

Memory Stick

Originally manufactured exclusively by Sony for Sony products, Memory Sticks are slowly starting to catch on. *Memory Sticks* (shown in the following) resemble a stick of gum and come in a variety of capacities up to 128MB.

Memory Sticks are smartly engineered. They're thin and narrow, like a stick of chewing gum, and they have a "self-cleaning" set of electrical contacts on the end—that means it's hard to damage the Memory Stick, even though the contacts are visible. Thanks to the card's unique shape, you'd have to try very, very hard to insert it into your digital camera incorrectly.

The real appeal of Memory Stick–equipped digital cameras is you can remove the Memory Stick and insert it into any other Sony Memory Stick–enabled device to access your images. Memory Stick products include VAIO laptops, digital picture frames, and the Clié handheld PC.

On the other hand, Memory Sticks were badly engineered from the start, designed to accommodate, as mentioned, a maximum of 128MB. As a result, Sony recently introduced a close cousin to the Memory Stick, called Memory Stick Pro. *Memory Stick Pro* cards come in capacities that range from 256MB to 1GB, with higher capacities on their way. Memory Stick Pro is a fast memory format, able to read and write data quickly enough to support DVD-quality video in real time. On the other hand, be careful when getting into Memory Stick territory. The vast majority of existing Memory Stick products can't accept Memory Stick Pro cards—you need to look for the Memory Stick Pro logo on new cameras. Older Memory Sticks work fine in new Memory Stick Pro products, on the other hand.

8

Secure Digital (SD)

The newest kind of removable memory, used in just a handful of digital cameras today, is called Secure Digital (and more commonly referred to by the acronym SD). *SD* is a modern take on the removable memory card problem and offers your digital camera high memory capacities in a footprint about the size of your thumbnail. SD cards are similar to MultiMediaCard (MMC) cards—both share the same overall dimensions (though SD cards are slightly thicker than MMC cards), and most mobile devices are designed to accommodate both formats interchangeably. The principal difference is data encryption: SD cards enable vendors to deliver copyrighted data to the end user while ensuring it can't be illegally copied.

Here's the important part: SD cards are likely to become a real success in the mobile storage battle. Palm, for instance, has standardized the SD card format for all its m-series PDAs, giving the format a huge base of operations. Just as important, the SD card is small enough to fit into every conceivable portable gadget, including very small digital cameras. As time marches on, I think you'll see SD become a popular digital camera format, especially because SD cards can hold large amounts of memory—currently 256MB and climbing.

xD

When it became clear that the SmartMedia card was ready for the Old Memory Card Home, Olympus and Fuji collaborated on a new memory card format, which they dubbed xD. The *xD card* is SmartMedia's more modern successor, and it appears in several Olympus and FujiFilm cameras—but, at press time, no models from any other manufacturers. That's not too surprising, because while the xD card carries the "price premium" you'd expect from a new product line, it offers few advantages over other, established memory formats like SD. xD is certainly the smallest memory card format on the market—which means it can be used to power some very tiny cameras—but it might be a format to avoid for the time being.

Floppy Disk and CD-R

Older Sony digital cameras used the floppy disk drive as a form of image storage. The advantage: floppy disks were ubiquitous. There were no confusing image transfer procedures because you just pull the floppy out of the camera and insert it into the PC's floppy disk drive. On the other hand, floppy disks only hold 1.44MB of data—a tiny amount compared to any other memory card format. Floppy disks are also fairly slow. Those disadvantages add up to cameras that simply couldn't take high-resolution images, and they suffered from a long lag between when the image was taken and when it was written to memory. These cameras are largely relegated to the dustbin of history, but Sony now sells cameras that write pictures to a recordable CD disc. These cameras suffer from all the same limitations as the floppy disk models. My advice? Avoid them.

Memory Card Glitches

I've heard from readers who complain that their SmartMedia cards sometimes seem to "die." If it's stopped working, what's the real problem?

First, remember that SmartMedia cards are pretty delicate. They're wafer-thin and have important electrical contacts exposed right on the surface. If you've damaged the card, which isn't altogether out of the question, it's now a really, really small coaster. Throw it away with the knowledge that you can replace it for just a few dollars.

An engineer from a memory card company has told me other possibilities exist as well. It seems that using the same SmartMedia card in multiple devices can change the formatting or fill the header information on the card with gibberish, rendering it unable to store digital pictures. So don't use the same SmartMedia card in your MP3 player and digital camera. In addition, when you get ready to transfer your pictures to your PC, don't use the Windows Explorer interface to copy the files—use My Computer instead. You can try to revive the card by using the Format command in the camera's menu system. But, if that doesn't work, you're probably out of luck.

And one more thing—this only seems to affect SmartMedia cards, so your CompactFlash, SD, and Memory Stick collection is probably safe.

Choosing a Memory Card Format

As mentioned, memory devices vary dramatically in size. In Figure 8-1 you can see the relative sizes of the most common memory formats.

Worth noting is this: in at least a few cases, you needn't choose between different memory storage formats anymore. Some camera makers include both CompactFlash and SmartMedia slots in some of their cameras. Not only does that mean you can pick a camera on features and not worry about whether you like SmartMedia or CompactFlash better, but you can also insert two memory cards in the camera at once and switch from one to the other when one card

FIGURE 8-1   Relative size of various removable memory cards

fills up. The Olympus E-20n (seen in Figure 8-2) uses just this system, eliminating the traditional confusion over competing memory card formats.

With all that said, what kind of memory card should you use? In general, I'd say choosing a specific kind of memory card isn't nearly so important as picking other camera features, like zoom, optical quality, and useful exposure modes. Of course, I'd definitely avoid cameras with floppy disk-, CD-R, and SmartMedia-based storage systems. I'm also inclined to avoid xD-only cameras, because those cards cost a bit more than comparable SD and CompactFlash memory. Memory Stick (not Memory Stick Pro) cameras are also a bit limiting because you're forced to use memory that's 128MB or less.

There's little compelling reason to prefer CompactFlash or SD. In my experience, CompactFlash cards are generally the cheapest on the market, and they're also available in higher capacities right now. But history has proven that prices drop and capacities go up for most memory cards, so don't get too hung up on that.

Bottom line? Buy a camera based on other features, and only use the kind of memory card it has as part of your last-look criteria.

8

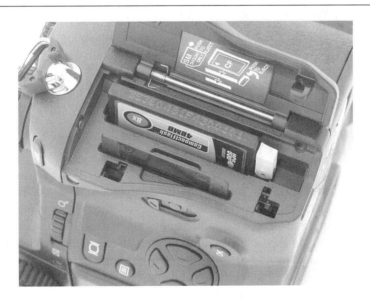

FIGURE 8-2   Most cameras use just one kind of memory, though some models—like the Olympus e-10 and e-20n—accept both SmartMedia and CompactFlash cards for more flexibility and storage space.

The Mystery of the Fifth Beatle

Everyone, it seems, stakes a claim to being the Fifth Beatle. This is an odd phenomenon that has perplexed me as well as other Beatles' scholars for many years. Here's a short list of the most prominent names sometimes awarded the coveted Fifth Beatle moniker:

- Billy Preston, close friend and occasional session musician
- Eric Clapton, close friend, guitar god, and occasional session musician
- George Martin, Beatles' producer
- Yoko Ono, wife of John Lennon
- Ravi Shankar, mentor to George Harrison
- Ringo Starr, often also acknowledged as the Fourth Beatle
- Stuart Sutcliffe, the actual Fifth Beatle in their early pre-EMI days
- Paul Rice, musician and writer widely acknowledged to be too short to be a Beatle

Transferring Images to the PC

No matter what kind of digital camera or removable media you use, eventually you need to get your pictures from the camera to a computer, where you'll be able to edit, print, and distribute them. Your digital camera comes with software for transferring images and a cable that you can use to connect the camera to your PC. For many users, this in-the-box solution is all they'll ever need. These days, the de facto standard for transferring images is via USB, though if you find a very old digital camera, it might come with a serial cable. And some high-end pro digitals use FireWire (also known as IEEE-1394).

Transferring Images with a USB Port

In the old days, most cameras used a serial connection cable to transfer pictures from the camera's memory to the computer. That's because most computers—both PC and Macintosh—have serial ports, so camera makers were assured their cameras would work with your computer, no matter what kind you have.

On the downside, your PC's serial port is slow, meaning it can take a long time to copy images from the camera to the computer. The serial port is also kind of stupid. It doesn't know when something is plugged into it, so you have to manually start the software needed to copy images. If you already have something in the serial port, you might also have to remove that device and disable its software. Most computer manufacturers recommend you shut off your PC before you insert and remove cables from the serial port, so that also entails a lot of rebooting.

TIP *If you're in the market for a new camera, you'll find they're virtually all USB based. You can discover a lot of used cameras with serial connections, though (like on eBay), and I emphatically recommend you avoid them.*

8

USB 2.0 Versus USB 1.1

The vast majority of computers and digital cameras use a standard called USB 1.1. You might hear about a new form of USB called USB 2.0, though, and it can be a bit confusing.

USB 2.0 is dramatically faster than its older cousin. Instead of 12 Mbps, which is the speed of USB 1.1, *USB 2.0* runs at a whopping 450 Mbps. So, if it used to take five minutes to transfer your digital images to the PC's hard disk, USB 2.0 will be able to do it in about ten seconds. Pretty cool, huh?

Unfortunately, for USB 2.0 to work, you need a computer with USB 2.0 ports (most new PCs sold in the last year have them) and digital camera that's USB 2.0-compliant as well (most digital cameras are still built around USB 1.1). If you use a USB hub to attach lots of USB devices to your PC, that must also be USB 2.0. If any one of those parts is USB 1.1, your image transfers will happen at the regular 12 Mbps speed.

On the plus side, USB 2.0 is 100 percent compatible with USB 1.1—so you can mix at match gear, albeit if any piece of the puzzle is USB 1.1, all the data is transferred at the slower USB 1.1 speed. USB 2.0 is a big step forward, but not everyone can take advantage of it.

FIGURE 8-3   Belkin's powered USB hub is just one of many options for connecting more USB gadgets to your computer's limited array of USB ports.

These days, USB is the standard connection system for digital cameras for two good reasons: they avoid most of the headaches associated with serial connections, and they transfer images a lot faster than the old, slow serial ports.

Not only is USB *hot swappable* (which means you needn't power off your PC to insert or remove the USB cable) but, typically, it'll automatically recognize your camera when you connect it and even launch the appropriate transfer software automatically.

In addition, USB ports transfer data at up to 12 Mbps. That's something like 50 times faster than data transfers with the pokey old serial port. In reality, transfers never reach that theoretical maximum speed, but it's a lot faster than serial nonetheless.

USB Glitches

Although USB is susceptible to fewer problems than serial ports, it can occasionally annoy you. The main problems? A lack of power and bandwidth, which can rear its ugly head when you try connecting a lot of USB devices to your computer. Consider these tips:

- *Add more ports.* Most PCs come with only two USB ports. If you have two USB devices connected to your PC, you're already out of ports. Solve that problem by buying a USB hub from the local computer store. A USB port typically turns one USB connection into four, as you can see in Figure 8-3.

- *Power the ports.* While some devices can get power from the USB port itself, many USB devices require more power than the USB port can deliver. That's why it's a good idea to use a *powered hub*—that's a USB hub that you plug into AC power. If your USB devices seem to work erratically or if you get warning messages in Windows, be sure to use a powered hub and keep the hub plugged in.

■ *Distribute your bandwidth*. Your PC probably has a two USB ports (though newer computers are beginning to come with more), each of which can transfer up to 12 Mbps of data. If you attach a hub to one of those ports, those four new ports in the hub still have to share the original 12 Mbps of data. If you put four data-hungry devices (like a digital camera, a video Webcam, a joystick, and a speaker set) on the same hub, they can overtax the USB hub and make it perform erratically. So, if you have a bunch of USB devices, I suggest you put a hub on each port and try to move devices around so the most power-hungry ones aren't all connected to the same port.

8

 Connect Your Camera with USB

If you have a USB-enabled camera and PC, the transfer process is easy. Here's a general overview of how to do it:

1. Start by installing the software that came with your camera. You need to install the software before you plug in the USB cable and the camera for the first time.

2. Connect the USB cable to your computer's USB port and to the camera. You needn't turn off your computer to do this, even if you have to disconnect an existing USB device to free up a port.

3. Turn on the camera and set it to its transfer mode. Connect the camera to AC power if you can.

4. The computer should automatically recognize the camera and start the transfer software. Now you can drag the images from the camera to a folder on the computer.

Transfer Shortcuts: Using Memory Card Readers

Just because your camera comes with a serial or USB cable, that doesn't mean you have to use it. *Memory adapters*, which are gadgets that let you insert a memory card and read images from it like a floppy disk, let you easily transfer images to the computer without messing with any cables at all. Using memory adapters has several advantages:

- You can conserve camera battery power because the camera isn't used in the transfer.

- You don't have to get to the back of your computer to connect or disconnect cables.

- Transfers might be faster with an adapter.

- You can avoid confusing transfer software because adapters let you drag-and-drop images directly to a folder on your hard disk.

Using a Memory Adapter

The kind of memory adapter you choose depends largely on the kind of removable memory your camera uses. In general, they're all more efficient than connecting your camera with a cable.

- **Desktop single-format card readers**   For $15 or $20, you can get a USB card reader that accepts whatever kind of memory card your digital camera uses. You can get readers for CompactFlash, SmartMedia, SD, Memory Stick, and even xD. The downside? If you ever need to read a different kind of memory card—like from a second camera or a digital music player—you'll need to buy a second card reader, which will eat up a second USB port and more desk space.

■ **Desktop all-in-one readers**   Just like cameras that are starting to accommodate more than one kind of memory card, readers are becoming more flexible as well. Universal readers can accommodate six or more kinds of memory cards, making it easy to read and write to cards for your digital camera, MP3 player, and PDA all from the same device. I use my 6-in-1 universal card reader from Dazzle all the time.

■ **Internal card readers**   For the ultimate in convenience, you can find card readers that fit in one of your PC's empty drive bays. Y-E Data (www.yedata.com), for instance, sells the excellent 7-in-1 reader that packs six kinds of memory card slots into a floppy disk drive. Replace your existing floppy disk drive and have access to any memory card (except xD) right from your PC.

Memory Card: Fact and Fiction

I've met people with some interesting misconceptions about digital film, so let me try to dispel some myths.

Removable memory cards are nothing more than digital storage for your camera. That means memory cards aren't designed to store images of a certain size. Some people mistakenly believe if they want to store images of a larger or smaller pixel size, they need a different memory card. Memory cards are completely standardized and interchangeable, and they don't particularly care what you store on them. In fact, you don't even have to put digital images on them at all. They'll hold sound files, text documents, and more. Your camera won't know what to do with files like that and, consequently, they'll ignore such files, but you can store anything on a memory card.

Differences exist among memory cards, though. The principal difference is speed-cards are rated at speeds like 2x (slowest), 4x, and 8x (fastest). The faster ones write data faster and are a good choice if you value speed when taking pictures. They're also good for high-megapixel cameras because large files take longer to record. On the other hand, faster cards cost more, and the speed benefits generally aren't measurable unless you have a digital SLR-other digicams don't take advantage of the faster performance.

Caring for Your Memory Cards

After you finish transferring images from the memory card to your PC, you no longer need those images. You can delete them to make room for more pictures. You can do this in two ways: you can delete them via the PC, use the camera's controls to delete the images, or reformat the card. If your memory card is inserted in the PC via some sort of memory card adapter, using the PC doesn't waste camera battery power, and that's a good reason to do it that way. If you don't have that luxury, a good idea is to plug the camera into its AC adapter, so you don't drain your camera's batteries.

To delete images from your memory card via the PC, you can usually just select the files and press the DEL key on your keyboard. It's just like deleting any kind of file from your PC's floppy or hard disk. But, if you want to format your memory card, only do it on your camera—not on your desktop PC.

To delete images using the camera's interface, you'll have to navigate the camera's menu system. Typically, you'll have the option of either deleting a single image or all the images on the disk at once. Be careful—this operation can't be undone.

NOTE *If you have some important images on your memory card and you don't want them deleted, you can usually use your camera to protect them. Check your camera's menu system for a feature called "protect" or "lock." That way, you can delete all the images on your memory card, and those specially protected images will remain until you explicitly unprotect them. In general, though, I suggest moving special images to your PC where you'll be less likely to accidentally delete them.*

In addition to deleting images from your memory cards, you should take other precautions to ensure your cards live a long and fruitful life. After all, memory cards can be expensive. Keep the following tips in mind:

- Avoid putting memory cards in direct sunlight.

- Don't put memory cards in your back pocket or other places where they can get bent or crushed. That's particularly true for SmartMedia cards and floppy disks, which can break with moderate amounts of force.

- Keep your cards empty whenever possible. All memory cards look alike, and the last thing you need is to put a memory card in your camera while you're on vacation only to discover it's still full of images you never saved to your PC from last time. Transfer images to the PC promptly, and then format or erase the card.

- Never write on memory cards or put any kind of sticker on them to track their contents. That can damage the card or the camera.

Recovering Lost Pictures

Have you ever accidentally deleted an important file, noticing it was gone an instant after you sent it irretrievably to the trash? All you can do is shout, "d'oh!"

The same thing can happen to pictures on a memory card. Thankfully, when you erase a card, the files aren't necessarily gone right away—the memory card simply "forgets" it's holding data. If you need to get back lost images, you might consider *Photorecovery,* a utility from LCTechnology (www.lc-tech.com). This simple program recovers deleted images, movies, and other data from removable memory cards. And, it works with any removable media, from SmartMedia and Compact Flash to Memory Stick and SD Cards.

Photorecovery scans the contents of a card, restoring lost files to a folder on your PC's hard disk as it goes. I've tried it, and it works. In fact, a friend recently

8

sent me a card he believed was corrupt—after he filled it with pictures, the PC reported no images were on board. I ran Photorecovery on the card and got a batch of photos back. My friend was quite grateful.

Just remember, if you plan to run Photorecovery on a memory card, do it before you use the card for anything else. Adding new data to your card can damage "deleted" pictures already on the card, lowering the odds that you'll get anything useful from the recovery process.

What are the odds you'll ever need this program? Pretty low, I suspect. But if you do find yourself with a dead memory card or lost pictures, Photorecovery might be worth a try.

Traveling with Pictures

It's one thing to travel with a memory card or two and a digital camera—it's quite another thing to have so many memory cards that your pockets jangle when you walk. But if you're traveling for a while, such as on a vacation trip, how can you have enough memory space to take all the pictures you need without running out

 Planning to Take Lots of Pictures

How many images can you fit on a memory card? You can use this handy chart to decide what size memory card—or how many memory cards—to take on your next family vacation. This chart assumes you're capturing JPG images in high-quality compression, but remember that your mileage may vary quite a bit depending upon how your digital camera processes its image—just use it as a general guide to picking memory card capacities:

	32MB	64MB	128MB	256MB	512MB
One-megapixel	91	182	356	731	1420
Two-megapixel	35	71	142	284	561
Three-megapixel	26	53	106	213	421
Four-megapixel	16	32	64	128	252
Five-megapixel	12	25	51	102	204

of room? Instead of taking a half-dozen 256MB memory cards, I have a better solution: take a storage device that you can use to transfer your pictures to, and then erase your card and start anew.

Several gadgets are on the market that store your digital images while you're on the road. These devices have memory slots to accept images from your memory cards and securely store your images until you can get home and transfer the data to your PC. Here are some you might want to consider:

- **Portable Digital Image Backup (www.ezpnp.com)**   This is my favorite gadget. It's a portable CD recorder that accepts AC power or AA batteries. Insert your memory card and press the Record button—the contents of the card are written to a folder on the CD-R, after which you can erase the card and continue shooting pictures. I like this device because, compared to portable hard disk, a CD-R is essentially indestructible—it won't break from rough handling.

- **eFilm PicturePad (www.delkin.com)**   This handheld, battery-operated gadget stores massive amounts of digital images and includes an LCD display that lets you preview your images while you're still on the road.

- **Nixvue (www.nixvue.com)**   *Nixvue* is a company that offers both kinds of storage devices—CD-R-based and hard disk-based solutions. The *Vizor* records images to disc, while the *Vista* is a portable hard disk with integrated LCD. The *Digital Album II* is a hard disk without the LCD display, but it has video outputs for connecting to a television.

8

Chapter 9

Keeping Images on the PC

How to...

- Use the My Pictures folder in Windows 98

- Organize your images in Windows

- Transfer, rename, and categorize your images to reduce clutter

- Use the special My Pictures folder in Windows Me

- Browse images visually with Paint Shop Pro and Image Expert

- Search images by keyword with Image Expert

- Use Quick View to see pictures without opening an image-editing program

- Install Quick View from the Windows 98 installation CD

- Estimate file size for TIF and JPG images

- Archive your pictures on CD-ROM

- Install a new hard disk for additional storage

In the previous chapter, we talked about how to get images from your camera or its memory card onto your PC. That's a good start, but if you're anything like me, you need some help getting it all under control. Digital images proliferate like bunnies and can be hard to organize. After just a few months, in fact, you might discover that your computer's hard disk is essentially full, and the unorganized mess within is largely a ton of poorly named, hard-to-decipher digital images that don't do anyone any good.

In this chapter, we'll talk about the essentials of getting your stockpile of digital images under control. You have a lot of things to consider: naming and arranging your images; using special software to better arrange and organize your pictures; and understanding the relationship between image size and file size, so you can predict how much space you'll need. And, because you might eventually need to add on to your PC's storage capability, we'll talk about how you can archive your images on media like CD-ROMs and additional hard drives.

Managing Your Digital Pictures

Keeping your hard disk organized is essential if you hope to find your digital pictures. In a sense, then, part of this chapter is a tutorial in managing your computer's life.

I know a lot of people who don't worry too much about organizing their hard disk. They just download images from their camera to some folder on their hard disk and assume they can find what they need later. The problem? The images from your camera typically have fairly obscure filenames, like pic00012.jpg or dsc0012.jpg (see Figure 9-1). It's impossible to determine the contents of an image from such an arcane filename. Imagine having hundreds or even thousands of files like this on your hard disk, and you start to get an inkling of the problem.

Organizing Your Images

Keeping your images organized isn't hard, but it takes a little planning. I recommend that you store your images in a single folder or set of folders, instead of spreading them all over your hard disk. Most versions of Windows have a folder called My Pictures for storing images, and I suggest you use it.Tip: If you're using Windows Me or Windows XP, you'll find the My Pictures folder inside the My Documents folder.

If you're using an older version of Windows and the My Pictures folder doesn't exist, create it yourself. To create a folder to store your images, do this:

1. Double-click the My Computer icon on your Windows desktop. You should see a window that displays all the devices and drives connected to your PC:

FIGURE 9-1   Your digital camera's code-like naming scheme for images is of no help
              when you want to find a specific picture.

2. If you're using Windows XP, double-click your My Documents folder (it
   might be called something like Dave's Documents or Betty's Documents).
   If you have an older version of Windows, double-click the C: drive. A
   window should open, revealing more folders.

3. If you don't see a folder called My Pictures, you can create your own.
   Right-click on an empty space in the C: drive's window. You should see a
   menu appear.

4. Choose New | Folder from the menu. A new, empty folder should appear in the C: drive window.

5. Now it's time to rename the folder. The New Folder text under the folder is highlighted, as the following shows. Type **My Pictures** and press ENTER. You should see the name of the folder change.

> **TIP** *If you click on the desktop before you have a chance to rename the new folder, just right-click on the folder and choose Rename from the menu. Then type the new name of the folder.*

You can store your images anywhere, but I think the My Pictures folder is a great place. It's easy to remember, and many graphics' applications will automatically look here for pictures.

Now that you have a main folder for storing your images, you might want to create subfolders, which are folders inside your main folder (like My Pictures) that let you organize your pictures more precisely. As you can see in Figure 9-2, I organize my images into a myriad of folders that help me find specific images by category, event, purpose, and genre.

Renaming Images

Now that you have an organizational system for arranging your images, it's time to think about filenames.

FIGURE 9-2   The more subfolders you use, the easier it should be to find the right image in a pinch.

I suggest that when you transfer your images to the PC, you immediately rename your images and categorize them into specific folders. Don't put this off till later! If you transfer images and opt to rename them later, you'll end up with a few batches of 30 images each that need to be renamed. The task will eventually get too daunting, and you'll have untold pictures with obscure filenames that need to be renamed.

Here's an easy strategy for renaming your images:

1. Open the folder in which your newly transferred images are stored.

2. If you're using Windows Me or Windows XP, you should be able to see a preview of the image in the folder. If you can't, choose View | Filmstrip or View | Thumbnails from the folder's menu. Look at the first photo and decide what you want to name it.

3. Click the photo, pause, and, after a second, click the image's name. Don't simply double-click, or the image will open. If you did this step properly, the filename should be ready to edit. Type the name of the file and press the ENTER key.

TIP
If this technique doesn't work for you, right-click the photo and choose Rename from the menu.

4. Repeat the process with the other images in the folder.

5. When you're done, you can drag images into an appropriate subfolder in the My Pictures folder and delete the empty temporary folder.

If you want a better view of a picture in the folder, you can always just double-click it. Windows will display it in the Windows Picture and Fax Viewer. You can use the scroll wheel on your mouse to zoom in and out when in the viewer.

9

If you're using an older version of Windows, you don't get the fancy image preview tools that Windows Me and Windows XP users see. Instead, you can access the contents of each image as you rename them by using the Quick View tool from the menu. Just right-click each picture and choose Quick View from the menu. Then close the Quick View preview of your image and rename the photo.

Finally, keep in mind that if you install certain programs, they can replace the built-in Windows picture viewer with their own picture viewing utility. If you install ACDSee to manage your images, for instance (see the section "Using Asset Management Software"), it'll substitute its own image viewer.

Faster Renaming

Ideally, you'll rename all your photos as you transfer them to your PC—that way, it's a bit easier to find them whenever you need a specific image. But let's be honest—sometimes that's just a bit too much work. If you simply want to change the name of your files from totally indecipherable —like P7281775—to something that reflects the overall theme of the batch—like Summer Vacation—then you can do that as well.

Select all the photos in the folder. You can do that by choosing Edit | Select All from the folder's menu, or you can click the first picture in the folder, scroll to the last image, and click again, holding down the SHIFT button on your keyboard. *Shift*

Selecting, as it's called, lets you choose all the files between the first and last click in a single action.

Only want to select a few images? Use the CTRL *key on your keyboard to Control Select method to choose only certain images. Or, select all the images, and use the* CTRL *key to deselect the images you don't want!*

Right-click one of the selected images—it doesn't matter which one—and choose Rename from the menu. Type a new name and press the ENTER key. Your pictures will all be given the new name, with a number in parentheses so you can tell them apart.

Working with Quick View

Quick View is a handy tool you can use to determine what's in a file when you're ready to rename it, and it's also handy for getting a quick look at pictures in general. But what is Quick View?

Quick View is simply a program found in Windows 95 and 98 that lets you see the contents of certain kinds of files just by right-clicking their icon and selecting Quick View from the menu. I think this is a lot easier—and faster—than opening a special graphics program just to look at a photo.

If you don't have Quick View in your menu when you right-click an image, it isn't installed. But fear not—Quick View is a utility that's included on the Windows installation disk.

Quick View is not included in Windows Me or XP because those operating systems (OSes) have much better image viewing tools.

Here's how to install Quick View on Windows 95/98:

1. Choose Start | Settings | Control Panel from the Windows Start menu. You should see the Control Panel window appear.

2. Double-click the Add/Remove Programs icon.

3. Click the Windows Setup tab. This contains a list of all optional software on the Windows installation disk.

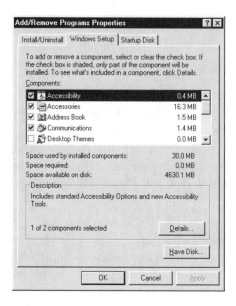

4. Click the entry for Accessories, and then click the Details button. You should see the Accessories dialog box appear. This contains a list of all the accessory programs in Windows.

5. Scroll down until you find Quick View and click on it, putting a check mark next to the entry. Then click OK.

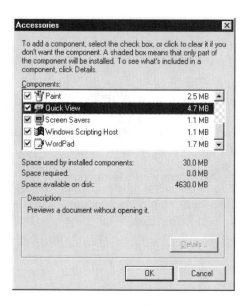

6. Click OK again, this time in the Add/Remove Programs dialog box. Windows might prompt you for the Windows installation CD. If it doesn't, insert it in your CD-ROM drive.

After the installation, you should have the Quick View entry in the context menu when you right-click on icons on the Windows desktop.

Locating and Cataloging Images

Even with a rigorous set of subfolders, it can get difficult to find specific images on your hard disk. My hard disk contains many hundreds of images, for instance, and even with descriptive filenames and lots of aptly titled subfolders, it can be a challenge to locate "that picture of the two wolves frolicking in the fallen leaves" I took two years ago. It's akin to finding a needle within a stack of other needles.

Filenames and folders are great, but there's no substitute for looking at your images. That's why I'm going to show you how you can catalog your images with a visual tool—software that lets you view your pictures directly, all at once, and open the one you need without delay.

Viewing Your Images with Your Image Editor

Many popular image editors make it easy to find your photos visually with some sort of thumbnail-based file browser. My two favorite image editors—Paint Shop Pro 8 and Adobe Photoshop Elements 2—have such a feature.

Using Paint Shop Pro's Image Browser   One great reason to use one of these programs is the capability to browse your images visually. Paint Shop Pro's Browse tool is seen in Figure 9-3. *Browse* lets you see the images on your hard disk graphically, with each image represented by a thumbnail. That means you can use Browse in two ways:

- If you want to edit or print an image, you can use the Browse tool to find an image visually, without needing to know the filename.

- If you just want to review your images, you can use the Browse tool to see your image thumbnails.

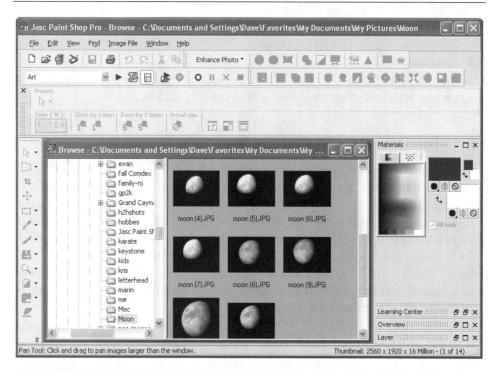

FIGURE 9-3 Paint Shop Pro lets you browse your hard disk visually.

Here is how to use Paint Shop Pro's Browse tool:

1. Start Paint Shop Pro.

2. Choose File | Browse from the menu. The Browse window should appear.

3. Use the folder tree on the left side of the window to find the folder you want to look in. When you click the folder, thumbnail images will appear on the right. To find My Pictures (where Windows XP commonly stores images), for instance, you would find it on the left, under Desktop, and click to see all the subfolders stored within.

4. To open an image in Paint Shop Pro, just double-click a thumbnail or click and drag it to the Paint Shop Pro workspace. The image will open, ready for editing, printing, or just viewing at a larger size.

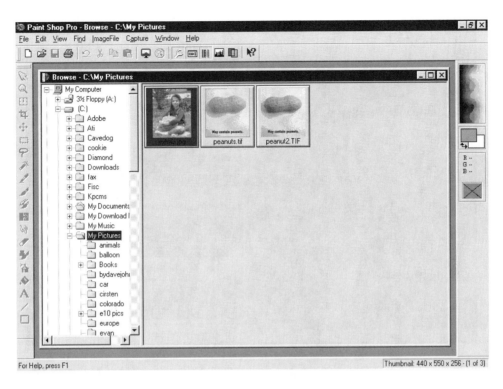

5. You can continue opening additional images from the Browse window. Close the Browse window when you're done with it.

TIP *You can right-click image thumbnails in the Browse window to perform many common operations, like print, rename, and rotate.*

Using Photoshop Element's Image Browser   If you use Adobe Photoshop Elements, you'll find a similar browse tool under the hood of that program as well. Just look for the File Browser tab at the top of the screen. Click it, and you'll get access to all the folders on your hard disk in a drop-down window. Navigate to your My Pictures folder (it's probably in My Documents) and you can surf around your images.

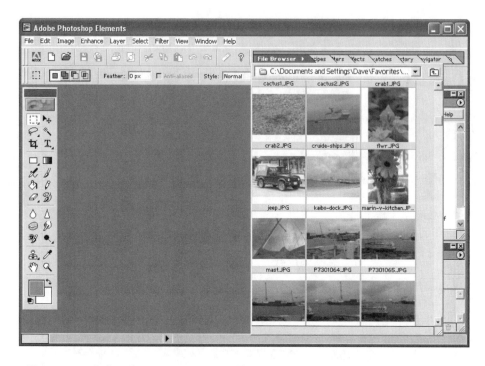

Be sure to notice that you can go "up" to the previous folder via the small Up Folder button atop the screen, and you can choose other, recently chosen folders from the folder drop-down menu as well.

When you're ready to work with an image, you can double-click to open it or just click-and-drag it to the Photoshop Elements workspace.

Using Asset Management Software

If your collection of digital images is large enough, you might feel constrained by the file browsers in programs like Paint Shop Pro and PhotoShop Elements. If you have a few thousand images in your library, consider a dedicated photo album program. You have a number to choose from, though, here are my favorites:

- **ExtensisPortfolio 6**   www.extensis.com

- **Adobe Photoshop Album**   www.adobe.com

- **ACDSee**   www.acdsee.com

- **Jasc Paint Shop Photo Album**   www.jasc.com

Using any of these programs, you can search for images visually, by keyword, or by filename. You can drag and drop images directly into your editor for modification or printing, and you can generate web pages based on your digital image thumbnails automatically, with little effort. A huge favorite among digital photographers is *ACDSee,* which combines ease of use with powerful cataloging tools and some basic image-editing features.

Portfolio, on the other hand, is the most sophisticated of these programs. *Portfolio* has the capability to automatically update its database with new pictures as they're added to your hard disk with no intervention on your part, and a small browser program sits in your System Tray, ready to find images at a moment's notice. Although it's the most expensive program in its class, Portfolio is the best for those who work with tons of photos, if for no other reason than its automatic update feature. With other programs, like Photoshop Album, you'll need to tell the program to locate new pictures every time you add some to your PC from a digital camera.

Adobe's Photoshop Album is perhaps the coolest of the bunch, though. *Photoshop Album* uses a clever drag-and-drop keyword system. Instead of painstakingly typing the same keywords into each of your picture's Properties boxes over and over, you create a bunch of "tags" in Photoshop Album, and then drag them on to pictures that should have that criteria.

In this way, you can quickly create a few dozen common tags (like family, kids, pets, vacation, and so forth) and associate multiple tags with each image. When you want to find a picture of your kids on vacation, select those tow tags and click the search button—it's that easy.

The program also has a great calendar-based search feature that lets you locate images according to when they were taken—just by dragging arrows around on a timeline.

9

Estimating File Size

So, you save a lot of images on your hard disk. How many can you pack in before you need more storage space?

That isn't necessarily an easy question to answer. That's because the most common file formats, like JPG, don't always save an image to the same file size. The size that any particular image takes up on your hard disk will vary, depending on how much color information is stored in the image. A single-color image, such as a graphic that's plain, solid blue, will compress dramatically to a miniscule size, while a complex image won't compress as efficiently. Nonetheless, we can make some ballpark estimates that will help you keep track of storage space if you want to.

Use Keywords

A *keyword* is a term you can use to identify the contents, theme, or style of an image. Suppose you have this witty picture, for instance:

May contain peanuts.

You might want to associate the following keywords with this image: **peanut**, **funny**, **macro**. When you search for all your pictures that have the work "funny" or "peanut" in their description, this image should appear in the list. Keywords are a manual operation, though. You need to decide what keywords to use and enter them all by hand in whatever program you use that supports this feature. But if your cataloging software supports keywords, a little effort up front can make it quite easy to find that proverbial needle in the haystack.

Calculating TIFs

Let's start with the easy file formats. Some file formats out there are considered lossless. (Recall from Chapter 7 that the term "lossless" means no matter how many times you open and resave the file, no loss of data will ever occur.) That's because the image isn't really being compressed in a way that destroys information in the original image. Every pixel is preserved forever. The most common lossless file formats are BMP and TIF files. To figure out how much space either of these files will take up, you can just use this equation:

File size in bytes = x-dimension × y-dimension × 24 / 8

In other words, take the pixel dimensions of your image and multiply them. Multiply that by 24 (because 24 bits of color information are associated with every pixel in the image), and then divide the result by 8, because we want the answer in bytes, not bits. Divide that answer by 1000 to get the answer in the more popular kilobytes.

Here's an example. Suppose you want to know how much space two dozen images will take up that were shot with your digital camera on its lowest resolution setting (which is 640 × 480). The camera saves its images in the lossless TIF format. The math would be

$$640 \times 480 \times 24 / 8 = 921{,}600 \text{ bytes}$$

Divide that by 1000, and you get 921KB—which is just shy of a megabyte. Multiply that single image result by 24 (the number of images you plan to shoot), and you get a total storage size of 22,118KB, or 22MB. That's a lot of space.

Calculating JPGs

That's all well and good but, most of the time, digital cameras shoot in the lossy file format known as JPG. JPG files can be adjusted to compress more aggressively—that makes the files smaller but the quality lower—or compress less for bigger, higher-quality files.

There's no easy equation you can use on JPGs, because the compression varies not only according to the image quality setting you use on your camera, but also according to the amount of color information, sharpness, and overall complexity of the picture. Nonetheless, I'll take a stab at it. In general, you can assume that JPG files will be about this size, depending on the quality setting:

JPG Quality	Compression
High (low compression)	Approximately 95 percent of the original TIF size
Medium	Approximately 75 percent to 85 percent of the original TIF size
Low (high compression)	Approximately 25 percent of the original TIF size

These are ballpark figures, but you would be able to store about 440 average JPGs in the same hard disk space that it would take to store full-resolution TIF files of the same pixel dimensions.

What does this say about how you should store your images? In general, high-quality JPGs are good enough for most applications, and they take up a mere fraction of the space TIFs or BMP files would consume. When you can, use the JPG format, and your hard disk will thank you. Be careful about using too much JPG compression, though. I recommend sticking with a fairly low compression level, or your image quality will suffer.

Archiving Images

Eventually, your collection of digital images could grow too large for your hard disk. If that's the case, you have a few choices:

- Delete nonessential images from your hard disk.

- Archive the images on another storage device, like CD or DVD.

- Add another hard disk for additional storage space.

Deleting images is the easiest route, but it has the least potential. You probably want to save many of your images forever, so you might not want to get rid of that many images. Instead, consider archiving your images to another device. If you have a CD-RW or DVD-R/RW drive, you can copy dozens or hundreds of images to a disc (depending on the file size) that will last more or less forever. CDs do degrade over time, but they will last for a hundred years or so—longer than the ink on many kinds of photographs. To be sure your images are protected, you can make a new copy of your CD or DVD every 10 or 20 years—or, more realistically, transfer the images to whatever technology is popular then, like nuclear bionic laser holographic kneepads. Or whatever.

A *CD-RW drive* is a kind of CD drive that can write to blank discs, while *DVD writers* come in several varieties—the most common of which is DVD-R/RW and DVD-RAM. Most of these drives come with software like Adaptec's Easy CD and DVD Creator (www.adaptec.com), seen in Figure 9-4, or perhaps Nero (www.nero.com). These programs let you simply drag and drop image files from the hard disk to the CD, and then "burn" the disk, a process that takes a few minutes to copy all the data to the CD. After it's done, the CD-R is playable in any computer with a CD-ROM drive.

If you have Windows XP and a CD-RW drive, you don't even need any additional software—just open a folder with images and select the images you want to copy to CD. Then click Copy to CD from the Picture Tasks pane on the left side of the folder. After a few moments, you'll see a balloon in the System Tray that says You have files waiting to be written to the CD. Place a black CD in

FIGURE 9-4   CD Burning software makes it easy to copy blank images to a CD.

your drive and open My Computer. Right-click the blank CD and choose Write these files to CD. It's a bit more complicated than using a program like Roxio or Nero, but it's free.

NOTE   *When you archive your images on to CD, be sure to use CD-R discs, not CD-RW discs. The two media are quite different, and CD-RWs are generally not readable on other PCs. In addition, data copied to CD-RW discs can be deleted, so it's possible to accidentally overwrite your images later. To be safe, always use CD-R media, which are cheaper anyway. On the DVD front, the same is true of DVD-R and DVD-RW; use DVD-R, which is cheaper, can't be erased, and is more universally compatible.*

Pixel Potential

If you photograph a plain white background, in JPG format it'll take up almost no space at all on your memory card or computer hard disk. That's because the JPG format stores information about the change in color information from one pixel to another and, if the image is all white, there's little change data to record. But what about a TIF? The same picture stored as a TIF will be much larger, because the file holds a space for all 24 bits of color data in each pixel. The TIF format isn't concerned about the colors in the image; instead, it's preoccupied with the potential colors that could be in the image. Even though every pixel is white, the TIF format has enough room to store any color in each and every pixel. TIF files compress quite nicely using a ZIP program, though, so you can save a file in TIF format and "zip it up" to e-mail it to someone.

Adding Extra Hard Drives

One other option you might consider is adding another hard disk. Hard drives get cheaper and bigger every year, and these days 80GB and 120GB drives are neither unusual nor are they particularly expensive. Some people install a second drive and dedicate it for images, video, music, and other multimedia files.

To see if your PC is a good candidate for a second hard disk, shut it down and open it up. Many computers have tool-free cases that you can open easily; other PCs require a small screwdriver to remove the side of the case. In either case, once the PC is open, check to see if there's a spare bay to mount the hard disk. You can mount it in one of the drive bays or, perhaps, on the bottom or side of the case, where there are some mounts for exactly that purpose. If there's somewhere to put a hard disk, it's easy to install yourself.

TIP   *If you don't want to mess around inside your PC, you can add an external hard disk instead. These days, USB 2.0 (discussed in Chapter 8) and FireWire (also known as i.Link or IEEE1394) hard disks are fast, inexpensive, and install in just minutes by doing nothing more than plugging in a cable. I highly recommend these sorts of external drives.*

Once you've found somewhere to put the drive, follow these basic steps:

1. Ensure the PC is off and you are fully grounded before proceeding. You can purchase a static grounding mat or a strap that attaches to your wrist at any local computer shop. Alternately, you can ground yourself by touching the metal cage surrounding the computer's power supply as long as the computer is plugged into the wall outlet. If you leave the computer plugged in for grounding purposes, be absolutely sure the computer is turned off before you open it and start working.

2. Remove the new hard disk from its packaging and review the instructions that came with it.

3. Configure the hard disk depending on how you're installing it and the sort of PC you have. If your computer is new, it might use *Serial ATA,* which is a faster, smarter, more modern way to connect hard disks. You can only connect one hard drive to each SATA cable, which is long and thin. These drives are a snap to attach. If you have an older PC with a traditional, wide ATA ribbon cable, you usually need to set the hard disk's jumper on CS (cable select).

9

4. Mount the drive in the PC. Connect the power cable and cable to the hard disk.

5. Without closing the case, turn on the computer. When the PC starts to boot, display the BIOS screen (usually by pressing the DELETE or F1 key as your computer starts to boot) and check to see that the computer recognizes the hard disk. If it doesn't, make sure you have set the jumper properly, it's connected to the correct IDE channel, and the power cord is fully inserted in the hard disk.

6. If all is well, shut down the PC and seal the case.

7. Finally, use the software that came with your hard disk to format the drive and prepare it for operation in Windows.

Install RAID to Protect Your Pictures

There's one problem with using a hard disk to store your digital photos—eventually, they all fail. No matter how new, fancy, or expensive your hard disk is, a day will come when it stops spinning. And when that happens, all your pictures—unless they're also backed up somewhere else, like on another hard disk or on a CD-R disc—will be lost and gone forever. That's why I'm a big advocate of using a RAID controller in your digital photo computer.

What, exactly, is RAID? RAID stands for Redundant Array of Inexpensive Disks. It is a combination of two or more hard drives, controlled in such a way that they act as one virtual drive. Long used just by large businesses, RAID systems have traditionally been too expensive and complicated for normal folk like us. That has changed, though, and RAID now offers a way to painlessly and securely back up 100 percent of your data (including digital images) in real time, with absolutely no effort on your part. No more delayed backups, tape rotation schemes, archives of CD-Rs, or forgotten data files. In many ways, RAID is the perfect backup solution.

There are many flavors of RAID, usually referred to as "RAID implementations" or "RAID levels." Large businesses have about a dozen RAID levels to choose from, each designed for some specific purpose. *RAID 6,* for instance, delivers "independent data disks with two independent distributed parity schemes." If you need that, you'll want to find a good book on RAID—I can't help you. I don't even know what that sentence means.

But more typical users can choose from three handy RAID levels. RAID 0 is called a *striped array* and it writes alternating blocks of data across two separate hard drives. The result? Two 120GB hard disks will appear as a single 240GB hard disk in Windows, for instance. And because the data is being distributed across multiple channels, data access is much faster than if you had a single, large hard disk drive. The downside, of course, is if either drive fails, 100 percent of your data is irretrievably lost unless you maintain a separate backup solution. RAID 0 is the most vulnerable way imaginable to store your data. And that's not our goal.

Instead, you want RAID 1. This *mirror array* treats two identical hard drives as a single drive and writes the same data twice, once to each physical drive. While there's no performance advantage like you get with RAID 0, there's no penalty, either. That's in stark contrast to mirroring data to a second drive using backup software, which uses system resources and slows your PC in a noticeable way. If one drive ever fails with a RAID 1 arrays, your PC continues functioning as if nothing ever happened, and all your images are preserved. Of course, you're warned during the PC's boot sequence if the RAID array isn't running perfectly, so you know it's time to replace the bad drive.

The final option, RAID 0+1, is the most expensive solution. Using an array of four drives, *RAID 0+1* stripes data to one pair of drives, while duplicating everything on the second pair. The result: higher overall performance, while also maintaining a real-time backup. The downside, of course, is you must purchase four identical hard drives.

To install a RAID system on your PC, you'll typically need a RAID controller card and two or perhaps even four *absolutely* identical hard disk drives—they should be the same brand and model number. Installing it isn't difficult, but if you aren't handy inside a PC, you might want to take it in to a shop for the surgery.

Note: If your RAID 1 hard disk is ever infected by a nasty virus or gets corrupted, both drives will be equally affected—so it isn't a bad idea to conduct periodic backups of your hard disk in addition. What RAID does is ensure you'll never get stung by a physical failure of your hard disk—and that's very reassuring, to say the least.

9

Chapter 10

Turning Prints into Digital Images

How to...

- Understand how a scanner functions
- Distinguish among different styles of scanners, like flatbeds and photo scanners
- Choose scanner resolution
- Shop for a scanner
- Operate a typical scanner
- Increase image sharpness
- Avoid moiré patterns
- Correct for uneven scan brightness
- Decide whether to use print or slide film

Most of this book is about how to take pictures with a digital camera, get those images on the PC, and edit, manipulate, share, and print them. But it would be a mistake to assume that everyone uses newfangled digital cameras all the time. A majority of photographers—both professional and casual—still use good-old 35mm cameras, and 35mm chemical film still sells like hotcakes in every grocery store around the world. I can vouch for that. In Honduras recently, ISO 100 film was hanging from clips in every neighborhood shop. It goes without saying that they didn't sell memory cards.

So, you might be wondering: how can I take my slides or negatives and get them onto my PC? That's a great question, because you probably have shoeboxes full of pictures that date back years and years, and it would be wonderful to turn them into digital images.

In this chapter, we'll look at bridging the gap between film and digital photography. I'll talk about scanners and how to get the best results from your analog images in the new world of digital. So, if you have slides or negatives and want to get them into your PC, take a look at this chapter. If you're already 100 percent digital and don't need any scanner advice, feel free to move along to Part III of this book. See you there.

Understanding Scanners

A *scanner* is a device that, like a photocopier, takes a snapshot of whatever document you lay on the *platen* (also called a scanning bed). A scanner doesn't just make a copy and print that document, though—it converts the data into bits and bytes and stores it on your PC in a digital image file, just as if it came from a digital camera.

In fact, a scanner is kind of like a digital camera that needs to remain stationary. Instead of a digital camera's rectangular, gridlike sensor (either a CCD or a CMOS chip) that captures an entire image at once (as I explained back in Chapter 1), a scanner uses a sensor with a single row of light-sensitive pixels. This linear CCD registers the light value of the image one "line" or "row" at a time, and that information is sent to the computer immediately and is flushed so that the next line can be read.

The resolution of the scanner is partially dependent on the speed and accuracy of the motor that steps the sensor past the document, or the document past the sensor, depending on the kind of scanner you have.

Several different kinds of scanners are around. You're probably already familiar with the most common kind of scanner, the flatbed. It's a good all-around scanner for most kinds of scanning jobs, but it isn't necessarily the best choice for photo scanning. Here's an overview of the kinds of scanners that are around:

10

- ■ **Flatbed scanner**   A *flatbed* is typically a long, narrow tray (usually either 8.5×11 inches or 8.5×14 inches) on which you place your document. An example is shown in the following illustration. The scanning head travels the length of the bed to create a digital image of the document. Different flatbed models connect to your PC in different ways; older models use a parallel port, others use a SCSI adapter or FireWire, and most modern models rely on USB. Flatbeds generally make high-quality images and [a few] accept options like automatic sheet feeders; so you can copy lots of pages at once. They can also scan almost any size document, from tiny business cards and 35mm slides all the way up to legal-sized documents. On the downside, they have a big "footprint," so they take a lot of space on a desktop. The major limitation of flatbeds, at least as far as photographers are concerned, is that they generally can't scan with sufficiently high quality to make good enlargements of slides and negatives.

- **Sheetfed scanner**   This sort of scanner does away with the traditional moving optics and flat scanning bed. Instead, *sheetfed scanners* pull documents through the unit—right past the stationary scanning head—to offer a compact scanning solution. You'll have a hard time finding a standalone sheetfed scanner, but they're commonly found in multifunction scanner/fax/printer devices. Of course, you can't scan thick objects like books or magazines unless you first separate the pages from the source. And some low-grade sheetfed scanners can potentially introduce imperfections in the scan because of the imprecise motor that pulls the page through. While this kind of scanner might be fine for text documents, I highly recommend you avoid it for photographic work.

- **Photo scanners**   Photo scanners are designed to scan just pictures—usually 3×5-inch or 4×6-inch pictures, though some also can handle prints as large as 5×7 inches. If all you need is the capability to convert 35mm prints into digital images, this is a decent solution. A few photo scanners even fit in an empty drive bay of your PC, taking up no room on your desktop at all. You insert the print in this kind of internal scanner much as if you were inserting a floppy disk in your PC. On the other hand, these scanners are completely useless for scanning anything except small pictures.

- **Film scanners**   This is the choice of serious photographers. Film scanners (like the one pictured in the following) vary dramatically in price—anywhere from about $200 at the low end to several thousand dollars at the high end—but they can give you outstanding results. *Film scanners* are designed to accommodate slides and negatives, and they can usually scan at a very high resolution—as much as 8000dpi—which gives you rich, detailed digital

Compensating for Tricky Lighting

Tricky lighting situations call for exposure compensation— like when taking a picture of subjects that are high contrast.

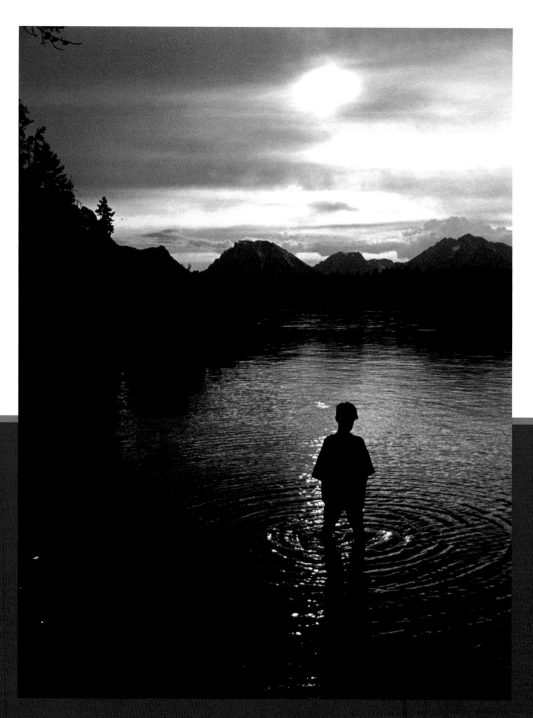

The only way to accurately expose a picture like this one is to take matters into your own hands—the camera's meter will be confused by the wide range of lighting in the scene.

Adjusting White Balance

Your camera's white-balance setting can be adjusted to correct for different light sources in a photo.

Using Histogram to Fix Contrast

The histogram displays the relative distribution of light and dark pixels in your image, and it can be used to help fine tune the exposure of your image back on the PC.

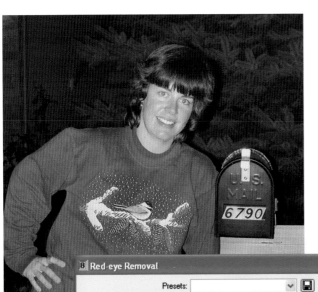

Fixing Red Eye

Even if your image editor doesn't have a handy red-eye remover like this one, you can do it yourself with a little careful painting.

Using the Layers Tool

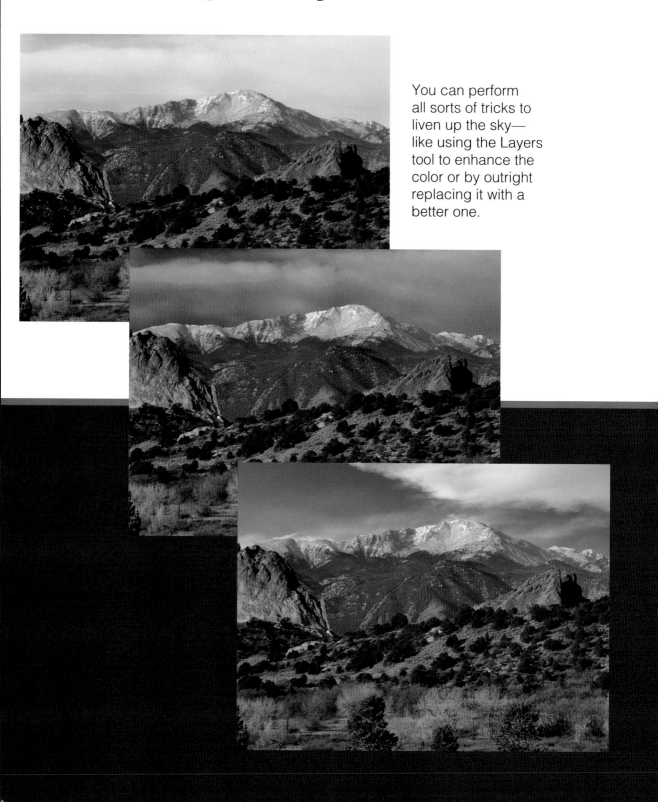

You can perform all sorts of tricks to liven up the sky—like using the Layers tool to enhance the color or by outright replacing it with a better one.

Creating Special Effects

Create your own special effects in about 10 minutes (larger image) with a digital camera and an image editor that would have taken hours of preparation with 35mm film (smaller image).

Creating Fantastical Pictures

You can take some fantastical pictures with the Layers tool in your image editor.

Two layers of the same picture—one color, the other black and white—
let you wow your audience with some eye-popping images.

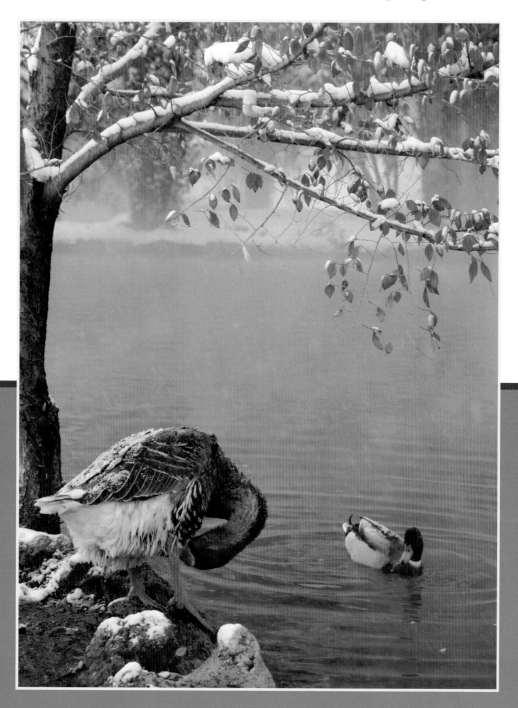

images that you can print at full enlargement sizes. Most film scanners—the affordable ones, that is—scan between 1800 and 2800 dpi.

How to ... Choose Resolution

10

Scanners come in a vast array of resolutions, from a paltry 300dpi all the way up to about 8000dpi. Which resolution do you need? If your printer is a mere 200dpi device—as are most inkjets—why would you ever need to scan a file at a resolution beyond 200dpi? In general, there are several principal reasons to choose a scanner with a higher resolution:

- High-resolution scanners typically capture greater detail in the images they scan, particularly in the lightest and darkest portions of the image, whereas lower-resolution scanners can't resolve detail in darker regions of the image.

- Higher-resolution scanners let you scan small images and print them larger than actual size. For instance, you can scan a small picture or a negative, and then print it larger than its original dimensions.

- You can scan an image at high resolution, and then crop it. The cropped and edited result will still have enough information to enlarge. On the other hand, if you scanned the image at just 200dpi initially, you would have to print the entire image without cropping.

Why go with lower-resolution scanners? That's easy—they're less expensive. Not everyone needs thousands of dots per inch. If your main goal is to scan images for web pages, for instance, even a 300dpi scanner could be as much as you need.

Shopping for a Scanner

So you want to convert your slides or prints into digital files and you need to purchase a scanner. You can look for a lot of features, but the most important things to consider when scanner shopping are the scanner's fundamental specifications, which I outline over the next page or so.

Resolution

Scanners are rated by the resolution at which they can convert documents into digital images. Inexpensive scanners are typically 600–1200dpi. Often, you'll see a rating like 1200×2400dpi. The first number is the optical resolution of the imaging system; the second number is the resolution of the step motor that moves the scanning head across the document. Because the optical resolution is always lower than the number of discrete steps the motor can perform, the first number—the actual resolution of the optics—is more important. You should use that number to compare scanners when you shop.

Color Depth

Inexpensive scanners might simply be 24-bit devices, meaning they can digitize as many as 16.7 million colors, which also happens to be about as many colors as the human eye can see. Most scanners sold today work at 30, 36, or even 48 bits per pixel, meaning they can distinguish among billions of colors. Those scanners with more than 24-bit accuracy have more colors to choose from when resolving dark regions, such as deep shadow.

This adds up to a high-quality image. If you're serious about scanning your photos, keep an eye on color depth and choose your scanner accordingly. If you're scanning snapshots or posting images on a web site, color depth isn't as important to you.

Dynamic Range

The concept of dynamic range is a bit complex, so a lot people often skip the topic entirely, much to the detriment of buying a quality scanner. I want you to know how to choose the right scanner, though, so we'll discuss the topic a bit. A scanner's *dynamic range* is a measure of how well the scanner can record changes in the brightness of the image it's scanning. It's measured on a logarithmic scale from 0 to 4, where 0 is pure white and 4 is very, very black (but not pure black, because the scale can extend past 4—by convention, we just use 4 as the upper end).

What the heck? Well, here's where we're going: the higher the scanner's stated dynamic range, the better it is at discerning shadows and subtle changes in dark colors. Because the scale is logarithmic (thought I wasn't going to explain that, didn't you?), every whole number change in dynamic range is a tenfold increase or decrease in light intensity, so a scanner that has a dynamic range of 4.0 is sensitive to a 10,000:1 range of light intensity in the scanned image. You can see what I mean in this graph:

Of course, no scanner is fully sensitive through the entire range from 0 to 4, so many scanners (especially the more professional, expensive models) describe their dynamic range in terms of DMin and DMax. Subtract the two to find the scanner's dynamic range. If a certain Nikon scanner has a DMin of .3 and a DMax of 3.6, its dynamic range would be 3.3.

So who should care about all this gobbly-gook? Anyone who scans slides and negatives. That's why you rarely see the dynamic range discussed for flatbed scanners—the dynamic range for those gadgets is usually pretty shallow, (around 2.4) and that's all you need to effectively scan prints. But slides and negatives store a very deep dynamic range and you'll want a film scanner to have the best dynamic range you can afford, else you'll lose all the details in your shadows and darker image regions. Only film scanners have sufficient dynamic range (usually 3.2 or higher) to make satisfying scans from film. This also explains why slide scanner attachments for flatbed scanners usually generate such awful pictures: the scanner's dynamic resolution is far too low to adequately capture slides and negatives with any modicum of accuracy.

Other Features

You might also want to consider other features, like convenience. Most scanners are fairly dumb; you need to activate them by choosing Acquire from the menu of your image editing program. Most scanners, though, place a button right on the front of the scanner, like the one in Figure 10-1. If you press it, the document in the scanner is automatically imaged for you. Some scanners even go this one better: they start the scanning software as soon as you open the cover to set a new document, or they feature multiple buttons on the front for automatic faxing, copying, printing, and e-mailing.

Are these features essential? Not in a million years. But they do make your scanner just a little bit easier to use.

Finally, you should also consider the scanner's interface. As I mentioned earlier, scanners come in all shapes and sizes, and while many connect with the USB or FireWire port, some connect with SCSI, too. Thankfully, the old parallel port scanners are largely extinct, so you probably won't have to worry about those much anymore. Which is best? USB and FireWire are the easiest, but old parallel scanners—if you find one in a bargain bin—can be slow and might conflict with your printer. SCSI is the traditional interface for high-end scanners and it's generally the fastest. But SCSI can be a challenge to install, and FireWire and USB 2.0 scanners are just about as fast. You'll need to open your PC and insert an expansion card in an available PCI slot, and SCSI software is finicky on some computers. Weigh all these issues before selecting a scanner.

FIGURE 10-1   A scanner button, like the one on this scanner, turns your scanner into a push-button appliance instead of a complicated peripheral.

   Almost all scanners that use a parallel port also include a "pass-through" port, so you can use your printer at the same time. Compatibility problems occasionally occur with certain combinations of PCs, scanners, and printers, but this system generally works without a snag.

10

Scanning and Correcting Your Images

Scanning is generally a straightforward process. Typically, you'll just need to access the scanner software from an image-editing program like Paint Shop Pro or Adobe PhotoShop, set the scanner to preview, and then scan the photo in the scanner. Figure 10-2 shows a typical scanner program.

Determining the Right Resolution

What resolution should you use to scan your image? Your scanner is probably capable of capturing images at a wide variety of resolutions—perhaps from under 100dpi all the way up to 3000dpi or so, depending on what kind of scanner you own. Which one should you pick?

In general, *scanning resolution* is a trade-off between file size and image quality. On the one hand, you might want to scan everything at the scanner's maximum resolution so you're prepared for anything, but that has practical

FIGURE 10-2   The Minolta Dimage software is typical of the software used by many scanners.

limitations. The files will be huge, which adds up to a lot of wasted disk space. In addition, large files slow your PC, sometimes dramatically so.

The solution is to attempt to match the scanned resolution to the resolution of the required final output. So, a newsletter that will be printed on a 300dpi printer, for instance, should incorporate images scanned at 300dpi. Use this table as a guideline for choosing the appropriate resolution:

Document	Scan Resolution
Fax documents	200dpi line art or grayscale.
Pictures for web pages	75dpi.

Document	Scan Resolution
Color or grayscale images for print	The easy answer is to scan at the resolution of the intended output, so a 300dpi printer would require scans at 300dpi as well. Images for inkjets should be scanned at about 200 or 250dpi.
	A more accurate method of printing to laser printers, however, is to look up the line screen frequency (LSF) and scan at twice that value. If you have a 300dpi printer, the LSF is probably about 70.
Line art for print	Scan at the printer's resolution (frequently, 300dpi).

But there are yet other wrinkles. Suppose you scan an image, but you intend to print it larger than the original. For instance, suppose you have a 3×5-inch picture that you want to print at 4.5×7.5 inches in a newsletter.

You need to scan it at a higher resolution to keep enough information to make a high-quality print. Otherwise, enlarging the scanned image results in a low-res, jaggy image. Use this formula for figuring out what resolution to scan:

Scanner resolution = final dpi × (intended image width / original image width)

So, let's say you want to print the 3×5-inch picture enlarged to 4.5×7.5 inches at 300dpi. The resolution would be

300×4.5 / 3 = 450dpi

You would set the scanner's control panel to 450dpi before scanning the image.

Likewise, suppose you want to crop a scanned image and only include a smaller detail of it in the finished product. If you end up choosing to enlarge the detail, you need to consider the dimensions of the cropped image at the outset—not the size of the entire image—and increase the scan resolution accordingly.

Tweaking Your Images

Today's scanners usually do a good job of reproducing photographs. Of course, you get what you pay for: a $1,000 scanner will create dramatically better images than a $100 scanner, almost without exception. But you can do some things to improve your images.

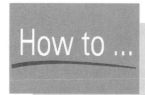 **Scan an Image with a Typical Scanner**

1. Start the scanner software. In Paint Shop Pro, choose File | Import | TWAIN | Acquire from the menu, as the following shows. The scanner software should appear.

2. Make sure the photo is properly positioned in the scanner, and then click the Preview button. After a few seconds, you should see the image on screen. It has been quickly scanned in low resolution, so you can adjust the image before the final scan.

3. Crop the image if you don't want to scan the photo in its entirety.

4. Adjust colors and brightness, if necessary. In this scanner program, there's an autoadjust tool, or you can tweak various color and brightness settings by hand.

5. Adjust the scan resolution. Scan the image at a resolution high enough for your final application (such as printing or web publishing), but don't overscan the image. You'll just waste disk space and slow the overall process.

6. When you're happy with the result, press the final scan button.

After the software is finished scanning the image, it'll either save it to your hard disk under a filename you specified, or open it for editing in an image program.

Sharpen a Soft Image

Some photographs are a tad soft to begin with. Others lose their edge in the scanning process because the scanner's focus isn't razor sharp. (Again, this is often an issue with the scanner's quality.)

Sharpening is a process your scanner software can use to increase the apparent sharpness of an image, as you can see in Figure 10-3. Sharpening filters typically increase the contrast along edges in the image, making the image seem sharper than it actually is. Some sharpening filters leave most of the image alone, only

FIGURE 10-3   The image on the right has had a sharpening filter applied to increase the apparent sharpness.

mucking with edges. Some sharpening filters increase the contrast of the entire image instead.

These days, the most popular sharpening filter is called *Unsharp Mask,* and it's typically built into scanning software as well as image-editing programs like Paint Shop Pro and Adobe PhotoShop. Do you need to use sharpening? Not always. Here's a guide to when to use this feature:

- Images with lots of edges and detail benefit more from sharpening than images that lack detail. Close-up pictures of people, for instance, are less likely to benefit from sharpening than a real estate profile of a house.

- High-resolution images benefit more from sharpening than low-resolution images because there's more detail for the sharpening filter to work with.

- Sharpening is more advantageous in printed images than in screen-based images.

- If in doubt, scan the image both ways and use the one that looks best. Too much sharpening can ruin an otherwise good image.

TIP   *You might want to disable automatic sharpening in the scanning software and sharpen the scan afterwards in an image-editing program instead. That way, you'll have more control over the process, and you can readily compare the before and after.*

Eliminate Moiré

You might encounter a problem scanning certain pictures: photos that have already been through the scanning process once before, such as newspaper and magazine images, could suffer from something called a moiré pattern. A *moiré pattern* is caused by the interference of your scanner's screening overlaid on top of the original screening pattern, as the example in Figure 10-4 shows.

To avoid this ugly moiré pattern, you can use the Descreening tool found in most scanners' control software. Descreening adds time to the overall scan, but it's necessary with these kinds of images.

Correct for Uneven Brightness

Some scanners have a lot of trouble evenly lighting the entire platen, and this sometimes creates images that are brighter in the center than at the edges. This problem seems to be getting worse, in fact, as some really cheap scanners hit the market. Usually, this isn't apparent, but it might be obvious with some photographs.

You can generally only avoid this problem in two ways. You can upgrade to a higher-quality scanner, or you can arrange your documents in the center of the scanner and avoid the edges. The disadvantage to this method is that it can sometimes be more difficult to ensure the document is placed squarely on the tray without using the edges.

10

FIGURE 10-4   The moiré pattern is caused by scanning not an original photo, but one that was originally in a magazine or newspaper.

Eliminate Scanner Aberrations

As with any optical system, you might need to clean the glass scanning bed occasionally; otherwise, it'll get dirty and the dirt will show up as smudges, streaks, spots, and lines in the scanned images. Use a damp cloth and wipe the surface of your scanner bed, but don't spray water or cleaning solutions directly on the glass. (They can leak into the mechanism through the edges of the glass.)

 Calculate Scanned Image Size

How much space will your scanned image take up on your hard disk? Some scanning software will tell you before you commit to the scan, others won't. If you're short on disk space, or you want to know if a few scanned images will fit on a Zip disk or a CD-ROM, you can use this equation to determine how large your scanned images will be.

File size = (resolution × horizontal size) × (resolution × vertical size) × scan mode

where size is measured in inches, and scan mode refers to the color depth you used in the scan:

Color Depth	Scan Mode
Line art	1/8
Grayscale	1
Color	3

Using this equation, you can see that scanning a full-color 5×7 image at 300dpi is about 9MB, but scanning that same image at 600dpi is over 36MB. If you're trying to carry images on a 100MB Zip disk, this formula comes in handy.

Surprisingly, dust can accumulate on the underside of the glass (inside the mechanism) after months or years of use. You might be able to remove the glass to clean it but—beware—that can void the manufacturer's warranty, so check first.

Slides, Negatives, or Prints?

I firmly believe that you'll get best results from your scanner if you start with slides. That's because the slide format is, at its core, the most accurate representation of what you *tried* to photograph to begin with. Negatives and prints have been tweaked by the photo shop, and they might not reflect what you intended to shoot. I do all my 35mm photography in slide format for exactly this reason. Given a choice, I recommend that you shoot on 35mm slides and scan those.

Slides have disadvantages, though. Most important, they have a fairly narrow exposure range and are less forgiving when used improperly. So, a photo that might look just fine when over- or underexposed on print film, might look terrible on slide film.

If you don't shoot slide film, my recommendation would be to go back to the original negative and scan that instead of scanning the print. That's because the negative has a lot more dynamic range than the print. And, if you have a film scanner, you can capture it at high resolution and crop it to your heart's content before printing. I consider print scanning to be a last resort.

10

Part III

Editing Images

Chapter 11

Quick Changes for Your Images

How to...

- Determine what the system requirements are to edit images on a PC
- Choose an image-processing program
- Open and edit images in Paint Shop Pro
- Change the resolution of digital images for e-mail, web, and other applications
- Change the number of colors that can be displayed in an image
- Save an image in a different file format
- Crop images to improve composition
- Crop and copy an image into a new file
- Create an irregular crop
- Rotate images taken with the camera on its side
- Fix a crooked image
- Change the brightness in an image
- Correct the color balance in a picture

One of the most exciting advantages of using a digital camera is the flexibility and control it gives you for tweaking and improving your images. Don't like your composition? Change it. You can crop your pictures just a little to subtly improve their appearance or radically change the look of a picture by turning its orientation from landscape to portrait. You can fix a crooked horizon, resize an image for e-mail, tweak the colors or brightness of an image—it's all up to you.

These are things that, until recently, you needed a darkroom and a whole lot of practice to do right, and every attempt would cost you money in photo paper and chemicals. These days, you can experiment endlessly. It never costs you a penny until you're ready to print the final result because it's all done with pixels on a computer screen. As long as you're careful not to save over the original file, you also never have to damage or change the original image.

In this chapter, we'll get started with image editing. This is the place to turn to for the most common kinds of corrections—simple things you can do to your images without learning a whole lot about the art and science of image editing. For more sophisticated things you can do to edit your images, check out Chapters 12, 13, and 14, which get into the topic a little deeper.

How Much PC You Need

You're probably expecting me to tell you that you should have the fastest PC you can afford—a 10 GHz Pentium 5 is just about right. Aside from the fact that computers haven't gotten that fast yet, you don't need quite that much speed. To be perfectly honest, you *should* work with the fastest PC you can afford. Image editing, especially with high-megapixel images, is a horsepower-intensive task. The more computer you have pushing pixels around, the more fun you'll have. A slow PC might frustrate you because it'll take a long time to perform editing operations and it'll even take a while to redraw the screen.

Here's what I think you should have, as a minimum, to do image editing without getting an ulcer:

- **Pentium III processor**   I used to do image editing on a 200 MHz Pentium (now known as a Pentium Classic), so it can obviously be done. But it's slow. A much better configuration: you should have at least a 1-GHz processor to push all those pixels around.

- **256MB of RAM**   Here's where spending a little extra can really pay off, though. If you upgrade to 512MB of RAM (which costs less than $100, and you can install it yourself if you want to), image editing will seem much faster, even on a slower processor. That's because high-megapixel images occupy lots of room in memory and, if they can't fit there, Windows stores parts of them on the hard disk. That can make something as simple as a screen redraw drag on forever. Is there value in having a gigabyte of memory? There sure is—if you have several large images open at once, your system won't slow down as it would with less memory. Many new PCs are now shipping with 1GB of memory (that's 1000MB), so 512MB certainly isn't an unusual amount of memory. Upgrade if your wallet can handle it.

- **60GB hard drive**   They're really cheap now, so you should have lots of room to store your images. The bigger the better but, unless you also want to make digital video, you probably don't need a monster 120GB hard disk. I wouldn't complain, though, if that's what you get. A second hard disk or a CD-RW drive for archiving old images can come in handy as well.

11

Choosing an Image Editor

Before you can get started editing images, you need an image editing program. Any one will do, at least at first. For the most part, all image editors give you the capability to do certain things, such as:

- Resize your images

- Apply paint to your image, using a set of brushes and other paint tools

- Add text and other graphics

- Delete parts of the image, which you can use to crop and change the composition

- Combine multiple images into a new composition

- Use tonal controls to change aspects of your image, like the brightness and contrast

That's certainly a quick overview of image editing, but the point is a lot of image editors are around that can get the job done. Which one is for you? Well, you might want to start with a free one. If your digital camera came with an image editor of some sort, you might want to give it a spin and see if you like the way it works.

Ultimately, though, you might be dissatisfied with the bundled software and decide to invest in a better program. You're likely to encounter two sorts of image editing programs: automatic and manual packages.

Automatic packages include a lot of wizards and automated processes to change your image for you. These programs can adjust the colors and brightness in an image, remove red eye in flash photography, and perform a host of other minor miracles without any real input from you. The downside, of course, is this: the final result isn't always what you expect and, often, such automated attempts to fix your photos don't quite hit the spot. Use them with care, and always remember you can use the Undo button to revert to the original image. These programs are really aimed at novices who don't want to learn the ins and outs of an image editing program, but want immediate results.

If you're reading this book, I suspect you're probably more interested in getting your hands dirty, so to speak, with a more manually operated image editing program. This sort of program gives you more control and power but, of course, you have to master the interface before you can see improvements in your images.

Perhaps the most famous image editor of all time is Adobe Photoshop, seen in Figure 11-1. The downside is the program has a somewhat steep learning curve. Another alternative is Photoshop Elements. I like the way Adobe has combined the best parts of Photoshop with a simpler interface that's designed for ordinary folks, not graphics professionals. Elements is a wonderful program.

Personally, I use and recommend Paint Shop Pro from Jasc (www.jasc.com). This image editing program has about 75 percent of the features found in Photoshop, but at a fraction of the cost and with a much simpler interface. Throughout the rest of this book, I'll generally use Paint Shop Pro or Adobe Photoshop Elements to illustrate techniques. Remember, though, you can use any software you like, but the actual mouse and keystrokes will differ somewhat depending on what program you choose to use.

TIP   *You can download a trial version of Paint Shop Pro from the Jasc web site at www.jasc.com and a trial version of Photoshop Elements from www.adobe.com.*

FIGURE 11-1   Photoshop is an outstanding program, but all of its features can be intimidating.

Throughout the rest of this book, I've mainly used Paint Shop Pro Version 8 to illustrate how to perform many common image editing tasks. You can use an older version of Paint Shop Pro or another program entirely but, remember, the menu items and tool locations will be different.

 Open an Image in Paint Shop Pro

Because I'm going to spend a lot of time in Paint Shop Pro over the next few chapters, let's take a quick look at how to use the program. Start Paint Shop Pro by choosing it from the Windows Start menu. You can open an image in Paint Shop Pro in three ways. Use whichever method you find easiest.

■ Choose File | Open from the main menu and navigate your way to the image you want to open in the Open dialog box. Double-click the file, or select it and click the Open button.

■ Choose File | Browse from the menu. The Browse window appears, which shows a set of thumbnails in the right pane and a directory tree of your hard disk on the left. The following shows an example. When you select a hard disk folder, its contents appear on the right. Just double-click an image to open it. The Browse window remains open in case you want to open more images in this way.

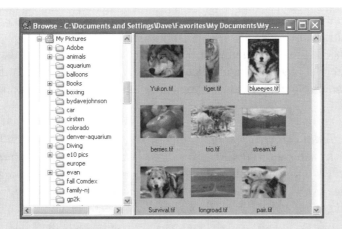

Open the folder with the image you want to open directly on the Windows desktop, and drag the image file from the folder to the Paint Shop Pro window. If Paint Shop Pro isn't on top, you can do this instead: drag the image file out of the folder and hold it over the Paint Shop Pro button in the task bar at the bottom of the Windows desktop. Don't let go of the file yet; just hold it there for a few moments. Paint Shop Pro should pop to the front. Finally, just move the file up to the Paint Shop Pro window and let go.

11

Changing the File Format

Much of the time, you'll only need to make minor changes to your images to get them into e-mail, on the Web, or into other documents and applications. In the next few sections, I'll show you how to make changes to the file itself, like resizing, changing the colors, and changing the file format of your digital images.

Shrinking Your Images

As Jebediah Springfield, founder of the animated city in *The Simpsons,* once said, "A noble spirit enbiggens the smallest man." If *The Simpsons* founder can make up a word, so can I—so this section is all about de-biggening your pictures.

Why would you want to do that? Well, high-res megapixel images are great, but they're just too big for many applications. Suppose you want to post some images to a web site, for instance. Or, say you want to e-mail some pics to friends and family. A 3.3-megapixel image, which measures about 2048×1536 pixels, is just too big for these kinds of applications. If you e-mail a 3.3-megapixel image to your friends, you'll lose friends fast. Files that big clog e-mail pipelines and take forever to download.

What you need is to de-biggen your images. In other words, shrink them to a manageable size that others can appreciate—to a size smaller than the computer monitor, for starters, so people can see your image all at once without panning around.

NOTE *Many digital cameras have the capability to resize images even before they're transferred to the PC. You should check your camera manual to see if there's a way to automatically make a duplicate, e-mail-size copy of images you want to share. That way, you can skip this de-biggening step when you want to e-mail or upload your pictures.*

How small is small enough? I suggest that for web-based or e-mail images, you shrink the file so its longest dimension—either length or width, depending on the orientation of the image—is no more than 600 pixels. Here's how to do it:

1. Open Paint Shop Pro and load the file you want to resize.

2. Choose Image | Resize.

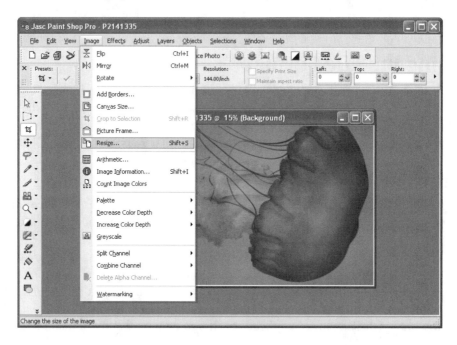

3. Because we want to make the image a specific pixel size, make sure Pixels is selected on the right side of the dialog box. We could also change the size of the image based on percentage or print size, but we don't need those options now.

4. Make sure the dialog box is set to resize all layers and to maintain the aspect ratio of the image (you can find these options at the bottom of the dialog box). Also set Resample using to Smart Size. This tells Paint Shop Pro to use the best algorithm for resizing the image to generate the best final result.

5. Finally, enter the new dimensions for your image. You only need to enter the height or the width and, because the aspect ratio isn't changing, Paint Shop Pro will fill in the other number for you automatically. Assuming you started with a 1024×768-pixel image, enter **600** for the width and you'll see the height change to 450 pixels.

6. Click OK to resize the image.

7. You should see the image shrink on the screen. You can now save your image over the original—destroying the original—or save it as a new file so you retain the original's larger pixel size. To save it as the old filename,

choose File | Save from the main menu. Otherwise, choose File | Save As
and give the image a new name.

 *You might have noticed that you can also make images bigger using this
procedure. Avoid increasing the size of your images, though, because all
you can do is stretch and manipulate the pixels already in the images. The
result is generally unattractive, especially if you enlarge the image too
much.*

 *Most image editors have similar features. If you want to resize an image in
Photoshop Elements, for instance, choose Image | Resize | Image Resize
from the menu and enter your changes in the Pixel Dimensions section
atop the dialog box.*

Changing the Color Depth of an Image

Sometimes you'll want to change the number of colors in an image. Every file
format supports a specific number of colors. JPG images, for instance, can display
16 million colors, the number needed for photo-realism. GIF, on the other hand,
supports just 256 colors.

Suppose you have a GIF image that you want to combine with a JPG for a special
effect (such as putting someone from one image into a scene in another picture). You'll
need to convert the image into a format that can accept more colors.

 *The JPG file format only works with 16 million color images. This means
even if you convert a 24-bit image into an 8-bit image, if you later save it
in JPG format, it'll automatically be converted a 24-bit image again.
That's usually OK because JPG files are quite compact.*

Increase the Colors in an Image

Here's how to increase the number of colors in an image:

1. Open an image in Paint Shop Pro. GIF and PCX can have just 256 colors,
   so load one of those if you have one on your hard disk.

2. Choose Image | Increase Color Depth. Choose 16 Million Colors (24 bit)
   from the menu.

3. The image will be immediately converted into a format that has the space for additional color depth.

Notice that the image didn't change visually. All this operation does is allow the image to display more colors if possible, but this process can't add more colors into the image all by itself. Suppose you had a four-color cartoon panel. By adding more color depth, you've created the capability to insert a photo-realistic image into the cartoon. We'll talk about how to do that kind of thing in Chapter 13.

 If you convert a 24-bit image to 256 colors, you've stripped away color information that can never be put back, even if you later resave it as a 24-bit file.

Decrease the Colors in an Image

Now let's consider the other possibility. Suppose you have an image with 16 million colors, such as a JPG. If you want to turn the image into a web graphic (like a push button, for instance), you might want to reduce the number of colors and save it as a GIF image. You might also want to reduce the number of colors to achieve an artistic effect or to save disk space (a BMP with 256 colors takes less space than one with 16 million, for instance).

The process for decreasing the colors in an image is similar to increasing the colors, though there's an extra step. Here's how to do it:

11

1. Open a JPG image in Paint Shop Pro.

2. Choose Image | Decrease Color Depth. Choose 256 Colors from the menu.

3. In the Decrease Color Depth dialog box, choose Optimized Median Cut and Error Diffusion, and then click OK. Those options will choose the best colors to give you the most accurate depiction of your image.

4. Click OK. The image should be rendered with fewer colors. Unlike the case of increasing the color depth in an image, in this case you should be able to see a difference because the image has to be painted on screen with fewer colors and, therefore, less accurately.

Some pictures look good enough in 256 colors to be converted from 24-bit without a serious compromise in quality. For the most part, though, I suggest sticking with a 24-bit format like JPG unless you have a good reason to use a less color-rich format.

Saving Images in Different File Formats

One of the most common things I do with my images is change their file format—usually from JPG to TIF. Why do I do that? Usually, to preserve image quality. Every time you resave an image in JPG format, it loses a little quality. TIF is immune from that kind of compression punishment, though, so as soon as I start to edit an image, I save it in the TIF format to (as they say in the zip-lock bag industry) lock in the image quality.

Why don't I just take pictures in TIF format right from the start? Well, even though my digital camera can take images in TIF format (as most can), it's an almost useless feature. Even with a large memory card, I can only take a few pictures in the huge, space-consuming TIF format, and it takes an enormous amount of time (a minute or so each) to save a TIF to the memory card. Because the image quality difference between TIF and high-quality JPG is quite small, I take the pictures in JPG format and convert them to TIF afterwards, when they're on the PC, if I plan to edit them. It's a compromise, but a sensible one.

> NOTE   *Just looking at a JPG file doesn't affect the image quality. You can open the file in an image editor, view it, and close it again without affecting quality—just don't make any changes and click the Save button. If you don't plan to edit an image, you can safely leave it in JPG format.*

You might want to change image file formats on the PC for a number of reasons. Here are some of the most common reasons:

■ You convert a JPG to TIF to preserve image quality before repeated edit-and-save sessions.

■ You convert TIF to JPG to save disk space or to make an image small enough to upload using the Internet.

■ You need to import an image into a program that doesn't support the file format the image is currently in, so you convert it into a file format the program does work with.

■ You want to save an image with features unique to the image editor you're using, such as with masks or layers intact. If you save an image in Paint Shop Pro as a .PSP file, for instance, you can retain special characteristics, making it easier to finish editing later.

For a more in-depth discussion of file formats, check out Chapter 7. Saving images in different file formats is easy, though. Just follow these steps:

1. Open the image in Paint Shop Pro.

2. Choose File | Save As from the main menu.

3. In the Save As Type drop-down menu, choose the file format you need.

11

4. If necessary, click the Options button to fine-tune the file format. The Options button lets you specify the amount of image compression, the number of colors the image will be saved in, and other properties.

5. Click OK to save the file.

After saving the file, you'll have two copies—one called myfile.jpg and one called myfile.tif, for instance. You can delete the older file or. if you might still need it, keep both copies. Of course, when you look at two files with the same name, but different file extensions on the Windows desktop, telling them apart can be hard. If in doubt, right-click the file and choose Properties from the menu. Verify the file extension before you possibly delete the wrong file. You can see how both Windows 95/98/Me (the dialog box on the left) and Windows XP (on the right) identify files in the following.

One-Step Photo Enhancement

Even advanced image editors with lots of manual controls often give you easy, one-step tools for improving your images. Personally, I'm enough of a purist to usually avoid these features. Sometimes, though, I'll try the quick-fix approach to see if it helps the image. If it does, great! I can save the image and get on with my day. If I don't like the results, the Undo button is one mouse click away.

What am I talking about? Check out Paint Shop Pro, which has an Enhance Photo button in the Photo toolbar atop the screen. Click it, and select the One Step Photo Fix menu item to make Paint Shop Pro run a slew of corrections on your picture, including color balance, contrast, and sharpness. You can also run these corrections one at a time by choosing them from the menu under Enhance Photo. Either way, they let you quickly optimize a picture with little to no effort on your own part.

 If you have Adobe Photoshop Elements, you can take advantage of a few Auto levels in the Enhance menu.

Improve Your Composition

In the world of 35mm photography, editing your composition isn't always easily done. To crop an image or change its composition, you typically need your own darkroom or a local photo shop with which you can work closely to dictate crop marks and reprint photos to your personal specifications.

Of course, exceptions exist. In many photo stores, you can insert your picture into a kiosk and the image is then scanned and displayed on screen. You crop the image on the screen and print the result minutes later. These image editing stations are just big, in-store versions of the image editing software you have on your PC.

In other words, you don't have to drive across town and pay money to do it in a store anymore. Now you have the tools to do it yourself at home.

Crop Your Image

I wouldn't be surprised if this were the single most common edit made to digital photographs. Because you can crop and recompose your images so easily on the computer, the need to compose your shot perfectly in the viewfinder is somewhat diminished. Instead, you can tweak the shot to your heart's content afterwards, when you have time to think about it and evaluate your options. In fact, the more megapixels your camera can shoot, the more cropping you can do. If you have a 2- or 3-megapixel camera and intend to mount your shot as an 8×10-inch print, you can't throw away many pixels. But if you have a 5- or 6-megapixel camera, you have lots of extra resolution to work with. You can discard a fair bit of your photo and still have sufficient resolution to print an enlargement.

Even if your shot is close to perfect to begin with, a little cropping can likely make it better. Here's how to do it:

1. Load an image into Paint Shop Pro. Adjust it so you can see the entire image onscreen at once. To do that, you might need the *Zoom tool,* shaped like a magnifying glass. Click it, and then click on the picture with the right mouse button to shrink it or the left button to enlarge it, until it comfortably takes up most of the screen. If you're not looking at a 100 percent magnification of the image, though, realize the image you see might be ever-so-slightly distorted from the actual image.

TIP *Even without using the Magnifying Glass, you can roll the scroll wheel on your mouse to change the image's zoom level.*

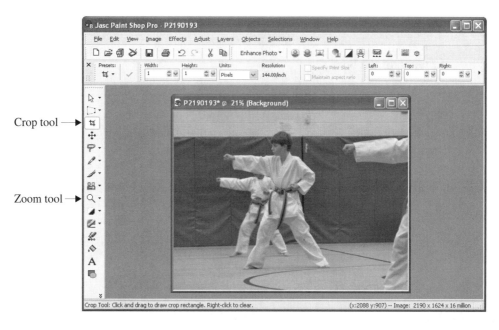

Crop tool →

Zoom tool →

2. Click the Crop tool, shaped like the thick frame.

3. Click in the image, and, holding down the mouse button, drag the crop tool until you've drawn a rectangular outline around the part of the image you want to keep.

4. To move the crop box around within the image, move the mouse inside the box, so you see the mouse pointer change into a four-way arrow. Click-and-drag the box around the image.

11

5. To change the size of the crop box, hold the pointer over the box outline. You should see a two-way arrow. Now click-and-drag to change the height or width of the box.

Resize crop marks

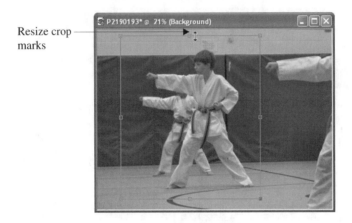

6. When your crop box represents the picture as you want it composed, click the check mark button in the Tool Options-Crop Tool dialog box. The image will be immediately cropped down to size, which you can save as a new file or save to replace the older image. Compare the original and cropped versions of this karate picture:

TIP

By default, the Tool Options dialog box is docked to the toolbars at the top of the screen. If you don't see it, it might not be activated. Choose View | Palettes | Tool Options. It should now appear on screen. Notice that this important dialog box changes depending on which tool you select.

Cropping by Cutting-and-Pasting

Not all image editing programs have a Crop tool. In fact, even in Paint Shop Pro there's another way to crop—one you should learn. In this alternate approach, you select and copy a portion of the image, and then paste it into a new image document. Here's how to do it:

1. Load an image into Paint Shop Pro and configure it so you can see the entire image.

2. Click the Selection tool (that looks like a dotted rectangle). Be sure the Selection Type is set to Rectangle in the Tool Options dialog box.

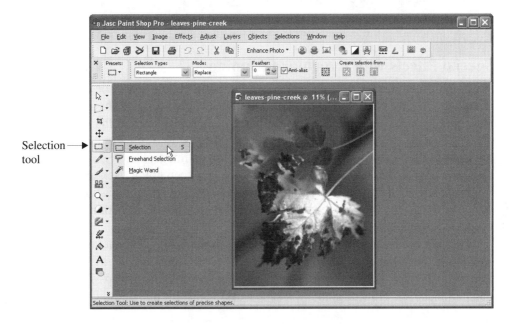

3. Draw a rectangle around the part of the image you want to keep. Note, you can't move or resize this selection rectangle in the same way you did with the Crop tool. If you don't like the result, right-click in the image to undo the selection, and then try again.

4. When your selection is complete, choose Edit | Copy from the menu. This copies the selected region into the Windows clipboard.

5. Choose Edit | Paste | As New Image. The selected region should appear in a new image window, which you can then save to the hard disk.

Using Cut-and-Paste

The Cut, Copy, and Paste tools are just like the ones in Microsoft Word and other programs, though you have a bit more in the way of options. These tools let you grab a selection—some part of the image—and paste it in a variety of ways. The most important options? You can paste the content of selections elsewhere in the same image (which lets you add a second copy of yourself to a photo, for instance) in another photo (so you can shake hands with Elvis, for example) or even into a new, blank image.

Special Effects with Irregular Cropping

Why would you want to use this process instead of the Crop tool? For starters, as mentioned, not all programs have a convenient cropping tool built in, so you might have to copy-and-paste your way to compositional excellence. But there are other reasons. You might want to create several new compositions, for instance, all based on the same original image. When you crop an image, the original data disappears. With the Selection tool, though, you can keep going back to the original image and copying different, even overlapping, parts and pasting them into new files. This is a way to make an unlimited number of new compositions based on a single photograph.

Last, but not least, you can make irregular crops with this technique—something that's not possible with the cropping tool. What do I mean? Check out Figure 11-2. Here, you can see I created an image by creating a crop of connected geometric shapes. How does this work? It's easy—just try this out:

1. Load an image into Paint Shop Pro and choose the Selection tool.

2. Draw a rectangular selection in the image.

3. Hold down the SHIFT key and add another selection to the image. The SHIFT key is a modifier that combines selections in the image.

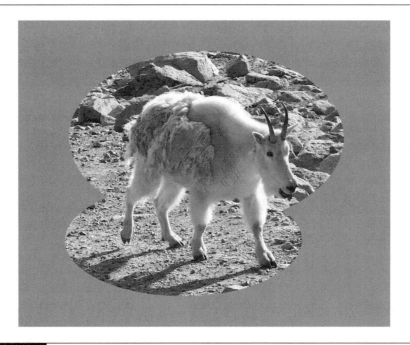

FIGURE 11-2   The selection tools let you work with irregular shapes.

11

4. Hold down the CTRL key and drag another rectangle in the image. Make sure this rectangle intersects at least part of one of the selections already in the image. The CTRL key is a modifier that removes overlapping selections from the image. You can use the CTRL key to take the edge off a rectangle or even to turn a selection into a "donut" by giving it a hole!

5. Keep adding and removing selections until you're happy with the result. Choose Copy | Edit from the main menu.

6. Now you need to create a new home for this image. Choose File | New from the main menu. In the New Image dialog box, make sure the width and height of the new image are at least as big as the selection you just made, and then click OK. You should see a new, empty window appear on screen. This is where we're going to paste our selection.

7. Before we do that, let's paint it. Click on the Fill tool (the overturning paint can).

8. Click on a color from the color palette in the upper-right side of the screen. Now click in the empty white image, and you should see it fill up with the color we just selected. In this illustration, you can see the Fill tool as it paints the entire image window a single color.

> TIP   *Left-clicking paints with the program's foreground color; right-clicking paints with the background color.*

9. Finally, it's show time. With the new image window still selected, choose Edit | Paste | As New Selection. The irregularly cropped image should move around under your mouse pointer. Decide where you want it in the new image, and then click. It will pop into the new image, with the strange shape clearly visible against the colored background.

That little exercise only scratches the surface of what you can do with selections in Paint Shop Pro (and other image editing applications). Here are a few other tricks you can try out:

■ *Create a vignette crop.* Have you ever seen oval-shaped images? This is easy to do with the Selection tool. Choose Ellipse from the Tool Options dialog box after you choose the Selection tool. When you make your selection in the image, it will be in the form of an ellipse that you can customize, depending on how you drag your mouse.

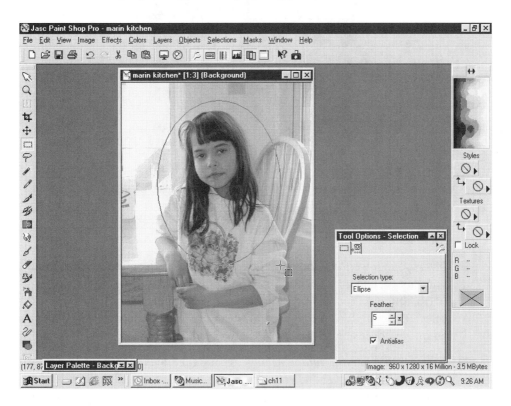

■ *Feather the edges.* When you paste an image into another image, you can smooth the transition from the selection to the background using the Feather tool in the Tool Options dialog box. The larger the number, the more feathering you'll get. Be sure to select the Feather option before you select your region, though, or it won't have any effect. In the following, you can see how I used a feather value of 40 to get a very fuzzy edge to this picture of my musical hero, Kristin Hersh, posing with some of her kids:

■ *Invert your selection.* One cool trick you can try is to create a selection in your image, and then choose Selections | Invert from the main menu (CTRL-SHIFT-I). You should find that you got the exact *opposite* of the selected region. It's an easy way to select everything except the middle of an image, for instance.

■ *Paste a selection into another image.* Using the Layer technique you'll learn about in Chapter 14, you can take a portion of two images and combine them in interesting ways. Consider the following image, for instance. I cut the fish from another picture using the freehand selection tool, and then I copied it into a picture of the diver as a separate layer. Because you can resize one layer without affecting the rest of the picture, I shrunk the selection until it fit in the lens of the mask.

Rotate Your Perspective

Not all your shots are going to be plain old, horizontal shots—especially if you took my advice in Chapter 3 and went nuts with camera position and perspective. If you have images from your camera that are sideways—you took the pictures sideways, so you have to turn your head to look at them on the PC—you should fix those images right away. It's a snap.

Some image editors, like Paint Shop Pro, even have one-click buttons for rotating your images to the left or right by 90 degrees. Here's what you need to do to fix a sideways (landscape-oriented) image:

1. Load the sideways image in Paint Shop Pro and decide which way it needs to be rotated—right (clockwise) or left (counterclockwise). Let's assume we need to turn the picture clockwise.

2. Choose Image | Rotate | Rotate Clockwise 90. The image immediately spins accordingly.

11

If your image editor doesn't have such a one-step rotate tool, it probably still lets you rotate by an arbitrary amount. You can even do that in Paint Shop Pro; choose Image | Rotate | Free Rotate and then specify how much you want to rotate the image in the Free Rotate dialog box. Typically, you'd click Left or Right and make sure the button for 90 is selected, and then click OK.

3. The image should rotate so it's oriented properly. If you made a mistake, choose Edit | Undo and try again.

You can also reorient your image in other ways. If you took the picture with the camera upside down, for instance (and stranger things have happened, trust me), you can choose Image | Flip from the menu. Likewise, you can flip it left-to-right, giving you a mirror image of the original shot, by choosing Image | Mirror.

Level a Crooked Picture

Nothing is quite as annoying as a crooked picture, especially when the horizon or some other straight line is visible in the image. A crooked shot can ruin an otherwise great picture. Even if the horizon is only off a little, it can be annoying, but you can use the principle you learned in the last section, on rotating sideways images, to fix this annoyance. Here's what you need to do:

1. Load the crooked image into Paint Shop Pro. Decide which way it needs to spin to correct the error and estimate by how many degrees. Most errors, even seemingly egregious ones, are typically less than 2 or 3 degrees.

2. Choose Image | Rotate | Free Rotate.

3. Specify the direction (left or right) and enter a number in the Degrees box. You can type in a decimal, such as .5 (which is half of a degree), if you want. Click OK to see the result.

4. Inspect the result. If you aren't satisfied, choose Edit | Undo and try again with a different angle of rotation. When you're happy, save the file.

 Don't apply rotation on top of rotation or the image quality will suffer. Undo the first rotation completely to get back where you started, and then apply a different rotation angle to get where you're going all at once. Any rotation effect will degrade the image slightly, but compounding rotation on top of rotation can wreck the image fairly quickly.

If you're using Photoshop Elements, there's a handier way to rotate an image. Right-click in the image and choose Select All. Then choose Image | Rotate |Free Rotate from the menu. You can now grab a corner of the image and rotate it in real time, making it easy to nail down the exact rotation needed to straighten the horizon.

When you're done rotating your image, be sure to crop it down a bit because the rotation probably introduced some unwanted background color in the corners of your picture.

11

Improve the Color and Brightness in Your Image

These edits require the most artistic skill, so I saved them for last. Fixing elements, such as bad color or poor exposure, in your pictures can be done, but it'll take some practice before you can make your images look right. Don't worry about that, though, time in your image editor is free and, if you stick with it, you can fix some badly mangled shots!

Set the White Point

Ask a serious photographer what's most frustrating about digital imaging and you'll get a short list of major gripes: the shutter lag when taking pictures, limited dynamic range, and goofy white balance. We've already talked a bit about all of these shortcomings and we discussed white balance adjustments in Chapter 6. Often, your digital camera will miscalculate your white balance and give you an image with a pronounced color cast. What does that mean? Not only won't there be a true white or black in your picture, but all the other colors will be a bit off as well.

Thankfully, you can fix the white balance of your photos in almost any image editor. You need to have a white point control and a swath of space in your picture that's white, black, or gray.

In Paint Shop Pro, load an image with something of a color cast and locate a part of your image with pure white or black, and then zoom in on it. Next, choose Adjust | Color Balance | Black and White Points. The Black and White Points dialog box should appear. Assuming you want to use a white region of the image to correct your photo, click on the rightmost dropper in the dialog box, directly above the white color box (you can use black instead, if you like).

Click the dropper in your image directly in the white region. Preview the change and, if you like the results, click OK to save your changes.

Incidentally, the process in Photoshop Elements is similar. To open the white point control, choose Enhance | Color | Color Cast. You needn't specify white or black in Elements. The program will figure it out. Click in the image, and then click OK to accept the changes to your image's color balance.

Brighten Gloomy Shots

Everyone has a stockpile of too-dark images. The flash didn't reach the subject or, perhaps, the camera underexposed the subject because of a bright background. Back in the first part of the book, I told you how to avoid those kinds of problems in the lens when you take the picture, but you can also repair some of the damage in postprocessing.

You can adjust the brightness in an image in three primary ways:

- You can use the Brightness control (in some programs, it's called *luminance*). *Brightness* raises or lowers the entire image's luminance value indiscriminately, whether or not all areas need it. On the other hand, if only one portion of an image needs to be brightened, you can select it using the Selection tool, and then add Brightness. When part of an image is selected, operations you perform on the image occur in the selected region.

TIP   *Use the Selection tool to add or remove brightness only where it's needed.*

- Alternatively, you can use the Gamma control. *Gamma* affects the midtones of an image more than the extreme bright and dark regions, which means you can brighten a dark skin tone without washing out a dark shadow nearby. Gamma affects a limited range of brightness in the image, so you can better target your changes.

- Finally, and the best way to tweak the brightness of an image, is by inspecting the histogram. The *histogram* is an intimidating-looking display that tells you the distribution of lights and darks in an image. It can be a powerful way to correct your shots—as long as you're willing to invest a little time to learn how to use it.

11

Correcting with Brightness and Contrast

Let's start with the brightness and contrast controls, though I suggest you don't rely on this technique often. Play with it, certainly, but I recommend you get familiar with the other two techniques—the gamma and the histogram—and use them.

The process for changing brightness in an image is similar, regardless of software, but we'll use Paint Shop Pro, as usual, for our example. Here's the general procedure:

1. Load the offending image into Paint Shop Pro.

2. Choose Adjust | Brightness and Contrast | Brightness/Contrast. The Brightness and Contrast dialog box appears.

3. Use the Brightness slider to adjust the image. You can see the effect of the change in your image immediately by clicking the Proof button, which is shaped like an eye. Auto Proof, to the left of the Proof button, leaves proofing on all the time, so updates are made constantly as you work the slider.

4. Typically, you'll also need to change the contrast in proportion to the brightness to keep the image from getting washed out. Experiment until you see the result you want.

5. When you're satisfied with the results, click OK. Your image will be updated with the new brightness value.

Better Corrections with Gamma

As I mentioned, the gamma control is often a better remedy for fixing an overly dark or an overly bright image. Personally, I tend to reach for the Gamma control first. I've found it's often the midtones in a picture that need enhancement, and brightness tends to wash out dark regions and increase the intensity of the highlights—overexposing them. The Gamma control, on the other hand, doesn't affect the brightest and darkest parts of an image, so you can't wash out shadows with this tool, for instance. So, as a general rule, you should see if gamma gets the job done.

To tweak the gamma, choose Adjust | Brightness and Contrast | Gamma Correction, and move the sliders (the Link control keeps all three colors in sync, which is the most common way to use this tool). Unless your image is poorly exposed, you shouldn't need to change the gamma value above 1.5 or below .5.

Fine-Tuning Images with the Histogram

The most precise and powerful way of correcting your images is with the histogram. The histogram is a graph that shows the relative amount of information stored in each color channel in your image or, in plain English, it displays how many pixels are dark and light in your image. The left side of the graph represents the darkest part of the image, while the right side is the lightest. A graph like the one on the left in Figure 11-3 has a lot of midtones, while the one on the right is mostly filled with dark pixels. We can use that information to tweak the brightness and contrast.

I use this Histogram adjustment technique on many of my pictures. I suggest you try doing the same. It only takes a few seconds and can improve almost any shot.

Most good image editing programs, like Paint Shop Pro, Photoshop, and Photoshop Elements, have a handy tool for adjusting the light levels in your image using the histogram chart and a few sliders. In Paint Shop Pro, it's found at Adjust | Brightness and Contrast | Histogram Adjustment. If you're using the full version of Photoshop, it's found in Image | Adjust | Levels. Finally, Adobe Photoshop Elements puts this control in Enhance | Brightness/Contrast | Levels.

No matter which program you use, this tool works more or less the same way. You simply want to move the sliders under the histogram to set the white and black points, stretching and optimizing the distribution of brightness information in the

FIGURE 11-3　Histograms tell a lot about the amount of color information in an image.

image. Paint Shop Pro throws in a gamma control into the same dialog box, which is treated separately (as the Curves tool) in Photoshop).

Suppose you have an image like the one in Figure 11-4. Here's how you would correct the image using the histogram Adjustment in Paint Shop Pro:

1. Because the histogram curve drops off before reaching the right side of the graph, that tells us there are few pixels with very bright colors. Consequently, you should drag the white point slider to the left to meet the point where the graph ends. That sets this point in the image as white and it should brighten the image. You should see the graph stretch as you drag the end points.

2. Do the same for the black point, if necessary.

3. Now use the gamma slider, if needed, to adjust the overall brightness level in the image's midtones.

Curious about how using the histogram can improve a run-of-the-mill photo? Check out Color Figure 4, which shows a before-and-after shot, along with the histogram setting that generated the improved image.

FIGURE 11-4   The Histogram Adjustment tool is a precise way to adjust brightness and contrast.

Add Snap to Your Colors

You can add life to washed-out, flat, or bland pictures in a few ways. One way is to use the Contrast control. Because bland pictures are often a result of low contrast, you can increase the contrast in the image and make the scene look much punchier. To do that, simply find the Contrast control and work the slider. In Paint Shop Pro, you can find the contrast in Adjust | Brightness and Contrast | Brightness/Contrast.

Contrast can also work the other way to good effect. Want to create some artificial fog? Just reduce the contrast in a picture by about 50 percent, and the image seems obscured by a dense fog.

Another way to improve your image is with the Saturation tool. *Saturation* increases or decreases the intensity of colors in an image, much like the saturation control on your television. Too much saturation can make the picture look like it was taken on Mars, but it can add life to an otherwise bland picture.

Do you have a people picture that's a little too red? This doesn't happen often, but it can occur when you take indoor pictures in artificial light. Back off on the saturation slightly to get a more natural skin tone.

In Paint Shop Pro, the Saturation control is found in Adjust | Hue and Saturation | Hue/Saturation/ Lightness. Experiment with the Saturation tool—it's fun. You can bleach all the color from your picture by reducing the saturation to zero, for instance, or hyperactivate the colors by going in the other direction.

Don't forget that programs like Paint Shop Pro also have automatic controls for many of these tweaks. You can find an automatic contrast adjustment, as well as an auto saturation tool, under the Enhance Photo button in the toolbar.

Correct the Color Balance

Quite often, the colors in some pictures won't come out quite right for some reason. Some cameras, for instance, tend to shift the whole image toward one end of the color spectrum under certain lighting conditions. You can change the color balance in an image in many programs as easily as sliding three controls marked Red, Green, and Blue.

To fix out-of-synch colors, open the color balancing tool in your image editing program. In Paint Shop Pro, you can find it at Adjust | Color Balance |

Brightness Only Goes So Far

You need to know the ugly little secret of brightness and gamma control. You can only take it so far because you can't add detail to an image that wasn't there when you originally took the picture. A black shadow, for instance, will only become gray as you continue to increase brightness—you'll never see the authentic Bigfoot creature that was hiding in the thicket of trees. That's why it's important to start with the best exposure you can, although you can always try enhancing it afterwards. You can sometimes salvage an otherwise throwaway image.

Red/Green/Blue. You'll see a dialog box in which you can slide the three primary color controls to the left (less) or right (more) to bias the colors in your photo. For best results, use the color balancing tool conservatively and be sure to preview your work before clicking OK. You'll rarely need to change the colors in your image by more than about 15 percent.

If your image is too blue, however, you won't necessarily get the effect you're looking for by backing off on the blue slider. Use this chart to fine-tune your image:

Problem	Solution (x is the amount you move the slider)
Too red	Decrease red by x, and then increase both green and blue by $x / 2$.
Too green	Decrease green by x, and then increase both red and blue by $x / 2$.
Too blue	Decrease blue by x, and then increase both red and green by $x / 2$.

Easy Color Correction with Variations

A better solution—unfortunately unavailable in Paint Shop Pro—is usually called the color variations control. Adobe Photoshop and Photoshop Elements both offer this powerful feature. Let's take a quick look at the Color Variations tool in Photoshop Elements because it's so useful.

If you have Photoshop Elements, open it and load an image. Then choose Enhance | Variations. You should see something like the screen in Figure 11-5.

Here's how you use this busy little dialog box:

1. Start by tweaking the brightness. If you want to make the image darker or lighter, click the appropriate thumbnail on the right side of the screen. All the images will immediately change to show you the effect of the change. (The Original thumbnail at the top left will remain the same, so you can compare your changes to it.)

2. Next, decide what color channel you want to change. If you want more red in the image, for instance, click the box marked More Red. The change will appear immediately.

3. Continue tweaking the image until you're satisfied with the result. At any time, you can revert to the original by clicking the Original thumbnail.

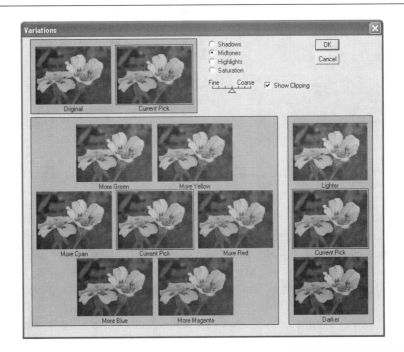

11

FIGURE 11-5   Use the subtle variations in color to fine-tune your picture, adding or removing just the right amount of color cast.

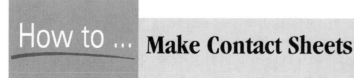 **Make Contact Sheets**

Film photographers like to file contact sheets of their photos. *Contact sheets* are sort of like cheat sheets that contain thumbnail views of their images, which makes it easier to locate and manage a large collection of slides or prints. My favorite tool for making contacts sheets is *ACDSee,* which lets you generate a page of thumbnails and print it or save the file to your hard disk for later editing and reference.

Other programs can make contact sheets as well. Photoshop and Photoshop Elements can do it, for instance. To start the contact sheet feature in Photoshop Elements, choose File | Automate | Contact Sheet II. The Contact Sheet II dialog box has fewer options than what ACDSee offers, but it's quite functional nonetheless. Photoshop lets you use the images' filenames as captions, for instance. After you select the appropriate folder and click OK, Photoshop processes each image, turns it into a thumbnail, and pastes it into the contact sheet. The process can take a while, especially if you have a lot of photos in the selected folder.

Chapter 12

Cleaning Up Your Images

How to...

- ■ Sharpen blurry images

- ■ Blur the background to enhance apparent sharpness

- ■ Use the painting tools in your image editor

- ■ Choose foreground and background colors

- ■ Make selections based on color, region, and by hand

- ■ Remove ugly red eye from flash photos

- ■ Eliminate distracting objects with airbrushing

- ■ Repair tears and scratches on photos

- ■ Create a panorama from a series of photos

In the previous chapter, we looked at easy and fast techniques you can use to gussy up your images—stuff like how to rotate or resize your images, correct bad colors, and even save them in different file formats.

But you can do so much more. In this chapter, we'll go one step beyond and learn how to fix your images with techniques that actually change reality. You'll see how to remove red eye caused by flash photography, for instance, how to sharpen (or blur) a picture, and how to airbrush away distracting elements from a scene and move elements around within a picture.

This chapter is filled with techniques that sit between what I would call elementary quick changes and special effects. We're not adding Elvis to your holiday pictures, but we're certainly going beyond color correction. Strap in and have fun with your images and your favorite image editor!

Sharpening Blurry Pictures

I know what you're thinking. Wow! I can sharpen my blurry pictures! Technology is great!

Well, let me begin by saying that as great as digital imaging is, you can never add detail or information into a picture that wasn't there to begin with. That's why I'm always amused when I see a movie in which the spy takes a surveillance videotape and enlarges the image enough to read the phone number on a piece of paper across the room. No matter how much they enlarge images in the movies, those Hollywood computers always seem to sharpen the focus perfectly.

With that said, there is some hope for your *slightly* blurry images. You can sharpen an image in two ways: a direct way, using the Sharpen tool in your image editing program, and an indirect way, which amounts to blurring the background so your subject doesn't look quite so bad. I'll show you how to do both.

As you might have guessed, you can combine those two techniques by doing both. But keep in mind that sharpening also can increases the digital "noise" in a photo and degrade the overall look of the photo.

Using the Sharpen Filter to Enhance Your Picture

The easiest way to sharpen an image is with the Sharpen tool. What the *Sharpen tool* does is increase the contrast between pixels, making the image seem sharper, as you can see by flipping to the middle of the book and checking out Figure 12-1. If the camera jittered madly while you took the picture, though, no amount of sharpening will hide the result.

Tech editor David Huss says that he sometimes adds a little noise to a slightly blurry picture to make it look sharper—and, indeed, it has roughly the same effect as the sharpen tool.

In most graphics programs, a few different kinds of sharpening filters are available. These are the most common options:

- **Sharpening**   This affects all the pixels in your image indiscriminately. Sharpen More is a common alternative, which is somewhat more intense.

- **Edge Sharpening**   This effect only increases the contrast along edges in your picture, where a lack of sharpness is most obvious. It is usually more effective than Sharpening, and it's less damaging to the rest of the image.

- **Unsharp Mask**   This variation of Edge Sharpening adjusts the contrast of pixels that neighbor an edge, in addition to the edge itself. This is the most common sharpening filter and, in fact, it's pretty standard practice for photographers to run the Unsharp Mask filter on most images that they scan into digital format from a slide or print.

In Paint Shop Pro, the Sharpen, Sharpen More, and Unsharp Mask filters are available from the Adjust | Sharpness menu.

12

FIGURE 12-1   A little sharpening can add an almost subliminal "punch" to your digital images—especially ones destined for print.

Which one should you use? Not all programs offer all three filters but, if you have a choice, Edge Sharpening is almost always more effective than the plain old Sharpening filter. Unsharp Mask works best of all, but it sometimes takes some tweaking on your part. You'll generally get to set at least three options, as you can see here:

- **Strength** Sometimes called Amount, this is the intensity of the sharpening effect.

- **Radius** This determines how many pixels around the edges are also affected by the filter.

- **Clipping** Also called *Threshhold,* this determines how different the pixels need to be before they're considered an edge.

> TIP *Start with 100 for Strength and 1.0 for Radius, and then watch the way the filter changes as you change Clipping. A Clipping of 0 is the most harsh effect; beyond about 30, changing Clipping has no real effect on your image. Likewise, raising Radius beyond 1.5 rarely has an attractive effect on your image.*

12

Blurring to Sharpen

Using the Sharpening filter is certainly one way to make your image look sharper, but there's another, more subtle, and more "artistic" way to enhance the apparent sharpness of your image—blur the background. This process works best when you're photographing something that's quite distinct from the background, like a portrait.

To blur the background of your image, you'll need to isolate the subject, so the blurring only happens in the rest of the picture. Once your subject is selected, you need to invert the selection so the Blur filter happens to everything except the subject. Finally, you can run the Blur filter on your image. In Paint Shop Pro, you

Undo a Big Mistake

Paint Shop Pro, like many image editors, has an extensive undo history you can use to fix a major boo-boo. If you spend 10 minutes making edits to a photo and don't want to choose Edit | Undo 25 times in a row to get rid of it all, do this:

1.   Choose Edit | Command History. You'll see a dialog box that lists all the operations you've performed, from the last back to the first (reverse chronological order).

2.   Scroll down until you find the point at which your unwanted edits begin.

3.   Click that first unwanted edit. All the operations from there back to the last operation you performed become highlighted.

4.   Click Undo. The image will revert to an earlier state.

can find Blur by choosing an option from the Effects | Blur menu. Once you've blurred your background, turn off the selection and save your image.

That's the quick overview. Here's how to pull off this feat of digital trickery:

1.   Load a slightly blurry portrait that you'd like to sharpen into Paint Shop Pro.

2.   Select the Freehand tool and set it to Smart Edge. Set the Feather value to about 5—that way the transition from the subject to the background won't be abrupt.

3.   Trace the outline of the subject's face or body, being careful to stay along the edge.

4. When you have completely selected the subject, choose Adjust | Sharpness | Unsharp Mask to sharpen the subject, but not to affect the background.

5. Next, choose Selections | Invert from the menu. This "flips" the selection so the subject isn't selected, but everything else is.

6. Choose Adjust | Blur | Blur More. You should see the background blur slightly. If you're not happy with the result, blur it again. In fact, you can repeatedly use the blur effect until the background is sufficiently blurred.

7. Finally, when the image is complete, choose Selections | Select None.

Hopefully, the subject now looks better, especially in comparison to the background. Compare the two images in Figure 12-2, for instance, for a look at this effect in action.

Painting on Your Pictures

Some of the techniques we'll be discussing through the rest of the book require a little, well…painting. And if you take a look at your image editor—especially a full-featured one like Paint Shop Pro or Adobe PhotoShop—you'll see a complete set of painting tools. These digital gadgets enable you to change the colors in an image on a pixel-by-pixel basis. How do they do that? Take a look at Table 12-1; there, you can see the most important tools in Paint Shop Pro's Paint toolbar. These are fairly typical tools as image editors go. You'll find their equivalent in most other programs.

12

FIGURE 12-2   Blurring the background can simulate a shallow depth of field—great for portraits—while also giving the impression of a sharper subject.

NOTE   *Paint Shop Pro stores several tools in each slot of the toolbar. Click the arrow next to each tool to see all the available options.*

Simulating a Shallow Depth of Field

You wanted to take a picture with a sharp foreground and a shallow background, but your automatic camera settings didn't cooperate. Well, it's easy to simulate the out-of-focus effect that a wide-open aperture gives your background by using the select-invert-blur technique we used to give the subject more apparent sharpness. You'll need to heap on liberal amounts of blur for this technique to work, though. You can run the Blur filter several times until you get the effect you like.

Tool	Description
	Pan This tool is used to move image windows around within Paint Shop Pro. It's a safe default setting to use because it won't do anything to your image if you click in the picture.
	Zoom Zoom into the image by left-clicking; zoom out by right-clicking.
	Crop We used this tool in Chapter 11. It lets you cut out unwanted bits of your picture.
	Selection We used this tool in Chapter 11 as well. It lets you select portions of an image for further editing.
	Freehand This is another way to select portions of an image.
	Magic Wand This tool selects a region for editing based on color. Because photos have lots of similar colors, you can click on a region and the wand will select everything nearby that's a similar color. It's an easy way to select, for instance, a person's face.
	Dropper This tool determines the color of the currently selected pixel and makes that the current foreground color for painting and editing.
	Color Replacer This great painting tool puts the power of many of the program's effects—like brightness and hue changes, effects filters, and more—into a brush so you can paint them on.
	Paint Brush This is just what it sounds like. It lets you paint on the image, not unlike the way you'd paint with a real brush. It's a lot more flexible than a real brush, though, because you can change features like the size and shape of the brush, as well as the amount of paint that you can spread at once.
	Airbrush You can configure this tool to splatter paint on your image like an airbrush.
	Clone Brush This tool lets you paint with pixels found elsewhere in your image, effectively cloning a part of your picture as you paint.
	Scratch Remover This automated tool erases scratches from scanned photographs.
	Eraser This tool lets you paint with the currently selected foreground and background colors.
	Flood Fill This tool pours paint into a region. The currently selected color will run right up to whatever color edges exist. Like the Magic Wand, you can set the color tolerance.
	Text This tool lets you write text anywhere in your image, in any color and any font. We'll talk about this tool in Chapter 14.
	Pen Use this tool to draw straight and curved lines in your image.

12

TABLE 12-1   Highlights from the Paint Tools Palette in Paint Shop Pro

Choosing Colors

So, let's say you want to do a bit of painting. We'll keep it simple: you just want to paint a solid-colored rectangle in the middle of an image. Before we do that, though, you'll need to know how to select colors in Paint Shop Pro.

Every imaging program has two important colors: the foreground color and the background color. These are usually displayed prominently on the screen (as in Figure 12-3) for easy access and reference.

The foreground color is the color you'll paint with when you use the left mouse button. The background color can often be used by painting with the right mouse button. The Eraser is one of many tools that use the background color. Note, the Eraser doesn't really erase anything; it just paints the background color (which can sometimes look like you're erasing).

In Paint Shop Pro, you can choose a color directly from the color palette by moving the mouse over the palette and clicking on the color you like. A left click selects the foreground color; a right click sets the background. You can also set these colors directly from an image; to do that, select the Dropper and click with it on the part of the image you want to grab the color from.

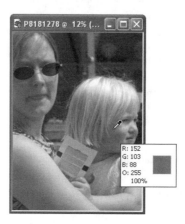

TIP   *Because colors can change from pixel to pixel in a digital image, you'll have better luck with the Dropper by zooming in for a close-up view of the region before you select a color with the Dropper.*

Applying the Paint

Once you've selected colors to serve as the foreground and background colors, it's time to lay down some paint. In Paint Shop Pro, do this:

Color Palette

Foreground color

Background color

FIGURE 12-3   The color palette is an important feature in most image editors because it lets you select colors for painting and editing.

1. Click on the Selection tool and make sure that the Selection style is set to Rectangle in the Tool Options dialog box.

2. Click and drag the Selection tool in the image to create a rectangle.

3. Click on the Flood Fill tool.

4. Set the fill style to solid color. To do that, make sure the solid round icon is selected, as the following shows. Also select None in the Tool Options Match Mode menu.

5. Finally, click inside the selection with the Flood Fill tool. You should see it fill with a solid color—the same one you selected in step 4. If you like, right-click in the selected rectangle as well. You should see it change to background color.

To paint freely anywhere in the image (as we're about to do in the rest of the chapter), you need to get rid of any selections. As long as a selection is in the image, you'll only be able to paint inside it; that's a powerful tool for making sure you only affect specific parts of the image. To turn off the current selection, choose Selections | Select None.

A faster way to eliminate selections is, with the Selection tool still active, to right-click the image.

Painting More Accurately

You've got the basics of painting down—selecting colors and clicking in the painting. But what if you want to paint a precise set of pixels? The rectangular Selection tool won't get the job done. Instead, you can rely on a few other tricks:

Paint Brush

For lots of close-in, delicate detail work, the old-fashioned Paint Brush is all you need. Select the Paint Brush, and you'll see you have a variety of options in the Tool Options dialog box. Of particular importance is the *Size slider:* by changing the size, you're specifying the number of pixels to be affected every time you click the image with the brush. To test this tool, select it, and then click-and-drag in the image. You can paint by drawing freehand lines or just dab the screen to make small dots of color.

Magic Wand

If you want to change the color (or perform some other kind of edit) on a region of the image that's somewhat similarly colored (such as a person's face or, in the case of the following illustration, someone's shirt), use the Magic Wand to select all the like-colored neighboring pixels. You can make the wand more or less sensitive to color changes by moving the Tolerance slider. To test this tool, choose the wand and click in a region of your image that has a somewhat consistent color. A Selection region will appear; you can then use Flood Fill or the Paint Brush in this area. You can hold down the SHIFT key and continue clicking to select a larger area of somewhat similar colors.

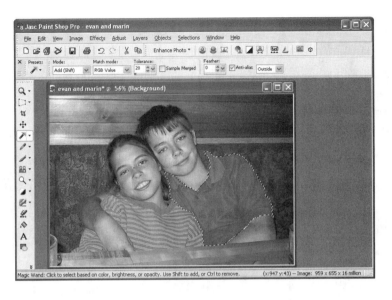

Freehand

The *Freehand tool* is a great choice when you want to select part of the image, especially when the part of the image that you want to select is irregular in shape and hard to select any other way. Perhaps the most powerful way to use the Freehand tool is to set it to Smart Edge mode. Here's how it works:

1. Select the Freehand tool and change the Selection Type to Smart Edge in the Tool Options dialog box.

2. Find a region that you want to select. Ideally, it should have a fairly well-defined outline because the Smart Edge tool will snap to high-contrast changes in the image.

3. Click the edge of the region and move the mouse pointer. You should see a box extend away from the point you clicked.

4. Following the outline of the region, click again on the edge some short distance away.

12

5. Continue clicking with the Smart Edge tool as you work your way around the region. When you reach your starting point, double-click to close the region into a complete selection.

Repairing the Evil Eye

Back in Chapter 4, we talked about how to avoid getting red eye into your pictures. Red eye, of course, is the phenomenon that occurs when the camera flash reflects off the subject's retina, because the pupils are wide-open in a dark room. If you have red eye, either because you didn't take the necessary precautions or because you've just scanned an old picture that has red eye, you can correct it on the PC fairly easily.

Using Automatic Red Eye Removal

First, check to see if your image-editing software has an automatic red eye removal feature. Some red eye removal software is completely automated: just draw a box around the eyes, and the software does the rest. Paint Shop Pro, for instance, has a great semiautomated process for eliminating red eye:

1. Open a photo that includes someone with a case of Evil Eye.

2. From the menu, choose Adjust | Red-eye Removal. You'll see the Red-eye Removal dialog box.

3. Move the image on the right around by dragging it with the mouse pointer until you see a red eye in the middle of the frame. (Don't try dragging the left side around because that's where you "draw" eyes.) Once you can see the eye, zoom in until it fills much of the frame.

4. Make sure that the Method is Auto Human Eye and select the proper hue for the person you're correcting. Then pick an eye color. Once everything is ready, click in the dead-center of a red eye and drag the mouse away from the center until you've covered the red with the new eye. You can resize and reposition the eye if needed.

12

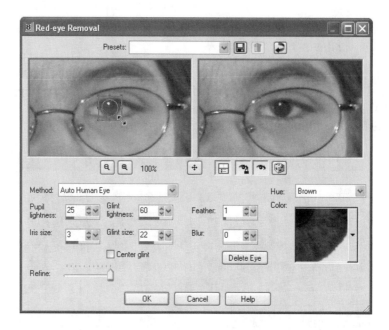

5. Repeat the process for the other eye. When both eyes are finished, click OK to close the Red-eye Removal dialog box and keep your changes. Check out Color Figure 5 for a look at how dramatically you can improve an image with this tool.

Removing Red Eye the Old-Fashioned Way

If you're using an image editor that doesn't have red eye removal built in, you'll have to take the red out yourself. It's easy, actually, and it doesn't even take a steady hand. Using Paint Shop Pro as our workhorse, here's what you should do:

1. Load the offending image and zoom way in so the eyes fill most of the screen.

2. Click the Magic Wand tool and click in the red part of the eye. Hold down the SHIFT key and keep clicking until you've selected all the red in one eye.

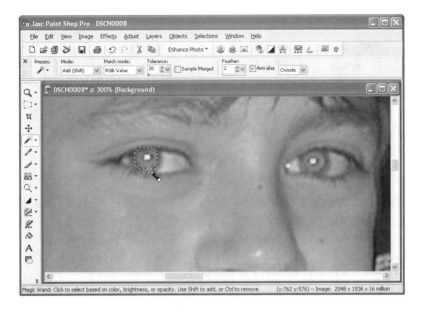

TIP *If the wand grabs too much of the image—like parts of the face outside the red—then the tolerance (found in the Tool Options dialog box) is set too high. You might need to adjust it to 15 or less.*

3. With the red area selected, select the Paint Brush or Flood Fill tool, and then choose a dark color, like black. Click in the selection to paint over the red.

12

4. Choose Selections | Select None from the menu and evaluate your work. If you can still see red around the fringes, you can take the Paint Brush and change the remaining to red on a pixel-by pixel basis. To do that, you might want to reduce the brush size to just a few pixels. (This setting is found in the Tool Options dialog box.)

TIP
Be sure to leave the white spot in the middle of the eye, or you'll have created a portrait of a space alien.

Notice that you don't have to do a perfect job to create a convincing eye—the detail is so small in most pictures that simply eliminating the red is enough to dramatically improve the picture.

Airbrushing Away Distractions

Have you ever taken a great landscape shot only to realize—far too late to reshoot the picture—that a telephone pole is in the middle of what should be serenity? Or a tourist in a loud shirt is right behind your family shot that you wanted to frame? Don't worry—this section will show you how to eliminate those kinds of distractions with a little digital airbrushing.

The tool at the heart of this magical process is the Clone tool. This handy feature, found in most image editors, lets you copy pixels from one region of your image to another. That means you can "airbrush away" distracting aspects of a picture—like power lines, hotspots, and so on—by duplicating a similar or nearby part of the image (see Figure 12-4). Typically, smaller and more-isolated distractions are easier to airbrush away than larger ones (or objects that cut through the main part of your picture); but if you're patient, you can get great results from a surprising number of photos that you thought you'd have to throw away.

To use the Clone tool in Paint Shop Pro just do this:

1. Click the Clone tool in the tool palette. It looks like a pair of paintbrushes.

2. You'll need to find a region in your image that's similar to the area you want to cover. If you want to airbrush away a power line that runs through the air, for instance, you can look for a nearby patch of sky that's similar enough so you can paint over the power line with this other section of sky.

3. Set the source for your cloning operation. In Paint Shop Pro, position the mouse pointer over the area you're going to steal color from and either right-click or hold the SHIFT key and click.

FIGURE 12-4   Paint away distractions with the Clone tool.

4. Move your mouse over to the area you want to airbrush and start painting. Don't try to cover the blemish all at once; paint a little, pick up the mouse, and paint again. This reduces the chances that a recognizable pattern will appear as a result of your painting.

12

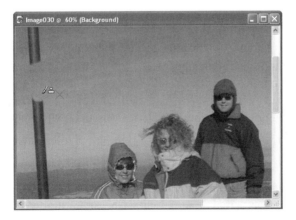

The Clone tool works best in small areas because you can start to tell something is wrong with the area you're cloning to if you paint over too large a region.

NOTE *The Clone tool has two different modes. In one mode, when you pick up the brush and paint elsewhere, the source stays where you put it: this is called Nonaligned mode. If you pick up the brush and start painting elsewhere, and the source moves the same relative distance from where you first started, this is the Aligned mode. Some pictures work better with one mode or the other. Experiment to see which is best in each situation.*

By the way, there's another way to solve this problem. If your blemish is small enough, just try using your image editor's Scratch Remover tool. It won't give you good results all the time (sometimes it'll look like the picture is "smeared" around the area where the tool did its work) but, often, this is the fastest, one-step way to improve your photo.

Clean Up Old and Damaged Pictures

An unexpected benefit of digital imaging and editing has been the capability to restore old pictures—heirlooms and keepsakes you might have written off as too badly damaged to be of much value anymore. Some of the techniques I've already mentioned can be used to fix these old prints on your PC. First, of course, you'll need to scan these images into the PC. I talk a bit about scanning in Chapter 10 but, basically, you'll want to scan your old prints at the highest resolution you have available. That'll make it easier to print them later. From there, it's just a matter of applying digital-editing techniques to repair them.

Remove Picture Scratches

After a particularly bad moving experience a few years ago, one of my wedding pictures got a few nasty scratches because of the way the glass broke and slid down the print. The image was essentially irreplaceable, so I turned to digital editing to make a repaired duplicate. You can take several approaches to fixing scratches, depending on where they are in the image, how prominent the scratches are, and their relative size with respect to the rest of the image:

■ In some cases, you can select and copy an undamaged area of the picture that's similar in color and overall texture to the damaged portion, and then paste it over the damaged area with a liberal amount of feathering to smooth the edges. This is particularly effective in fairly uniform backgrounds, such as the sky.

- Another alternative—and the more common solution—is to use the cloning tool (see the earlier section on airbrushing for more details). Select the cloning tool and use a nearby, similar, but undamaged, section of the image to paint over the mar. Remember to use short, dabbing motions to paint, or you'll introduce an undesirable pattern into the image.

- Finally, you can use the automated scratch remover found in many image editors. Paint Shop Pro's Scratch Remover (it looks like a trowel) lets you drag a selection box over a long, straight scratch. It then removes the scratch by painting over it with nearby colors automatically. This technique doesn't work well for wide scratches or scratches that curve or bend—it's off to the Clone tool for those.

Remove Dust, Dirt, and Digital Noise

Your images can be filled with little specks that come from grainy, high-speed 35mm film, from bad scans, or from using a digital camera in very low light. Whatever the reason you get specks on your image, most image editors have a Despeckle tool. In Paint Shop Pro, you can find it at Adjust | Add/Remove Noise | Despeckle.

Make a Panoramic Photo

A *panorama* is an image that's wider than the ordinary images produced by your camera, such as the one in Figure 12-5.

Panoramas are typically used to take landscapes because they provide the wide, sweeping vistas that look so impressive. You can take a panorama of anything, though—a school play, the inside of your home, or another scene. The key to making something into a panorama with a digital camera, though, is that you'll need to take two or more images and "stitch" them together on your PC. That means the scene shouldn't change much between photographs, or you won't be able to match them. So, if you're taking a landscape, for instance, the same cars, people, and other objects shouldn't move as you rotate your camera and take successive shots.

I first talked about panoramas back in Chapter 6. In that chapter, I explained how you can use your camera to take the panorama's raw ingredients—the individual shots. In this chapter, we'll pick up where we left off and talk about how to stitch those together on the PC.

FIGURE 12-5 You can connect a number of images to make a wide (or tall) panoramic shot.

As mentioned in Chapter 6, taking a panorama involves two steps: photographing the scene and stitching the images together afterward. When shooting the pictures, keep these tips in mind:

- You need to take a series of pictures that overlap. Try to get 30 percent to 50 percent of each image to overlap into the next picture to make it easier to stitch them together. Scenes with lots of movement are a poor candidate for panoramas because the computer needs to look for similar regions in common from one picture to another. A little movement is fine, but the scene should be essentially static.

- To keep each image's perspective identical, you'll need to keep the camera's rotational axis the same. In plain English, that means you need to take all the pictures from the same location. Don't drift a few feet as you photograph, and take the shots on a tripod if possible.

- Avoid using a wide-angle lens because this can distort the images and make it difficult to line up edges.

Now it's time to make the panorama. There's a hard way and an easy way; which way you choose depends on how much enthusiasm you have for delicate editing and how much money you have to spend on yet another image-editing program.

If you're game for doing it the easy way—and that's the method I highly, highly recommend—you need to purchase a panorama program that automates the entire process for you. Several programs are around that do the stitching for you. If you're interested, check out any of these:

- Adobe Photoshop Elements (includes a stitching utility)

- Jasc Paint Shop Photo Album (includes a stitching utility)

- Ulead Cool 360 (www.ulead.com)

- ArcSoft Panorama Maker (www.arcsoft.com)

Using any of these programs, all you need to do is drag-and-drop the individual images in the proper order (see Figure 12-6). The software matches the edges all by itself, and does a good job even with low-quality digital cameras, wide-angle lenses, and other technical difficulties.

FIGURE 12-6   Automatic panorama software is a convenient way to stitch images together into impressive panoramas without the muss of lining up images by hand.

The Resolution Advantage

Not all panoramas are photographed just to take wide, scenic landscapes. Sometimes, you might want to photograph a subject in sections so you can get more pixels for a high-res print.

What am I talking about? Consider a situation in which you want to make a 20×30-inch poster-sized print, but your two-megapixel camera doesn't have remotely enough resolution to make a large picture. You can still get the shot, as long as you're trying to photograph a stationary object. Shoot it in sections, and then stitch the individual segments together on the PC using a program that lets you create a panorama from a grid of horizontal and vertical images, like ArcSoft Panorama Maker. When you're done, you'll end up with a much higher-resolution image because it'll have a lot more pixels than a single photo would have—and that you can make a poster from. Figure 12-7 shows how I took six sequential

FIGURE 12-7   You can stitch several smaller images together to make a huge print.

photos of my car—each one measuring about 3.3 megapixels—and ended up with a huge, super high-resolution 8-megapixel shot that's plenty big for just about any print I could possibly want to make.

Make a Virtual Reality Panorama

The panoramas we've talked about so far are very wide or tall images that go beyond the ordinary aspect ratio people expect to see when they look at a picture—that's what helps make them look so striking. You have another option entirely.

Perhaps you've seen virtual reality movies on the Web or in online encyclopedias like Encarta. They present a scene in a small window that, when you click-and-drag the mouse inside, spins around so you can see a full 360 degrees, as if you were actually there. When you think about it, isn't that just a 360-degree panorama in which you only see a small piece at once? Indeed, that's the secret behind these VR movies. And that means there's nothing particularly magical about them. You can make your own VR movies and share them in e-mail or on the Web. The most common format for these interactive panoramas is Apple's QuickTime, as the following shows.

To make your own VR movies, you need to take a series of images that can be assembled into a complete 360-degree panorama. You also need special panorama software. The best—and most affordable—such programs that I've managed to find are Ulead's Cool 360 and ArcSoft Panorama Maker. Both of these excellent program let you create panoramas and save them in QuickTime format, which most people can view on their computer without any additional software (if they don't already have QuickTime installed, it's available free from Apple' web site if not). Panorama Maker even has an option to let you save your VR movie as a web page, which makes it easier to post on the Web.

Stitching Photos Together by Hand

If you don't have an automatic stitching program, you can still make a panorama by hand. It just takes a bit longer (and your results won't be quite as good as what you get from most automated software).

Here's how to do it:

1. Calculate the finished image size by finding the size of your individual images. If you don't know the resolution of the individual shots, load one into Paint Shop Pro and choose Image | Image Information from the menu. Close the image after you've determined its size.

2. Create a blank document by choosing File | New. For image size, make sure it's the image width times the number of images (such as 640×3 images, or 1920 pixels). For height, make it about 50 percent bigger than the starting image height, such as 720 pixels for a 480-pixel image. This gives you some room to maneuver if the images turn out to have some vertical offset, and you'll crop out the extra white space at the very end. You'll want the image type to be a 24-bit image (16 million colors).

12

3. Add the first image to the panorama, working from left to right. An easy way to do that is to leave the Browse window open and simply drag each image, as you need it, into the new image.

4. Take the next image and add it to your panorama document. As you add the images, line them up with the image to their left. If you use a program like Paint Shop Pro that supports layers, you can make the new image somewhat transparent to help you see where it should line up with the previous image. For a quick introduction to layers, see the sidebar "Combining Images with Layers."

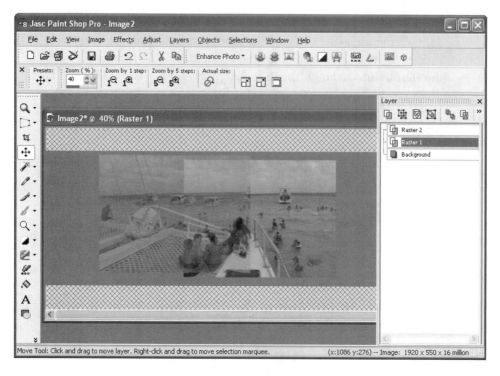

5. Repeat this process until all your images are inserted and lined up.

6. When you're done, be sure you reset all the layers to 100 percent, or they'll look transparent in the final image.

7. Use the Crop tool to crop the new panorama so any irregular tops and bottoms aren't in the image.

8. Save your file.

Improving Your Sky

I bet if you browse through your photos, you'll find many of your outdoor photos lack a certain punch—the sky is washed out, cloudless, or otherwise a little boring.

There's a good reason for that. When you compose a photograph, you usually concentrate on the primary subject and pay little heed to the sky itself. Because the sky is a lot brighter than your subject, the camera overexposes it and your sky ends up looking at least a little bleached. Even if the sky is properly exposed, it sometimes just doesn't cooperate, and you'll have a cloudless, boring sky that

Combine Images with Layers

More sophisticated editing tasks, like combining multiple images in a panorama, benefit from the Layers feature found in Paint Shop Pro and other image editors. Here's the basic idea: your picture can be made up of many different images and selections, each occupying a different layer. Each layer has its own unique characteristics, including transparency. So you can add a ghost to an image by using the image of a person in a layer with a high level of transparency.

You can add images to a picture in layers in two ways:

■ Drag images directly to an image window from the Browse window.

■ Use the menu option: Edit | Paste | As New Layer.

Once an image is considered a layer, you'll need the Layer Palette dialog box to control it. If it isn't already on screen, choose View | Palettes | Layers.

The layer palette shows you all the layers in an image. To vary their transparency, double-click on a layer in the list in the Layers Palette and vary its opacity. To make a lot of layers easier to manage, you might also want to rename them with more descriptive titles than Raster 1, Raster 2, and so on.

12

doesn't match the mood you were trying to get. By adding some snap back into to your skies, you can dramatically improve your so-so photos.

Multiply Your Sky

The easiest way to fix a bleached sky is to multiply it. What does that mean? Well, we're going to open a photo, select the sky, and copy it the clipboard. Then we'll paste copies of the sky back into the image, using a seldom-used tool to *multiply* the colors in each layer of sky to produce deeper, darker colors. If even a little blue is peeking through your sky, this technique is ideal because it's so easy to do.

For starters, find a picture with a weak sky, perhaps like the following one. Skies rarely come more anemic than this one, so let's see what we can do with it. Open it in Paint Shop Pro.

Now try these steps:

1. Click on the Magic Wand tool in preparation for selecting the sky. The *Magic Wand* is one of my favorite selection tools because it grabs parts of the photo that share similar colors. Set the tolerance in the Tools Options dialog box to about 20.

2. Click the Magic Wand squarely in the middle of the sky: you should see selection marks appear around a big blotch of sky. Use the SHIFT key and click all around the sky until you've selected the entire thing, without also grabbing any non-sky parts of the picture.

3. Make sure you've selected the entire sky—you can zoom in and pan around the image to double-check. When you know you have it all, copy the selected sky to the clipboard by choosing Edit | Copy from the menu.

4. Next, choose Edit | Paste | As New Layer. You can tell two copies of the sky are in the picture because you can grab the top sky layer and drag it around. Position the new sky so it lines up perfectly with the original sky underneath.

5. Now for the magic trick that makes all this effort worthwhile: the multiply effect. Choose Layers | Properties from the menu and you'll see the Layer Properties dialog box. Set the Blend Mode to Multiply. Click OK.

12

As soon as the dialog box disappears, you should see the colors in your sky immediately deepen. If you don't think that was enough of a change to suit you, don't worry. Here's where your artistic judgment comes in: because the sky is already copied into your clipboard, you can continue to paste new layers of sky into your image until you get the deep and colorful effect you're looking for. Using this technique, you can transform an anemic, pale blue sky into an angry, stormy scene in minutes.

Every time you paste in a new layer, be sure to set the blend for that new layer to Multiply, or the added layers will have no effect on the color of the sky.

Replace the Sky

The multiply technique isn't the only way to punch up a lame sky. You can also steal the sky from another photo, as I'll show you how to do now.

For starters, though, you're going to need a great photo of the sky. When I see a pretty blue sky, a swirling, cloudy day, a stormy afternoon, or a beautiful sunset, I grab my camera and start shooting. Use the Exposure Lock feature on your camera to set the exposure based on the sky or simply fill the entire frame with sky—either way, you'll capture all the color and intensity that you see through the viewfinder in the final image.

Shoot your sky shots with your camera's highest resolution because you never know what resolution you'll eventually need. You might also want to take some pictures in Landscape mode and others in Portrait mode, so you have a selection of skies for any situation. Store your collection of sky images in a special folder, and you'll always have options available when you want to replace a bland sky.

Evicting the Old Sky

Ready to try this technique? Load a picture with a weak sky in Paint Shop Pro. Then follow these steps:

1. Just like last time, use the Magic Wand with the Tolerance set at a moderate level (like 20) to select the sky in the photo.

2. After the sky is completely selected, choose Selections | Invert from the menu. You should see that the foreground is now selected and the sky isn't selected.

3. Copy the selected foreground to the clipboard by choosing Edit | Copy from the menu.

4. Check the image's resolution by choosing Image | Image Information from the menu. If you need to, write it down. You'll need that information in a few steps.

5. Open the image with the substitute sky in Paint Shop Pro.

6. Choose Image | Resize from the menu and fill in the proper numbers in the Pixel Size boxes to resize this image to match the original.

7. Making sure the new image is still selected, choose Edit | Paste | As New Layer from the menu. You should see the foreground from the old picture appear in the new sky photo.

8. Drag the image around as needed until it's positioned properly in the frame. If you like the results, save the new image. You're done! You can see three versions of the same picture—with an ordinary sky, a Multiplied Sky, and a Replaced Sky, all in Color Figure 6.

Let Someone Else Do the Work

Sure, after reading this book, you can do almost any kind of image edit yourself. But there might be times when you'd like a professional to do it for you instead. Or, perhaps you think a professional-quality edit might make a good gift for a friend. In either case, check out a web site called Image Edit and Art (www.image-edit.com).

This site offers professional tweaks and changes to digital photos for a small fee. Here's how it works: you upload the digital image you'd like to change and pick from their extensive list of services. Red eye removal, color adjustment, blurred backgrounds, restoration, wacky caricature filters . . . it's all here. Within a day, the folks at the site e-mail you a price quote. If you choose to pay, it takes a few days to get the work done. They do nice work, but let me be clear: there's almost nothing they do that you can't do yourself, especially if you're armed with this book and a decent image editor. That's why I think that buying a gift certificate (yes, they sell gift certificates) as a holiday gift for your digital-imaging neophyte is a better use for the site.

Come to think of it, you should give a copy of this book to all of your friends and relatives who own digital cameras for the holidays! See that? Now I'm even giving you handy gift ideas.

12

Chapter 13

Creating Special Effects

How to…

- Simulate a Hollywood-style blue screen effect

- Create Chroma-Key effects like a news-show weather map

- Create perfect selections using masks

- Insert friends and family into pictures of celebrities

- Take science fiction shots of laser battles

- Shrink your friends and put them in jars

- Make double exposures

- Add artistic and paintlike effects to your photos

- Decolorize your photos

- Colorize black and white photos

When I was a kid, I remember going to the movies and being wowed and amazed by special effects—stop motion, blue screen, animated laser combat, matte paintings—and while I'm sure a lot of people were just thinking things like "wow" and "cool," I was thinking "I wish I could do that." I was intrigued by the possibilities of trick photography, and I wanted to be able to do it myself.

Such special effects have always been possible for anyone with the time, money, equipment, and determination. I had none of the above. But when I got my first image-processing program back in 1987, I realized I could finally do what I'd always wanted to—special effects and trick photography on a budget.

Indeed, digital photography opens a lot of doors for us mere mortals. In this chapter, I'll tell you how to do some of the tricks that can make your images go beyond simple reality. You might not want to try all the techniques in this chapter, but I think there's a little fun in here for just about everyone.

Using a Hollywood-Style Blue Screen

What's a blue screen? Well, *blue screen* is the generic term for a technique in which action is photographed or filmed in front of a solid-colored backdrop.

Did you know?

Blue Screens Aren't Always Blue

Hollywood has traditionally used blue screen to do special effects because it was easier before the age of computers. Movie makers could apply a red filter to a scene with a blue background, and the result would be a black matte that was easy to replace with different film footage. But, on the PC, it doesn't matter what color you use for a backdrop, as long as it's a unique color that doesn't blend in with other parts of the scene you're trying to preserve.

Later, in postproduction, special-effects' technicians substitute a different scene in place of the blue screen. So, a scene that looks like it happened in midair or in France or on the moon actually happened in front of a blue tarp. Separate footage is added in place of the tarp, and voilà. That's movie magic.

We can achieve the same kind of results ourselves. It helps to use a real blue screen—a solid-colored backdrop that you can "paint out" afterward with a different image—but it's also possible to achieve good results with no preplanning at all.

Make a Weather Map

Let's start with the kind of shot we plan ahead for, which makes it a tad easier to get good results.

First, think about the evening news. You've seen the weather forecaster stand in front of a map of the United States and point to cold fronts a million times before, but have you ever thought about how that bit of TV magic happens? Obviously, the forecaster isn't standing in front of a real map. Instead, it's a blue screen—a solid-colored rectangle. The engineer uses a technique called *Chroma Key* to replace the rectangle with video from another source. What happens is this: the engineer selects the color of the blue screen and identifies it as a "key." The second video source then overwrites anything in the scene that has the key-valued color.

You can create your own Chroma Key weather map effect yourself. Here's how to try it.

How to ... Use Chroma Key Effects in Your Photos

1. Start with a piece of solid-colored board. Hobby stores sell foam boards in a variety of sizes and in a number of bright, primary colors. I use them frequently for projects like this. I have boards in several different colors, so I can choose one that's differently colored than my subject—that makes the technique easier to apply. Tack the board on a wall or have your subject hold it, like this:

2. Because the board is a relatively solid color, we should be able to select all of it quite easily with the Magic Wand tool. Choose the wand and click in the board. You should see a selection appear around it.

3. If the board isn't selected in its entirety, hold down the SHIFT key and click in the region that didn't get selected in the previous step. Repeat as necessary, until the entire board is selected.

4. Open a second image in Paint Shop Pro. This will be the image we insert into the first image as a sort of weather map effect.

5. With the second image selected, copy the image to the clipboard by choosing Edit | Copy.

6. Choose Edit | Paste | Into Selection. You should see the second image pasted, or Chroma Keyed, into the first image.

13

You can use this technique in all sorts of ways. You can make a window look out over an unusual vista. You can have a plain board become a famous painting. You can use it to create your own news or weather effects. Experiment—it's fun and easy to do.

Blue Screen Without a Screen

As I mentioned, in the movies they need to film in front of a special color matte to know which pixels to eliminate from the final scene. Our lives would be easier if we could always shoot in front of a blue screen, too. You could simply use the Magic Wand tool to select the whole background with just a few clicks. But because we don't live on a sound stage, sometimes it's a slightly more convoluted process to get a blue screen effect using our image-editing software.

Suppose we want to place a subject in a completely different scene than the one in which it was photographed. In the movies, an actor would be filmed in front of a blue screen, and then a matte, or a second video source, would be substituted in place of the blue screen in postproduction. Here's how we can do it in Paint Shop Pro:

1. Open the image of the person or subject that will be transplanted into another scene.

2. Create a selection area around the entire subject you want to transplant to another scene. Most of the time, the Freehand tool set to Smart Edge works best, but you might also have good results with the Magic Wand.

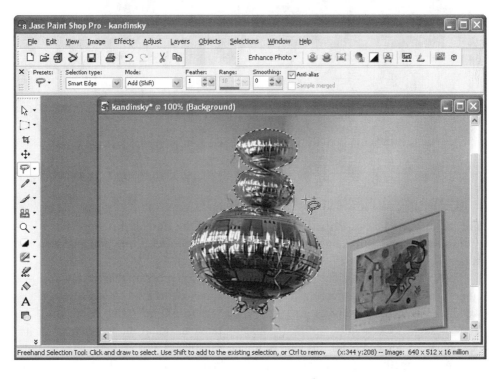

3. When the selection is complete, choose Edit | Copy from the menu.

4. Open the second image.

5. Choose Edit | Paste | As New Selection. The selection should appear in the second scene. Reposition the selection until it looks about right, and then save the finished image with a new name.

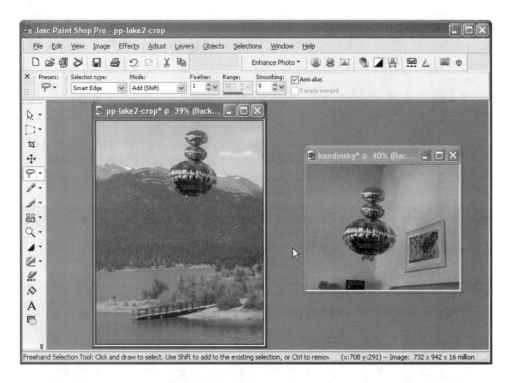

Fine-Tuning the Selection

The technique I just described works fine a lot of the time, but it's just not accurate enough to create a truly convincing special effect. You can get even better results in other ways.

First, you can invest in a professional edge-detection program that largely automates the process of creating accurate selections for this kind of special-effect work. One of the best is a program called Knockout from Corel (www.corel.com). You can see Knockout in Figure 13-1. This program can isolate individual hairs on a person's head—it's great for this kind of image transplant.

Another method: if you have Paint Shop Pro 8, you can use the *Background Eraser* to delete the background from around the subject of your image, making it easy to copy and paste it into other images.

The Background Eraser works well, often able to leave individual hairs on someone's head intact, while deleting unwanted backgrounds from around them. Select the Background Eraser from the tool palette. The only setting you generally need to set is the eraser's size; it shouldn't be too large, for reasons you'll see in a moment.

FIGURE 13-1   Knockout is a masking program that lets you precisely cut a subject out of a scene.

13

Click on the image and you'll see a dialog box asking your permission to promote the target image to a full layer. Click OK (you might want to select the option to always take this action automatically). Now position the brush near the edge of the subject you're trying to isolate. Click, hold, and paint away the background. Be careful not to get more than half of the brush over your subject, or you'll erase a bit of that, too. If the brush is too large, make it smaller so you can control how much of it covers your subject at any moment. Work in bits: click, erase a little, and release the mouse. If you try to do the whole image in a single stroke, but you make a mistake, the Undo button will set you back to square one and you'll have to do it all over from scratch. It's best to work in sections to avoid having to redo your work because of a glitch. On the other hand, it pays to remember that painting the Background Eraser with the right mouse button restores the erased area.

The Background Eraser works kind of like the Magic Wand, erasing regions of similar color. It works best when a clearly defined edge is between the subject and background you're trying to erase. After you're done erasing the background, just select the image and you can use it any way you like.

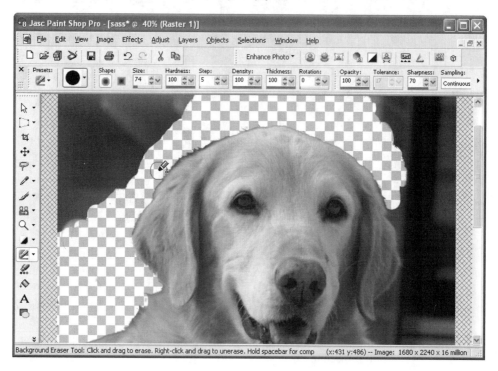

Using Masks Finally, you can make your own masks. A mask is similar to a selection; just like the regular Selection tool, *masks* isolate the area you want to change, or protect from change, when you apply color, filters, or other effects to an image.

Masks are significantly more powerful than ordinary selections, though. They have three attributes that selections don't offer in most imaging programs:

■ A mask is a 256-level grayscale image that sits on top of your picture. People usually treat a selection area as either on or off, but a mask can be used to select the degree to which an effect will occur. Black parts of the mask block all edits, white parts allow changes to occur at 100 percent strength, and gray areas are something in between. It's as if you were spray painting a model in your basement and using some sort of mask to block unwanted paint. In this case, though, the mask is made of a porous material like gauze that lets you control how much paint gets through.

■ You can fine-tune the mask with ordinary paint tools. In many applications, a selection area is only as accurate as your ability to draw with the mouse—it can't be edited—but you can create a mask, zoom in, paint pixel by pixel, and make sure it looks exactly the way you need it to look. In some applications, though, you can change the boundaries of a selection after it's created, essentially turning it into a mask. In Paint Shop Pro, choose Selections | Edit Selection and you'll find you can "paint" on the selection just as if it were a mask.

■ You can create a mask, and then save it to disk, meaning you can reuse it in many different images.

That said, let's talk about how to use a mask. Usually, unless your selection area is well defined with a narrow range of colors conducive to using the Magic Wand (such as if you're trying to enclose a solitary object against a high-contrast background), a standard selection is only as accurate as your ability to draw with the mouse. Thus, let's see how to turn a selection into a mask and fine-tune it with painting tools.

1. Load the image you want to use as the basis for your mask.

2. Draw a selection area around your subject as accurately as you can. But don't spend all day on it because we'll use the mask tools to fine-tune the selection.

3. Turn the selection into a mask by Selections | Edit Selection.

4. Now you can fine-tune the size and shape of the mask using ordinary paint tools. If you choose a paintbrush, for instance, you can edit the mask, pixel by pixel if necessary, until it perfectly matches the subject you're trying to duplicate. You can use the Zoom tool to get a close look and alter the paintbrush's diameter to get just the right amount of detail. It's not quick and easy, but it works, even for including single strands of hair from a person's head.

TIP *Regardless of the color your program uses to display the mask, the mask is just a grayscale image, and you need to paint with black, white, and shades of gray. Use white to erase the mask and black to paint the mask. If you want to manually insert various levels of transparency in the mask, use levels of gray.*

5. When the mask is just the way you like it, convert it back into a selection area by choosing Selections | Edit Selection.

6. From here, you can save it by working in the Selections | Load/Save Selection menu.

13

Shake Hands with Elvis

Now the moment you've been waiting for—the opportunity to combine pictures of yourself or friends with famous celebrities and historical figures. It's not all that hard, especially now that you know the basic principles from working with blue screens. Let's suppose your friend, Kristen, has always wanted to meet Elvis. It's too late to set up a meeting, but you can do the next best thing. In the following steps, I'll show you how to combine a picture of her with an old shot from the Nixon administration (see the finished product after step 7).

1. First, you need a suitable picture of Kristen—one in which she's more or less the same size as Elvis. Load the picture of the King into Paint Shop Pro and choose Image | Image Information to find out how tall Elvis is in the selected image.

2. Armed with knowledge about Elvis, load the picture of Kristen and crop her so she's only seen from the waist up—like Elvis—and resize the image, using the Image | Resize menu, until she's about the right height.

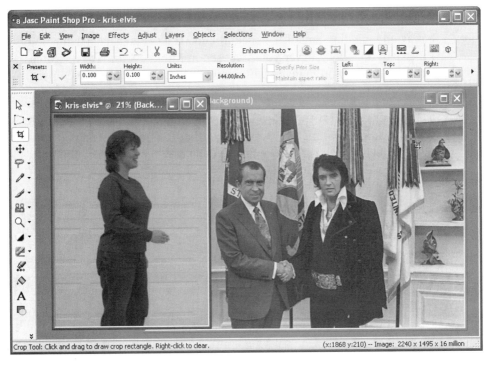

3. Now for a little housecleaning. You need to erase as much of Nixon as you reasonably can, using the Clone tool and techniques covered in Chapter 12. In this case, I copied the flag to Elvis's immediate left over the flag that was immediately behind Nixon, and then I copied the surrounding wall to get rid of as much of the former president as possible. I don't have to erase all of him because we're going to position Kristen over part of this image. This is what it looked like when the image was getting close to good enough to paste in Kris:

13

4. Now for the tricky part. You need to use a selection tool to copy Kristen, but avoid including any of the background. You can use the Magic Wand, Freehand tool—whichever you're most comfortable with. Try the Smart Edge tool, which often gives fairly good results in situations like this.

5. Once she's selected, it becomes obvious that the transition from Kristen to the background is too sharp to be believable. That means it won't look realistic in the final picture. Use the Feather tool to smooth out the edges of the selected region. Choose Selections | Modify | Feather, and then choose a value of about 4 pixels.

6. Copy Kristen to the clipboard, and then switch to the other image. Choose Paste | As New Layer. Kristen will appear onstage next to Elvis. If she's not quite the right size, use the Image | Resize control to change her size (use the Percent option) and be sure to deselect Resize all Layers so only Kristen changes size.

7. Position Kristen in the new image, arranging her so their hands meet.

8. There's something a bit squirrelly about their handshake. If you arrange the image so Elvis's arm appears over Kristen, you can mask her badly cropped appendage with a bit of Nixon's leftover hand and create a slightly three-dimensional effect—she's in front of his left shoulder, but behind his arm. To do that, copy Elvis's arm to the clipboard and paste it back into the image as a new layer, exactly over the old arm. The only difference is it'll end up lying over Kristen's hand, making it look more like they're in the same picture.

To make the illusion more convincing, you can try to sharpen or blur Kristen a bit to match the original Elvis photo before you copy-and-paste her. The CIA might know it's a fake, but it's probably fine for your purposes.

Shoot a Sci-Fi Firefight

When I was in college, I took my geeky love of *Star Trek,* added a dose of photography, and came up with a hobby that could pretty much only be done around 3:00 A.M. Although it didn't help my grades much, it was a lot of fun to create special effects like phaser blasts and disintegration halos. The best part? It was all done "in the lens," which means you can try it yourself if your digital or 35mm camera supports very long exposures. You can compare techniques and see if the digital way is easier, here's how I did it in college:

1. Set the camera up on a tripod in total darkness and start a long exposure.

2. Using a flash, expose the subject (like someone holding a phaser) and the target person. The flash needn't be mounted to the camera—you can just take a flash unit and hold it in your hand, flashing the subject once or twice.

3. Get behind the subject, and, pointing a flashlight directly at the camera, walk to the target of the phaser blast, trying to keep the flashlight moving in a straight line so it traces what will look like a solid laser beam on the film.

4. Outline the target with the flashlight, again pointing it at the camera.

5. If you want to make the target look like he or she is disintegrating, ask the subject to leave the scene, and then flash the rear wall once.

6. Stop the exposure.

That's a lot of work, and the results are often hit or miss. Against all odds, you can sometimes get a half-decent one, as in Color Figure 7.

The Disintegrating Subject

With a digital camera and a program like Paint Shop Pro, you can create this special effect a lot more scientifically. Here's an alternate way to create a similar image:

1. Take a picture of two people posed to be the aggressor and the target. *Star Trek* clothing is optional.

2. Load the image into Paint Shop Pro and immediately store a copy of the image in the clipboard by choosing Edit | Copy.

3. As a first step toward making the target glow, carefully create a selection region around the subject, and then set it to get bigger. To do that, choose Selections | Modify | Expand and select perhaps 10 or 20 pixels. Then feather the selection in the same way—choose Selections | Modify | Feather and set the feather to 5 or 10 pixels.

4. Now it's time to add an effect to make the subject glow. Choose Adjust | Brightness and Contrast | Brightness/Contrast and jack the brightness up to maximum. Click OK, and you should see a pure white region where the subject used to be.

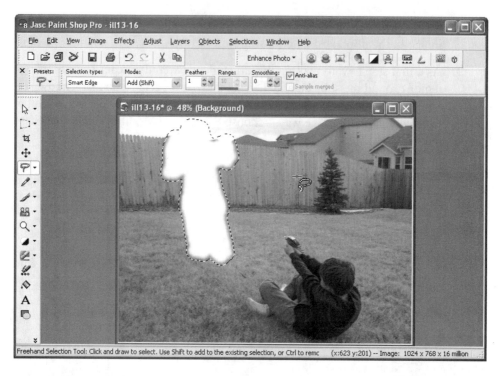

5. Next, add the copy as a new layer into your image. Choose Edit | Paste As New Layer. The glow should disappear because the copy of the original, unretouched image is now on top.

6. Double-click on the top layer to open the Layers Properties dialog box (shown in Figure 13-2), and then reduce the layer's transparency until you get the effect you like—it'll probably be in the neighborhood of 20 percent to 40 percent.

You can also do variations on this. To get the target to disintegrate, take two pictures using a tripod so you have identical framing. In one image, include the subject; in the other image, just shoot the background without the subject. When you combine the images using the layer strategy I previously discussed, it'll look like the subject is evaporating.

FIGURE 13-2 When you layer different images in an image editor, you can usually specify the transparency or opacity of each layer as you can see here.

13

The Laser Blast

We've now made a pretty convincing disintegration scene, but what about the phaser blast? As I already mentioned, using a flashlight is an inexact science—it's hard to get a straight line, as you can see in Figure 13-3.

With a paint program, though, you can get a perfectly straight beam. In most paint programs, holding down the SHIFT key while you draw a line locks the brush into following a perfectly straight path.

In Paint Shop Pro, click on the Paint Brush icon in the tool palette, and then select the color you want from the Materials Palette. Position the paint brush where you want the beam to start, and then left click. Hold down the SHIFT key, and click on the end point. The program draws a perfectly straight line between the two points. You can see how this particular shot came out in Color Figure 7.

FIGURE 13-3   It's fiendishly difficult to "draw" a straight line through the air with a flashlight doing this the old-fashioned way.

Put Your Kid in a Jar

Have you ever been impressed by the fanciful digital art in magazine ads that depict the impossible or the far, far-fetched? I can't promise that you'll soon be able to photograph a cow driving your car or aliens posing with your dog while it plays the piano, but let me show you how easy it is to something both cute and clever—we'll trap your kid in an old mayonnaise jar. Hopefully, when you see how easy it is to pull this stunt off, you'll want to make up a few clever gags of your own.

This is going to be easy. We'll take a few pictures and combine them in layers within Paint Shop Pro, resizing them to achieve the effect we want. Do this:

1. Start by finding a nice, big jar (when I tried this shot, I used a clear plastic peanut butter jar, but a mayo jar or any large, clear container is ideal). Photograph someone peering inquisitively into it.

2. Next, take the person who'll be trapped inside the jar and pose him or her in front of a big backdrop. This is where a blue screen style background (discussed earlier in the chapter) comes in handy, but you can also use a basement wall or some other background of uniform color. Don't have anything like that? Just shoot the picture outdoors and we'll deal with it.

13

3. Load the two images into Paint Shop Pro, but bring the trapped kid to the front. We'll work with this picture first.

4. If you managed to photograph the subject in front of a blue screen-style background, it'll be easier. Use the Magic Wand tool until the entire background is selected, leaving just the kid. Using a subtle feathering in the Tool Options dialog box can help you out later.

5. When the background is entirely selected, choose Selections | Invert from the menu.

If you have an irregular background to content with, you might want to use the Background Eraser or SmartEdge selection tool instead of the Magic Wand.

6. Once the subject is selected, copy it to the clipboard by choosing Edit | Copy from the menu.

7. Bring the jar photograph to the front and choose Edit | Paste | As New Layer from the menu. Your kid should appear onscreen in the photo.

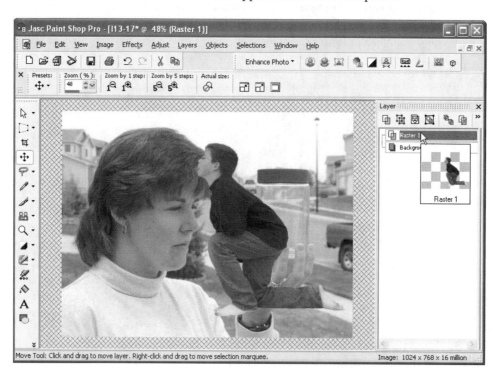

8. Now it's time to shrink the new addition down to size. Choose Image |
Resize from the menu. In the Resize dialog box, remove the check mark
from Resize all layers (it's near the bottom). In the Percent of original
box, enter a number you think will reduce the subject to fit in the jar.
Try, for instance, 20 percent. Another option: you can use the Deform
tool in the toolbar and right-click-and-drag to keep the proper
proportions.

9. Click on the subject and drag it on top of the jar. If it fits, fine. If not,
return to the Resize dialog box and fine-tune its size until it fits
properly in the jar.

Once you tweak the size and position of the captured kid, your photo is done, as you can see in Color Figure 8. You can also try other things, though, to improve the photo:

- Try to photograph both pictures with similar lighting to make a more believable picture.

- Be careful about the angle from which you shoot the jar-kid to match the jar's perspective in the first photo.

- Select the jar, copy it to the clipboard, and paste it on top of the jar-kid as yet another layer. By varying the transparency of the jar (see the next section, "Make a Double Exposure," for details on how to do that), you can increase the illusion that the subject is, indeed, inside the jar, not just pasted on top of it. You can see an alternate version of the jar photo (also in Color Figure 8) using this technique.

Make a Double Exposure

Now let's return to Earth for an easy trick that mimics double-exposure photography. In the world of 35mm photography, double exposures are fun, but hard to do well. You can go for far-out stuff that combines two completely different kinds of subjects or a simple artistic effort like the double-exposed flower in Figure 13-4.

The good news is that double-exposure shots in digital photography take seconds to do and don't require any of the elaborate planning or in-your-head exposure calculations you'd need to do with film. And you can combine any number of photos into your multiple exposure. Here's how:

1. Load two photos you plan to combine in Paint Shop Pro.

2. Make sure they're both the same pixel size by choosing Image | Image Information from the menu. If one is larger, resize it so they're the same size.

3. Select one photo and choose Edit | Copy to put it in the clipboard.

4. Select the other photo and choose Edit | Paste | As New Layer. You should see the first photo appear over—and completely obscure—the selected photo.

5. If the Layer Palette toolbar isn't already on the screen, open it by choosing View | Palettes | Layers.

6. In the Layer Palette, double-click the top layer, and then drag the transparency slider for Layer 1 back from 100 percent until you can

FIGURE 13-4   A double exposure like this one can add an ethereal quality to your photograph.

start to see the underlying image. Setting the slider at 50 percent will give you equal amounts of both pictures, though you might want one of the images to be significantly more prominent. If so, drag the slider back and forth until you get just the right multiple-exposure effect.

When you're happy with your multiple exposure, save the image. As mentioned earlier, you can see the final version of a double exposure-style image of a flower in Figure 13-4. To get this shot, I took one photo in sharp focus and a second exposure with the flower completely out-of-focus, and then combined them. I kept the out-of-focus image mixed back around 35 percent.

Paint Like Van Gogh

An easy way to transform your images into unique works of digital art is with the filters that are built into image-editing software like Paint Shop Pro and Adobe PhotoShop. A *filter* is graphics-talk for a tool that lets you edit or manipulate your image. It's called a filter because when you run it, software changes your image according to a specific mathematical process, filtering the original data in a certain way to deliver a modified image. A common and relatively boring example of a filter is *sharpening,* which adds contrast to the pixels in an image, increasing the apparent sharpness.

13

Plug-ins Expand
Your Image Editing Options

Many image editors, including Paint Shop Pro, can use something called a *plug-in,* or a *plug-in filter,* which are filters originally designed for Adobe Photoshop. Photoshop filters have become something of a standard in image-editing software, and many programs can use these filters. You can download filters from the Web, purchase them in stores, or get them with other image editors. Back in Chapter 6, for instance, I talked about a program called *LensDoc,* which lets you straighten images that got distorted because of wide-angle and fish-eye lenses. Well, LensDoc is a plug-in for Photoshop. It's a filter that processes your image within an image editor.

Filters can do a lot more than just sharpen (or blur) your images, though. Hundreds of filters are out there, and many programs (like Paint Shop Pro) come with a few dozen. The best way to find out what a filter does is to experiment. I say that because it's one thing to read an explanation of the filter, but it's quite another thing to process a picture with each filter to see the effect. In general, you probably won't use many of these filters very often. But it pays to try them out, because you never know when a certain effect will be just what you're looking for. Table 13-1 provides a quick summary of the most common filter types you might run across.

Filter	Description
Blur	Blur filters average nearby pixels to give the impression of blur, poor focus, or motion.
Sharpen	Sharpen filters increase apparent sharpness in an image by increasing the contrast between pixels, either throughout an image or only along edges.
Edge	Edge filters typically enhance and trace edges—regions defined by high-contrast borders between pixels.
Noise	Noise filters can add or remove "noise" in an image. Noise manifests itself in digital images as specks of high-contrast color, like snow in a TV transmission.

TABLE 13-1   Common Filter Types

Filter	Description
Geometric effects	These tools let you distort and skew parts of an image. They're good for displaying an image in a different perspective. You can change the orientation of an image in three dimensions or perhaps distort images within circles, cylinders, and other shapes.
Artistic effects	This is the general name for a slew of filters that do everything from add bas relief, watercolor, charcoal, mosaic, and more to your images. This is where you should go when you want to make your image look like it was hand-painted or give it a unique, nonphoto-realistic look.

TABLE 13-2   Common Filter Types *(continued)*

There's no limit to the kinds of effects you can achieve with filters, though beware: many of them are somewhat clichéd. Use your judgment when applying them. Check out Figure 13-5. Here you can see the original strawberries, as well as what they look like with Brush Stroke, Stained Glass, and Colored Pencil filters applied. In Paint Shop Pro, you can find all of these effects—and many others—in the Effects menu.

13

FIGURE 13-5   A variety of artistic effects are applied to the same original image (shown in the lower-right corner).

FIGURE 13-6　A blurry portrait (left) transformed into art (on the right) with a plug-in.

Lots of companies sell add-on plug-in filters for Photoshop and other graphics programs. More plug-in packages are available for Photoshop, Photoshop Elements, and Paint Shop Pro than I have room in this book to list, but I'll mention two. *Jasc's Virtual Painter,* for instance, includes a dozen effects like pastel, silk screen, pointillism, and watercolor that help you look like an old-world painter. See Figure 13-6 for a low-light portrait, which was simply unusable because of camera shake, that's been transformed into a pretty watercolor via Virtual Painter.

Xenofex 2, from Alien Skin Software (www.alienskin.com) is another great program. It includes 14 filters that add lightening or a gorgeous blue sky to your images, or transform an image into a TV-style graphic, complete with old-fashioned, picture tube-esque curved edges and video scan lines. You can add burnt edges to a picture, shatter it like broken glass, or turn it into a virtual jigsaw puzzle. And that's only about half the effects. Figure 13-7 shows a night photo that's been transformed with the addition of an oversized moon (added via Paint Shop Pro's Layers feature, plus lightening and a TV effect from Xenofex 2.

Decolorizing Your Pictures

This effect is a lot of fun. Surely you've seen television commercials in which everything is black and white except for one item—a person, perhaps, or the featured product—which is in full color. It's an effective trick because your eyes are drawn to the color image in a sea of gray.

On television, this effect is typically done with two cameras. On the PC, though, we can do it after the fact with a single image—you didn't even have to have this effect in mind when you originally took the shot. Best of all, it's not

FIGURE 13-7   A creepy sci-fi look after just a few minutes in an image editor with filters

hard to do. It's particularly easy if your image editor supports layers. The basic idea is this:

- Stack two copies of the image in separate layers.
- Convert one to grayscale.
- Select most of the image in the color version.
- Delete the selection, leaving a small color subject on top of the grayscale image.

Specifically, here's how to do it in Paint Shop Pro:

1. Open the image you want to use and make a copy of it by choosing Edit | Copy. Don't paste it anywhere yet; just let it stay in the clipboard.

2. Select the image and convert it to a grayscale picture by choosing Image | Grayscale. Then turn the image into a 24-bit file by choosing Image | Increase Color Depth | 16 Million Colors.

3. Rename this image's layer to Grayscale so it's easier to keep track of. To do that, double-click the layer in the Layer Palette and change the Name in the Layers Properties dialog box. In this illustration, you can see the layer has been renamed.

4. Now add the color image on top of this one. Select the image and choose Edit | Paste | As New Layer. You can prove it worked by sliding the transparency control of the top layer until you can see the grayscale image peeking through. Now the second layer sites on "top" of the grayscale layer, as you can see in the Layer Palette dialog box:

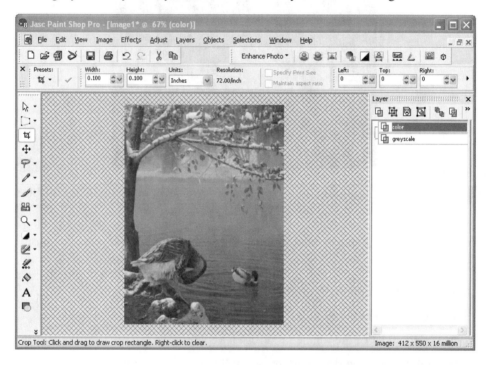

5. With the new color layer selected, use the Selection tool to trace out the subject you want to keep in color. Trace as carefully as possible. If you need to, use the background eraser or create a mask to fine-tune the area, and convert the mask into a selection.

6. When you're done, choose Selections | Invert to select everything *except* the color subject. (If you've used the Background Eraser, skip down, because the background is already gone.)

7. Choose Edit | Cut to cut most of the color image away.

8. Choose Selections | Select None to finish.

You should now have a grayscale image with a single element in color, such as the one in Color Figure 9. Save the image with a new name.

Colorizing an Image

Now let's try the opposite technique: instead of taking color away from your picture, let's add color or change the colors in your photos. Colorizing digital images—or even old back and white photos you've scanned into your PC—is easy, though it takes a little artistic skill to do well. Some folks use the colorizing technique to see what their car or basement walls would look like painted another color, while others want to enhance old photos they found tucked away in a family photo album. Whatever your motivation, the mechanics of colorizing your photos is easy. Try this:

1. Start by loading a picture into Paint Shop Pro and selecting just the part of the image you want to colorize. If you're trying a new paint scheme on your car, use the Magic Wand tool to select the car's body without also capturing the windshield, chrome, or surrounding background. If you want to paint the basement, select the walls. As usual, you should fine-tune the Magic Wand's Tolerance setting and use the SHIFT key to select the entire region.

2. Now click the Flood Fill tool and, in the Tool Options dialog box, change the Blend mode from Normal to Color.

Another Kind of Colorizing

You can create an interesting work of art using the Colorize tool. Colorize converts your image into a picture with uniform hue while maintaining the original brightness levels, and that means you get a monochrome image that isn't grayscale. Instead, it's bluescale, redscale, or whatever-scale you happen to choose. Want to get an image that looks like it was photographed through night-vision goggles? Try to colorize it with a hue of 75 and a saturation of 80. But keep experimenting—some images can look dramatic when rendered in just a primary color.

3. Left-click in the color palette to select the color you'd like to paint.

4. Click anywhere in your selected region, and you should see the color change without losing any of the underlying texture in the selected region. In other words, you've changed the color of your subject.

Adding Digital Motion Blur

Life is full of little paradoxes. They bother to tell you the nutritional information on the wall at McDonalds, for instance. And, in the world of photography, people often try to capture the essence of motion in pictures, which are by their very nature totally static, two-dimensional, and frozen in time.

That's what makes motion-themed photos so compelling, though: the notion that you can somehow capture motion and freeze it for all eternity on an unchanging computer screen or sheet of photo paper. Back in Chapter 3, we talked about motion blur techniques when you actually took the picture; now let's add it digitally after the fact. My guinea pig is a rental car that I came to call the Maruti of Horrors on my scuba vacation in the Cayman Islands last year.

In the following photo, the Maruti is parked on a side street in Georgetown, but we'll make it look like it's moving using two different techniques.

These two digital techniques correspond to the different ways you can photograph movement. One way to shoot a moving vehicle is to make the camera perfectly stationary and let the vehicle blur as it moves through the frame. The other method involves panning the camera with the moving vehicle. As you take the picture, the vehicle will be sharp and focused, while the background will be blurred. We'll start by blurring the vehicle.

Blur the Subject

For starters, we need to select the vehicle. To do that, click the Freehand tool and make sure it's set to Smart Edge. Work your way around the vehicle, selecting little pieces at a time, until you get all the way around to where you started. Double click to close the selection and encase the entire vehicle.

We're not done yet. When you see motion blur—whether in a photo or in a Mighty Mouse cartoon—blur lines tend to extend beyond the rear of the moving object. This means we need to select the area in the picture that's behind the Maruti. It's easy enough to do: just hold down the SHIFT key as you start selecting more real estate.

When you press the SHIFT key, you should see a small plus sign (+) appear atop the lasso pointer onscreen. Position the lasso at the top rear of the canvas cover, and then click. Now move the mouse straight back and click again at the

13

very left edge of the photo. Move the mouse down until you're parallel with the bottom of the rear tire, click, and then position the mouse over the tire where it meets the ground. Click, and the space behind the vehicle should become a part of your selection. The selection now looks like this:

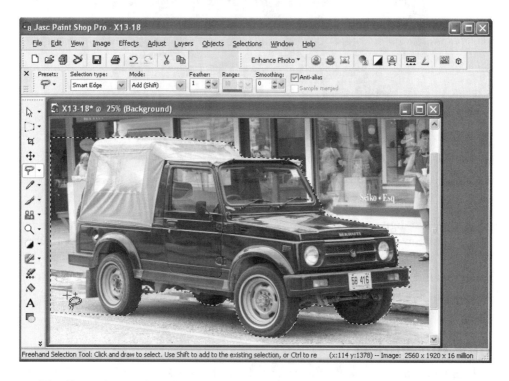

Finally, we're ready to blur. And this part is pretty easy: in Paint Shop Pro. Choose Adjust | Blur | Motion Blur from the menu. The Motion Blur filter blurs your picture, but only in one direction, giving the impression of movement. For my example, I'd set the Angle control to 270 degrees, so it's pointing directly left, maximize the Strength (100 percent) and click OK.

I've ended up with this example of motion blur:

Can the image be improved? You bet! A little less blur would be a good start—unless you're intentionally going for a comically unrealistic effect.

13

Blur the Background

That was a good start, but a more common blur technique is akin to panning (see Chapter 3). For that, I only want to blur the background and leave the subject intact. To do that, select the subject using whatever technique you prefer. But, because we want to apply motion blue to the background, we need to invert our selection—that will select the entire background, leaving the vehicle itself unselected. Choose Selections | Invert.

When you're done selecting the vehicle, it's time to apply some blur. Choose Adjust | Blur | Motion Blur. Again, set the Angle and Strength, and then click OK.

You'll should see a pretty plausible example of motion blur (as in the following illustration), but it's not perfect. Notice that you can still clearly see the background through the front of the windshield, and it's not one bit blurry. That's easy to correct. You could right-click anywhere on the image to eliminate the current selection, and then use the Smart Edge Freehand tool to select just the portion of the windshield that looks directly into the storefronts. After you complete the selection, apply the motion blur again.

One final touch: our wheels should be spinning, but they're not. A ten-second solution to this glaring error is to select the two driver-side wheels, and then add some plain old blur to them by choosing Adjust | Blur.

Chapter 14

Working with Text and Creating Projects

How to...

- Add text to digital images
- Fill text with color gradients
- Fill text with other images
- Create text drop shadows
- Turn images into wallpaper for the Windows desktop
- Add small images to letterhead in Word
- Create greeting cards on the PC
- Make your own newsletter

Over the course of this book, I've shown you how to do all sorts of things to your images—everything from the mundane—like sharpening, cropping, and brightening your images—to adding sophisticated special effects like Chroma Key and abstract effects.

Sometimes, though, all you want to do is add a caption or turn a picture into a birthday card. In this final chapter on image editing, let's talk about the various ways you can add text to your images to turn them into true multimedia works of art. I'll even show you some simple tricks for creating stuff like Windows wallpaper, greeting cards, and letterhead with your images.

Adding Text to Pictures

If you're used to using a word processor like Microsoft Word, you might be surprised to find that some image editors don't let you type directly on to the canvas as if you were writing a letter to your Mom.

Instead, a program like Paint Shop Pro requires you to type your text into a dialog box, and then paste that text into the image. In fact, the Text tool in Paint Shop Pro plays by a few unusual rules:

- Unlike some image editors, such as Adobe Photoshop Elements, you can't type directly onto the image. Instead, you need to type your text in a dialog box, and then transfer it to the image when you finish. You can see the Text Entry dialog box used by Paint Shop Pro in Figure 14-1.

FIGURE 14-1 The Text toolbar and the Text Entry dialog box let you specify the style, color, and size of the text you add to a digital image.

- The color of the text will usually be painted in the currently selected background color, so make sure it's set to the right color before you click the Text tool.

- Text is an editable object when you first position it. That means you can position it, stretch it, transform it, and so on—but, depending on which mode you insert the text, it might only be editable initially. If you change tools and do something else, that text typically becomes a permanent part of the image.

14

Add Text to a Picture in Paint Shop Pro

1. Change the background color to whatever you want the text to be.

2. Click the Text button in the tool palette. The mouse pointer will change to the letter *A*. In the text toolbar, set the Create As menu to Floating or Vector. Set the font and size as well, but you can adjust those in a moment.

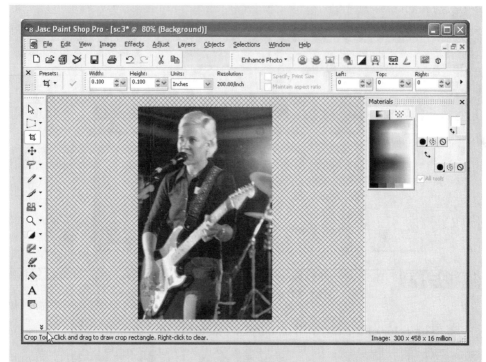

3. Click in the image where you want the text to be positioned. The point that you click will be the lower-left corner of the text box.

> **NOTE** *The timing of these steps vary in different programs. In Adobe Photoshop, for instance, there's no text box at all. In older versions of Paint Shop Pro, you don't see the font selections until you click the image.*

Special Effects with Text

You can do a lot with text in an image—so much more than pasting letters down in some primary color. Attractive text, in fact, is what makes or breaks documents like posters and greeting cards. A lot of text tricks are so easy to do that you can experiment and create your own. I' have a few you might want to start with, though.

Create Picture-Filled Text

One of my favorite tricks is to make an image show through the text, as if it were a digital stencil. Look at Figure 14-2, for instance. As you can see, I've made the word "Flying" from a photo of a bird in flight, and the word "Tiger" from, well, a tiger.

4. When the Text Entry dialog box appears, type your text into the space provided. You can adjust the font and size by selecting the text in the box, and then changing its characteristics from the toolbar.

5. Click Apply. The text should appear in the image at the place you positioned it in Step 3.

This is an interesting exercise in creating an eye-catching picture, so let me show you how to do this yourself.

1. Open the image you want to show through the text. Click the Text icon in the tool palette.

2. Set the Create As menu in the text toolbar to Selection. This will create the text as a selection instead of as solid-colored text. Set the font and size in which you want the text to appear. You'll need to make the text big and fat for this effect to work. For starters, I suggest you choose a font like Bauhaus.

14

6. For the moment, the text is treated as an object you can edit. You can reposition the text by dragging the box 'in the center of the text box. If you selected Vector text, you can also resize the text by dragging the small boxes in the sides of the text box.

FIGURE 14-2   You can convey the spirit of a word using patterns from pictures as stencils.

3. Click in the spot where you want to grab the photo as text, and then enter your desired text.

> **TIP** *In Paint Shop Pro, the spot you click becomes the lower-left corner of the text.*

4. Click OK. The text appears as a selection in the image. You can also reposition the text by clicking-and-dragging its center point. The pointer will change to four arrows when you can drag it.

5. Copy the text to the clipboard by choosing Edit | Copy.

6. Open the image to which you want to add the text.

7. Choose Edit | Paste | As New Selection from the menu. The text should appear in the image.

8. Position the text to your liking and choose Selections | Select None.

14

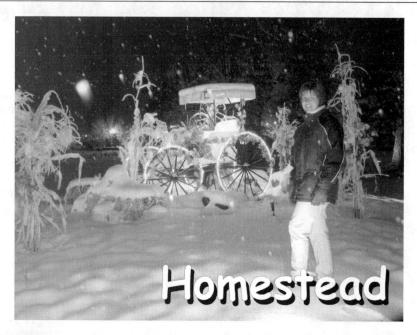

FIGURE 14-3   Drop shadows are a great way to lead the eye to text in the image.

Add Drop Shadow

Drop shadows, seen in Figure 14-3, are a cool embellishment that can add a lot to
the visual appeal of your text. They can even make it more readable, particularly
on certain kinds of images. Some programs come with a drop shadow tool built in,
making it a snap to add drop shadows to your text. But, if your program doesn't
have a drop-shadow feature, you can achieve similar results simply by making two
copies of the text in different colors and arranging them by hand, so they look like
text and shadow. Try this:

1. In the Materials Palette, set the background color to black. This will be the
   color of our shadow text.

2. Click the Text button in the tool palette and enter the text, font, and size.
   Select the Vector option in the Create As menu.

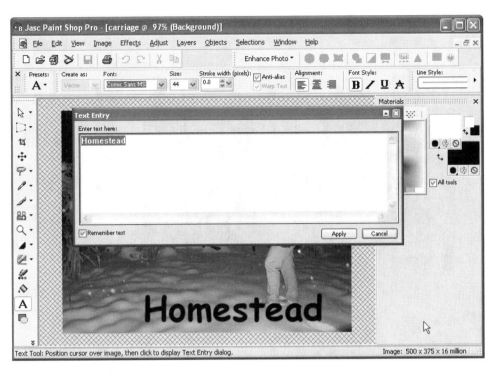

3. Now, click the image to specify where you want it to appear. The Text Entry dialog box should appear. Enter your text, click Apply, and then position the text precisely where you want it in the finished image.

4. Now go back to the color palette and change the background color to white.

5. Click the Text button in the tool palette again. In the Text Entry dialog box, don't change anything. You'll want the font, size, and text to be exactly the same as the shadow text we've already entered.

6. Click in the image. You needn't be precise about where the text will go right now because we'll move the text with the mouse in a few steps. Type your text, and then click OK to paste the text into the image.

7. Position the mouse pointer over the center of the text, and then drag the text until it's positioned over the shadow text, offset just enough so it looks like a drop shadow.

14

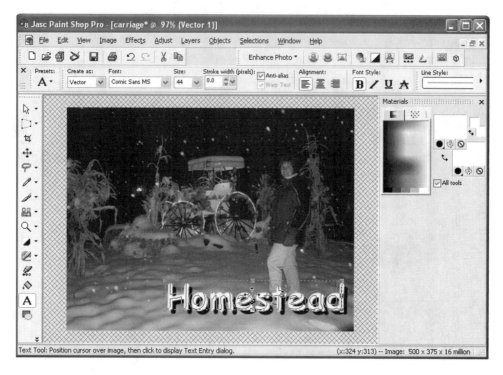

8. Choose Selections | Select None.

Combine Image and Drop Shadow

This last text trick is so simple you're going to say it's hardly a trick at all, but I'm including it to show you how easy it is to come up with cool effects with little effort. The effect: text filled with a picture, like we've already done but, this time, the underlying picture is the same as the text. How can you see the text at all, you wonder, if it's filled with the same image as the background? The text is bordered—on two sides, at least—by a dark drop shadow. Check out Figure 14-4.

Here's how to do it:

1. Change the background color to white using the Materials palette.

2. Click the Text button. Make sure the Stroke and Fill styles are set to solid color, and then choose Selection in the Create As menu. Set the font to taste.

3. Click in the image to specify where the text will be pasted.

4. Enter the text, and then click Apply to paste the text into the image.

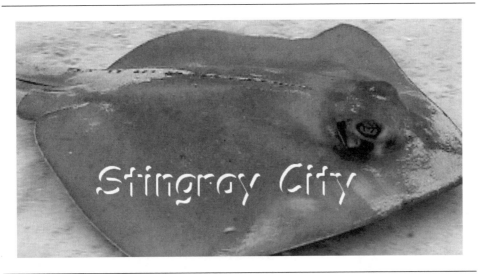

FIGURE 14-4   This effect is subtle, but one of my favorites.

5. You should see a selection shaped like the text. Grab the text and drag it a
    short distance. In place of the text, you should see lettering that will serve
    as your drop shadow. Don't move the text too far or the image text will get
    "lost" in the surrounding image.

Projects for Your Digital Images

Now that you know how to edit, manipulate, and embellish your images, you probably
want to apply those skills by using images in projects that go beyond e-mailing images
to your friends. One of the benefits of digital images, of course, is the ease with which
you can incorporate them into projects like posters, greeting cards, newsletters, and
business cards. Let's take a look at how you can get started doing this yourself.

Using Digital Images as Wallpaper

Let's start with something that's not only easy, but also can make your PC a bit more
fun. Your Windows desktop can display any kind of image as long as it's been saved in
a JPG, GIF, or BMP format. If your desktop still has that same old blue background,
you can use an image from your digital camera to brighten things.

To display your image on your desktop, do this:

1. Make sure your image is in JPG, BMP, or GIF format. As you know by now,
    most digital images save images in JPG format, so you're probably ready to go.

14

If you're using Windows 98 or later, you can select a JPG or a GIF image. If you have an older version of Windows, you can only use a BMP file.

2. Right-click the desktop and choose Properties from the Context menu. The Display Properties dialog box appears.

3. On the Background tab, click the Browse button to choose the image (If you have Windows XP, that button is on the Desktop tab).

4. If you want the image centered in your display, choose Center in the Display drop-down menu. If you'd prefer the image to repeat itself all across the display, choose Tile instead.

5. Click OK to close the dialog box.

NOTE *You might want to resize the image in a program like Paint Shop Pro to match the screen resolution you run on your PC. That way, the image will take up the entire screen. The original resolution of the image should be close to your desktop size (or bigger). If you start with a small image, the result will often be quite ugly.*

If your image is too small for the display, it'll either be tiled to fill the screen or centered in the display with a lot of blank desktop around it. For photographs, I think centering looks good—tiling photographs just looks busy and annoys me (see Figure 14-5). Of course, you can experiment and arrange your display any way you like.

FIGURE 14-5   The same image shown centered, tiled, and stretched

Adding an Image to Letterhead

If you use Microsoft Word and send a lot of letters, you might want to try this next project—creating your own personal letterhead with an embedded digital image. Here's what to do:

1. Open Microsoft Word. If you don't already have a new blank document open, click the New Document icon in the toolbar.

2. Design the letterhead any way you like. You should set your formatting to single space and try to keep your text smaller than about 11 points.

3. To insert an image from your digital camera, choose Insert | Picture | From File and locate the image you want to include. The image will appear in your document.

14

4. To make the image easier to move around and position on the page, you need to put a frame around the picture. Right-click the image and choose Format Picture.

5. Click on the Layout tab and choose Tight.

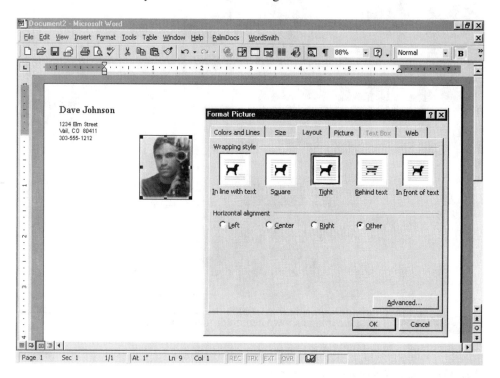

6. Click OK.

7. Position the image in the letterhead region of your document, such as to the left of your name. Notice how the text moves to accommodate the image.

8. Finish the letterhead by drawing a thin horizontal line under the text and image (see Figure 14-6). To do that, activate the drawing tools by clicking the Drawing icon in the toolbar. Then click the Line tool and drag out a horizontal line, holding down the SHIFT key at the same time. The line will snap to the horizontal automatically.

Creating Your Own Greeting Cards

You can make greeting cards using your computer in two ways: the easy way and the not-as-easy-but-still-not-very-hard way. The easy way is by using one of the

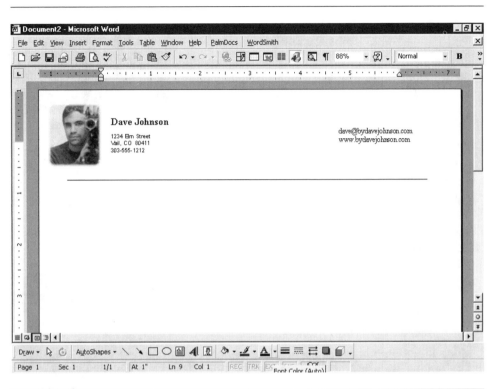

FIGURE 14-6   Images can make your letterhead quite elegant (unless it's a picture of me... Use that at your own risk).

many greeting card software packages on the market (see Figure 14-7). Not only can you import your digital camera images into these programs, but they also come with a considerable collection of clip art and premade card templates.

   If you don't have one of those programs, you can still make your own greeting cards in a page layout program or Microsoft Word. Because Word is the lowest common denominator—almost everyone has it—let's create a card in that. Before we get started, though, it's worth pointing out that you can make a greeting card on the PC in two common methods: the single-fold and the dual-fold.

   Single-fold cards are simply made from 8.5×11-inch paper or cardstock and folded once down the middle, so the card measures 5.5×8.5 inches. This is a slightly oversized card, but it's a good size and the one I usually use. The alternative is a dual-fold card that's folded once lengthwise and again widthwise, for a card that measures 5.5×4.25 inches. The disadvantage to this kind of card is it's a bit small and it has a potentially amateurish double-fold along one edge (see Figure 14-8).

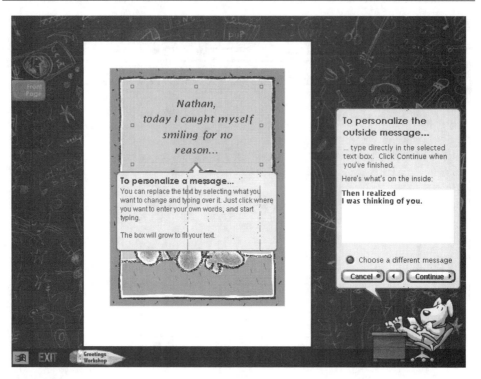

FIGURE 14-7   Programs like Microsoft Greetings Workshop let you import your own digital images into their greeting card templates.

Single-fold

-side	one-
Back	Front

-side	two-
	Inside Right

Dual-fold

	Front
Inside Right	Back

FIGURE 14-8   You can make either single-fold or dual-fold cards on your PC with almost any program.

You can't make dual-fold cards in Word because that kind of card requires one of the panels to be printed upside down. So Word is best at single-fold cards, as in this example:

1. Open Word and create a new document.

2. Change the document into a landscape orientation. Choose File | Page Setup. The Page Setup dialog box appears.

3. Click the Paper Size tab and select Landscape from the orientation section. Click OK.

4. Now we need to give the document two columns. Each column will be a panel on the finished card. Choose Format | Columns.

5. In the Columns dialog box, select Two and click OK.

6. Now you can enter your text. The left column on the first page is the rear of the card. If you want to, you can add something to the bottom of the rear panel like commercial greeting cards have. Press ENTER enough times to get to the bottom of the page.

7. Now it's time for the front of the card. That's the right column on the first page, so press ENTER to get there. You'll probably want to insert an image there using Insert | Picture | From File. You can place text above or below the image, or you can integrate the text in the image in a program like Paint Shop Pro first. Be sure to experiment with large and stylish fonts for this card.

 Create Gifts From Pictures

14

Many web sites and local photo stores can take your digital images and use them to create all sorts of interesting gifts, like coffee mugs, T-shirts, refrigerator magnets, jigsaw puzzles, and even food (your picture can be added in edible food dyes to cookies, cakes, and candies). Sites like ClubPhoto.com, ofoto.com, and PhotoWorks.com all offer these basic services. If you're shopping for a picture-apron or you want to eat some vacation shots, check out these web sites.

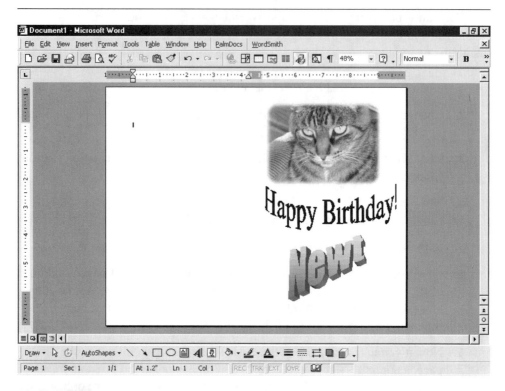

FIGURE 14-9 Word can be used to make "quick and dirty" greeting cards, though a dedicated graphics or card program is a better bet.

Microsoft's WordArt is a cool way to dress up a greeting card in Word. Choose Insert | Picture | WordArt to insert WordArt into your project. WordArt lets you turn plain text into a fancy 3-D piece of art, as seen in Figure 14-9.

8. The inside of the card is on the second page. The left inside panel is the left column, and the right inside panel is the right column. Enter text and images as necessary to lay out the card you want to create.

9. When you're done, you need to print your card manually so it doesn't print the second page of the document on a second sheet of paper. To do that, you have two choices:

■ Only load a single sheet of paper in the printer. When the first page is printed, turn the paper over and load it back in for the second pass, *or*

■ Change the printer settings. In Word, choose File | Print. Choose
Properties to open the Printer Properties dialog box and change the
printer's paper source to Manual (your printer's dialog box might
not look exactly like this one:

TIP *If you're printing on an inkjet printer, make sure you wait for the first
side to dry before turning the paper over and printing the second side.
See Chapter 15 for more information on printing.*

14

Create a Newsletter

Equipped with Microsoft *Publisher* or a similar page layout program, you can
create professional and attractive newsletters for the office, family, or your
club or organization. Publisher comes in most versions of Microsoft Office,
and I highly recommend it for generating your own newsletters (as well as
business cards and other projects). Publisher is a wizard-based program. All
you have to do is follow the directions to set up the overall look and feel of
your document, and then fill in the text and replace the placeholder images
with your own pictures.

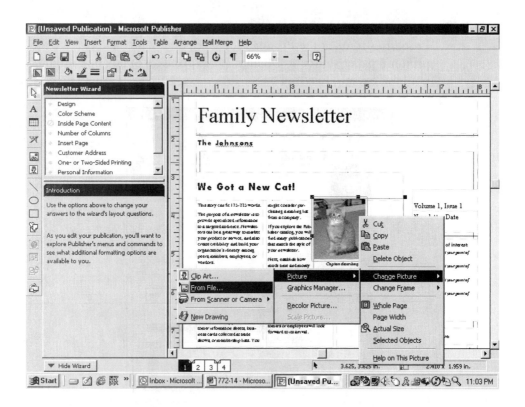

Make a Magazine Cover

At gift time, I believe photos are some of the most personal and most appreciated gifts you can give. But just handing someone an 8"×10" photo lacks that certain *je ne sais quois,* as the French like to say. So I like to do things with my pictures that are a bit unusual. The next time a birthday rolls around, here's a clever gift you can make all by yourself, without any help from a bakery: a framed mock magazine cover featuring your guest of honor.

This is' easy to do. All you need is an appropriate, high-resolution photo and an image editing program to make some surgical changes. Then send it to the printer and it's ready for framing. Because this will eventually be printed on an ink jet printer at 8"×10" size, you should start with a 2- or 3-megapixel image. For our example, I'm going to make the debut issue of *Kristen* magazine using this image:

1. Our first order of business is to give our picture a magazine-like outline. Load it into your image editor and add a blank border area around your image. You can make it any color you like but, for my picture, I think a nice fire-red border will be very magazine-ish. In Paint Shop Pro, there's an easy way to do this. Choose Image | Add Borders, and then choose a color from the color box in the Add Borders dialog box. Next, enter a border dimension. If you're using a 3-megapixel image, you might need about 100 pixels of border to get the right effect, but experiment until you see something you like. Be sure to set the border to symmetric, so all four sides are the same. Click OK to create the border. You should see a red border added around the outside of the image.

2. What's a magazine without a catchy title? Mine will be called *Kristen* magazine, after all, it's the place people go when they want to read all about Kris. Click the Text button and adjust the font style, size, and color. Set the Create as to Vector. Click in the upper half of the picture, more or less where the title should end up. You'll then get the Text Entry dialog box. Type a title,

14

and then select it with your cursor, drag the text around the screen, and even change its size. If you want to get fancy, you can even rotate it by clicking-and-dragging the small box to the right of the center of the text.

3. From here, it's all up to you. Add some "cover lines" to your magazine to make it look more like a real publication. Add an issue date, some revealing new feature, and more. If you're ambitious, you can photograph a bar code from a real magazine with your digital camera and paste it into the cover. My first draft looks something like this:

Part IV

Using Your Images

Chapter 15

Printing Your Pictures

How to…

- Choose the printer that's right for you

- Distinguish among laser, inkjet, and dye sublimation printers

- Shop for a printer

- Match resolution to print size

- Choose the right kind of paper for your print job

- Print an enlargement with Paint Shop Pro

- Configure your printer for paper and quality

- Determine what side of the paper to print on

- Care for prints after they come out of the printer

- Send your images to someone else for printing

A lot of the time, it all comes down to this: no matter how versatile the digital medium is, a digital camera isn't very useful unless you can make prints. Great prints. Prints that look every bit as good as what you can get from a 35mm camera and the local photo shop.

If that sounds like something you would say, you're in luck. Recent advances in print technology have made it possible to make your own prints that look just as good as what you can get from a 35mm camera. In some ways, the results can be better. With a digital image, you can tweak it so it looks exactly the way you want it to, and you can print it any way you like, from wallet size all the way up to near-poster 13×19 inches.

In this chapter, I'll talk about everything you need to know to get great prints from your digital images. When you're done, you'll be able to frame your creations, and no one will be able to tell that the pictures came out of a computer printer.

Using the Right Printer

Not all that long ago, there was a time when computer printers had a reputation for, shall we say, substandard output. Of course, everyone thought the printers looked pretty good at the time, but there was no way anyone would mistake what came out of a computer printer for a real photograph. Printers couldn't depict enough colors.

The resolution was too low. Obvious bands of different intensity colors ran through images like Venetian blinds on a window. And those were just the most vexing of the output problems.

Then, a few years ago, it all started to change. Around the same time that scanners became affordable and digital cameras began to hit the scene, printer manufacturers had new incentives to make their products work better. By the late 1990s, most mainstream printers could create passable prints from computer images, and the top-of-the-line printers made prints that were essentially photo-realistic.

In the last few years, not a lot has changed dramatically. For most practical applications, it's not possible to make prints look any better to the casual viewer, so printer manufacturers have turned their attention to other aspects of digital printing, like making the prints last longer before they fade. I'll discuss this area in more detail in the section "What to Look For."

Choosing a Printer

Before we get started printing, let's talk about the printers themselves and how to choose the right one. Buying a printer isn't an easy decision because not only are many different brands of printers competing for your attention—and lots of different models from each manufacturer—but you also have to figure out what kind of printer you want. If you're serious about printing digital images, I suspect you'll want an inkjet printer. But, to be sure, let me tell you about the variety of printers you can choose from.

Laser Printers

Laser printers are like specialized photocopiers. Using the digital image in the computer's memory as a template, they electrically charge a piece of paper. The printer then allows *toner*—a fine ink-like powder—to come into contact with the paper. (See Figure 15-1 for a look at a typical toner cartridge.) The toner sticks to the paper in places where it has an electrostatic charge and, finally, the toner is permanently melted into the paper by a hot fusing wire.

Laser printers have a lot of advantages. They can print quickly (many personal laser printers can generate as many as eight or ten pages per minute), and the toner lasts a long time, yielding a low cost per page. My HP LaserJet 1200 prints about 3000 to 5000 sheets of paper for each $80 toner cartridge. Those advantages add up to a good all-around office printer that handles most common print jobs pretty well. Personal laser printers can be had for between $100 and $500, with many excellent models priced under $300.

FIGURE 15-1 A laser printer's toner cartridge is generally good for several thousand prints.

Unfortunately, laser printers tend to be better at printing text than graphics. That's mainly because most laser printers are black-and-white devices, able to generate just shades of gray. Color laser printers are available but, because they're priced at $750 and up, they're more expensive than many people want to invest. Even if you could purchase a color laser printer, I wouldn't recommend it for printing digital images for framing. Color laser printers tend to produce output that don't look much like traditional photo prints and, thus, they don't look good framed. They also limit you to a print size of 8×10 inches.

Laser printers can certainly be used to print images, and they can do it well, as long as your needs don't include color. You can print a large quantity of family newsletters with a laser printer faster than with an inkjet, for instance.

Inkjet Printers

If you want to print images, I think inkjet printers are the best all-around printing solution for most people. They produce excellent color output, but can also print text at a reasonable speed—as long as you don't need to print a lot of it.

Inkjet printers are, in some ways, a simpler technology than laser printers. Simply put, they work by spraying microscopic droplets of ink onto paper. You can see an inkjet's internals—complete with ink cartridges—in Figure 15-2. Of course, it gets a lot more complicated than that. Printer manufacturers exert a lot of effort making sure that the dots are small; that they combine with other dots to mimic thousands of

FIGURE 15-2   The print head slides back and forth across the page, spraying dots of ink as it goes

distinct colors; that they dry fast enough so they don't spread, run, or smear; and that the paper is optimized to handle the ink's chemical characteristics. It's a highly technical business.

Nonetheless, we generally don't have to worry about most of that stuff. What matters is that they create stunning output and they're pretty affordable, typically running between $50 and $500 (though professional-caliber inkjets can cost more than a thousand dollars).

I often run into people who are concerned about inkjet quality based on experiences they had with older printers from the late 1980s or early 1990s. But, as I mentioned earlier, those fears are relatively unfounded today. Inkjet technology has improved to the extent that it can be difficult to distinguish between a 35mm print and a quality inkjet print made on photo-grade paper. My walls are covered with digital images that I've printed, matted, and framed (see Figure 15-3). No one can tell the difference.

Dye Sublimation Printers

The smallest segment of the printer market is occupied by dye sublimation printers (also called *dye-subs* for short). Look inside a dye-sublimation printer, and you'll see a long roll of transparent film that appears to be sheets of red-, blue-, yellow-, and gray-colored cellophane. The film is composed of solid dyes corresponding to the four basic colors used in printing: cyan, magenta, yellow, and black (CMYK).

15

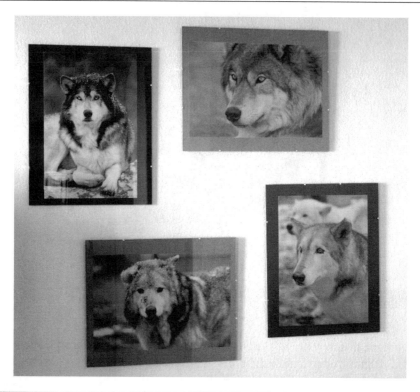

FIGURE 15-3   These pictures were printed on the Epson Stylus Photo 1270.

The print head heats as it passes over the film, causing the dyes to vaporize and permeate the glossy surface of the paper before they return to solid form. Because the dye gets absorbed and goes just below the surface of the paper, the process is called *dye-sublimation.* Because the color infuses the paper, it's also less vulnerable to fading and distortion over time. Dye sub printers also create "continuous tone" images—they have no dots whatsoever, something you tend to get with inkjet printers. Bottom line: the results from dye-sub printers are nothing short of stunning—they typically look just as good as 35mm prints and even magazine photos.

The downside is this: dye-sub printers aren't' not much good for printing text, so your dye-sub printer will have to be a second printer, which you only use when you're expressly printing photos. For me, a bigger disadvantage is that dye-sub printers typically only create 5×7-inch or perhaps 8×10-inch prints—nothing larger. Kodak sells several dye-sub models that print 4×6-inch prints; Sony's DPP-EX5 does the same. Also, the selection of printer models is much more limited and much more expensive. You can find some printers in

Do You Need Two Printers?

I have two printers. I use an HP LaserJet 1200 for routine text printing—I do a lot of that—and an Epson Stylus Photo 1270 for all my image printing.

Do you need two printers? It might seem a bit decadent at first, but it's really not, depending on how much printing you do. Both inkjets and lasers are reasonably affordable these days, but an inkjet alone will lead to slow and comparatively expensive routine printing. That's why I have one of each.

If you do have two printers, you can alternate between them by using a bidirectional switch box. (Parallel port switch boxes are available at most computer stores. Also, make sure your printer will work with a switch box—not all do.) If your printers connect via the USB port, you don't need to use a switch box because you can connect each printer to its own USB port. Or if you have two PCs in your home, you can connect one printer to each PC, and then network the PCs together with a home networking kit. That lets you print to either printer from either computer.

the $300–$500 range, but full-page, 8×10-inch prints require bigger printers that tend to start at $1,000. These printers are more commonly used in the professional arena, where publishers can inexpensively make test prints that show what output from the final printing press eventually looks like.

Make no mistake: output from dye sublimation printers looks great. But, given all the disadvantages, I think you're better off choosing an inkjet. And, because pictures from inkjets look so good—just about as good as from a dye-sub—there's hardly a reason to choose otherwise.

What to Look For

OK, so now you know you want to buy an inkjet printer. At least, that's the assumption I'm making. If you don't agree with me, you're shopping on your own. Actually, I'll talk about laser printers as well. I hope you're happy.

Where do you start? Walk into a store and all printers tend to look more or less the same. And, in my humble opinion, salespeople are not particularly helpful unless you already have a pretty good idea of what you want. So use this checklist to help choose your printer:

■ **Resolution**   Resolution is measured in dots per inch (dpi), and virtually all laser printers print at 600 or 1200dpi. In the inkjet world, resolution varies quite a bit, though better printers will typically be advertised as either 2880dpi or 1440dpi. Don't be fooled, though—they still print around 200–300dpi. Most inkjet printers, regardless of the thousands-of-dots-per-inch rating on the box, have a much lower effective resolution. I explain why in the section "The Right Resolution."

- **Number of colors**   This is irrelevant for a laser printer, of course, but when inkjet shopping, look for a printer that uses a pure black cartridge instead of mixing all the other colors to mimic black. (The result is a muddy gray-brown instead of black, and these printers use up their ink exceptionally fast.) Better inkjet printers use five or more independent ink color cartridges to create more realistic photo prints, but four cartridges (black plus three colors) is the absolute minimum you should accept. You can also save money on replacement inks by buying a printer that has separate cartridges for each color. That way, when one color runs low, you don't have to replace all the inks at once.

- **Speed**   You should pay attention to the printer's speed, measured in pages per minute (ppm) and resolution. Slow laser printers run at 8ppm; the fastest are around 24ppm. Remember, inkjets print much more slowly; color is their selling point, not speed.

- **Eyeballing the prints**   No matter what the specs say, a printer is only as good as the prints. Try out printers in the store before you buy. Most computer stores have demo models set up that spit out prints when you press a test button. And, as I mention in the section "Working with Paper," remember, the paper is just as important to print quality as the ink and the printer itself.

- **Ease of use**   Once you get the basic specs down, you might want to consider some less-tangible factors like ease of use. Most modern printers connect to the desktop with a USB cable instead of a parallel port connector, for instance. Most good printers also come with status monitor software that lets you get important information about your printer—like how much ink is left—right from the Windows desktop. If you have a notebook PC or a handheld computer, you might want to print directly to your printer via the wireless infrared port. Few printers have infrared support, however, so you'll have to shop around. An emerging feature is Bluetooth printing. *Bluetooth* is a wireless networking standard that cell phones, PDAs, laptops, and other gadgets can use to exchange data. Epson is one of the first printer companies to directly support Bluetooth printing, and it sells a Bluetooth adapter for a handful of its inkjet printers. Other companies, like AnyCom and MPI, sell Bluetooth adapters for common printers.

■ **Direct printing**   Many printers let you connect your digital camera directly to the printer—or insert the camera's memory card into the printer. This lets you circumvent the PC for fast and painless printing.

■ **Size and capacity**   Although most major manufacturers like Epson, Canon, and HP all make good printers that generate excellent results, they differ dramatically in terms of what kind of paper they can print on. Most printers print up to 8.5×11 inches. You'll have to buy a wide-format printer if you want to create 11×17- or 13×19-inch prints.

■ **Dye versus pigment**   If you're shopping for an inkjet printer, you should know that most models use dye-based inks, while higher-end designs sometimes rely on pigment-based inks. If you're concerned about generating prints that are highly resistant to fading, investigate pigment-based printers. On average, you'll find that run-of-the-mill (dye-based) inkjets can make fade-resistant prints last for 10 to 20 years. Pigment-based printers generate prints that last for 100 years. On the other hand, cheaper dye-based inks are brighter and more vivid than more expensive (but longer-life) pigment-based inks.

Printing Your Images

So you're all ready to print. You've downloaded your pictures from your camera to your PC. You have a printer connected to the computer. All you need to do is print. Let's talk about the things you need to ensure great prints.

The Right Resolution

The resolution of your image is one of the two most important factors that determine how good your pictures look when printed. Printers do vary but, in general, you can use this rule of thumb:

15

Type of Printer	Resolution (in dpi)
Laser	300 or 600
Inkjet	150–300

Experimentation is key, though. Choose a high-quality image and sample it at several different sizes. Print each one and compare them to see where the quality threshold lies with your printer. In other words, what minimum resolution do you need to eliminate obvious pixels and jaggedness from your prints?

Let's assume that 200dpi is about right for your printer. Suppose you want to print an image on an inkjet printer. To determine how big your image should be before you print it, just multiply the output size (in inches) by 200. The following chart illustrates the minimum dimensions of your image for a variety of common print sizes with an inkjet printer:

Print Size (inches)	File Size (pixels)	Camera Resolution Needed
4×6	800×1200	1 megapixel
8×10	1600×2000	3 megapixel
11×17	2200×3400	6 megapixel
13×19	2600×3800	10 megapixel

Wow. Surprised? It takes a lot of pixels to make high-quality prints. So what does that chart mean—that you need a 10-megapixel camera to make a 13×19-inch print with a wide-format inkjet printer?

Well, yeah, that's exactly what it's saying. But there's good news: you can cheat. Many printers will still give you great results, even if you feed them an image that's underpixeled. In other words, suppose you have a 1600×1200-pixel image. You might still get quite decent results by printing it at 11×17 inches or perhaps even 13×19. Try it out and see.

NOTE   *Right now, high-end digital cameras top out around 6 megapixels. But if you have some 35mm slides or negatives, you can scan them into your PC at much higher resolutions than any digital camera is currently able to capture.*

Increasing Print Size with Genuine Fractals

Need to print an image at a certain size—like 8×10 inches, for instance—but don't have nearly enough pixels to make the picture come out sharp? You might want to try a program like Genuine Fractals, from a company called Lizard tech (www.lizardtech.com).

Genuine Fractals digitally enlarges your image, while preserving quality using a complicated mathematical procedure that does a pretty good job of reducing noise and digital artifacts. Three versions of Genuine Fractals are available.

■ **Genuine Fractals LE**   This version costs just $49, but it has a key limitation: it won't input an image any bigger than 1500×2100 pixels, and it won't let you enlarge the image to a file size any bigger than 64MB. That makes this version affordable, but means you can only use it to work with images that are 3 megapixels or less.

■ **Genuine Fractals**   The primary version of Genuine Fractals, this program has no file size limits—in or out. It costs a healthy $159, though, making it only worthwhile for folks who print their pictures really big, very often.

■ **Genuine Fractals PrintPro**   Intended for print professionals, it includes the capability to work with file types average digital photographers will never see, and it costs $300.

Using Genuine Fractals is a piece of cake. It appears in the Save As type list when you choose File | Save As from any plug-in compatible program, like Photoshop or Paint Shop Pro. When you open your saved Genuine Fractals file, you can choose how much to enlarge it via a dialog box that looks like this:

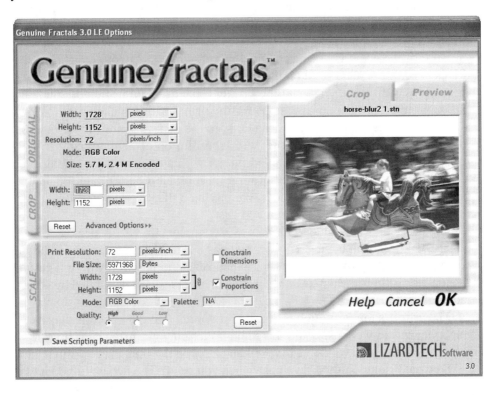

Remember, while Genuine Fractals does a bang-up job of preserving detail when enlarging pictures, it's not magic. There's a limit to how well you can print a low-resolution image, so have realistic expectations when using this program. Nonetheless, Genuine Fractals often lets you make surprisingly good enlargements from smaller images.

15

The Real Resolution of an Inkjet

Confused? I said earlier that inkjet printers come in resolutions up to 2880dpi, yet now I claim they print at 150 or 250dpi. Which is it? How can one number be so different from the other?

I agree: it is confusing. The simplest answer is that printer companies aren't being entirely honest with you. The resolution they advertise on the box isn't a measure of how many pixels per inch (ppi) the printer can accurately lay down on paper. If it were, 2880dpi ink jets would be capable of printing photos around professional magazine quality, and that's clearly not the case. So something else must be going on.

Indeed. Here's the deal: the advertised resolution of an inkjet printer is a measure of the accuracy of mechanical systems like the step motor that drives the print head around on the page and the precision of the nozzles themselves. Certainly, you want the printer to be as accurate as possible, but, remember, it takes several steps for the print head to make even a single dot on the paper—and it's the dots, in the end, that limit the printer's maximum resolution. So, an ink jet with a resolution of 2880dpi isn't necessarily a whole lot better than an ink jet with a resolution of 1440dpi. Visually, prints made with one printer might look a bit better than the other, but certainly not twice as good. It's like buying a 3GHz computer. It's faster than a 1.5GHz PC, but it's not twice as fast.

Put another way, a printer with a lousy step motor can visibly degrade the quality of a print. But buying a printer that has a 10,000dpi resolution via the way that companies like Epson measure that sort of thing today, will only result in more perfectly formed pixels. The pixels themselves will be limited by other factors.

The printer's top resolution is, indeed, important, but other factors play an important role as well: using the sharpening filter on your image and choosing the right paper can have just as much of an effect on the final print quality.

So what resolution should you use when you print? The honest-to-goodness dpi of most ink jet printers is still in the range of 150–300dpi. If you start with a sharp image and plan to use high-quality inkjet paper, you might see a small difference in image quality if you feed the printer a 300dpi image. But the difference will be small, and you can generally get decent results with as little as 200dpi. If you send images of lower resolution to the printer, you'll be able to tell the difference.

Too Much or Too Little Resolution

As I already mentioned, a 4×6-inch inkjet print typically requires an 800×1200-pixel image to start with to avoid pixels and jagged edges in the final image. That's almost twice the resolution that a VGA-resolution 640×480-pixel digital camera can muster. What happens if you print an image that doesn't have enough pixels for the size you want to achieve? You get something like Figure 15-4.

If the output size isn't as important to you as having a sharp, quality print, then just print the image smaller. Cramming those pixels together on paper in less space will make the print sharper.

In reality, you might still get adequate results printing even a 640×480-pixel image at 4×6, even though that only works out to 100dpi. If you look carefully at the finished print, you'll find that you can see jagged edges where there weren't enough pixels to fill in. For best results, pick a size that lets you print around 200dpi, or whatever resolution best matches your particular printer.

That's what happens when you print too few pixels for the size you're shooting for. What about too many pixels? Can an image that's too high-res ever be a problem? The answer is generally not. Too many pixels isn't really a problem, though it does make your image file bigger than it has to be, and it can potentially bog everything down. The bottom line is this: if you pack more

15

FIGURE 15-4   This sort of thing happens when you try to print a low-resolution image too large.

pixels than you need into an image—above 200dpi, for instance—odds are good that you won't improve image quality very much. Instead, you'll just make the file bigger, which takes more storage space on your hard disk and can slow down the printing process.

Test your own printer by generating prints in high-quality mode at 150, 200, and 300dpi. Use these to figure out what the resolution threshold of your printer is, and strive to use that setting as often as possible.

Of course, all this advice is specifically for someone who wants to know how much resolution an image needs to print well at a certain output size. If you just want to print an image and don't care how big it turns out, just print it. Most image editors have an option to let you print the image at full-page size or at the image's normal size. If you choose normal size, the image will print smaller than full page and probably look just fine. It's only when you force the image to print at a certain size that the image's original resolution becomes important.

On the other hand, you should set the print size yourself whenever possible, If you allow the printer driver to resize the image on its own, it'll usually just scale the image and introduce a lot of pixelization in the process.

Understanding DPI

Some image editors and print programs use dpi instead of, or in addition to, pixels. And I've found that a lot of people are flambuzzled when it comes to understanding the relationship among resolution, dpi, print size, and pixels. What, really, is a dialog box telling you when it says an image is 4 by 6 inches, 72dpi?

The important thing to understand is that measurements like "4 by 6 inches" are meaningless while the image is still on a PC. A computer deals only in pixels. An image can be 640 by 480, 1280 by 1024, or 2240 by 1680 pixels, for instance. And the "size" of the image on a computer screen depends on two things: the screen size of the Windows desktop and the zoom factor of the application displaying the image. If you show a 640 by 480 pixel image on a Windows desktop that's only 640 by 480 itself, the image takes up the whole screen. If you show it on a PC that's using a 1280 by 1024 pixel screen, then the image will be tiny, because all the pixels are small and o many of them are in the display.

Zoom can also be a factor. Some image programs automatically fit images to the screen, shrinking them as necessary. Other programs try to display the image at full size, which can result in images that you have to pan around to see properly because they're larger, pixel for pixel, than the computer screen itself. The bottom line: when still in the virtual world of a computer, the only image size that has any real meaning is the number of pixels used to create it.

Only when you're getting ready to print a picture does a size like "4×6 inches" have any meaning. If you assume there's a one-for-one relationship between a pixel and a printed dot, then the size the image prints at is determined by dividing the number of pixels in the image by the dpi rating you hope to print with.

Consider the same 2240×1680 pixel image. It can make a

- **7.5×5.5 inch print**   When set to 300dpi (ideal for a color laser printer)

- **15×11 inch print**   At 150dpi (such as for a inkjet)

- **31×23 inch print**   When set to 72dpi (on a computer screen), if displayed at full size

Remember, dpi and print size is just a way to measure how large you can print a digital image—the numbers that really tell you the true size of the image are the number of pixels.

Working with Paper

Here's a common scenario: you see great, photo-realistic prints in a computer store and think, "that's the printer for me. It's only $150 and it makes outstanding pictures!" So you buy the printer and bring it home. But when you get the printer set up and send your first few images to it, you're devastated. The output is horrible. The prints look flat and lifeless. The paper curls. What went wrong?

Paper for Laser Printers

If you have a laser printer, you might be wondering what kind of paper is appropriate for that printer as well. I suggest you use ordinary 20-pound laser or copier paper. Decent laser paper shouldn't cost more than about $7 per 500 sheets (a ream). I'd be reluctant to buy really inexpensive paper ($3/ream or less) because loose paper fibers in budget-priced paper can, over time, clog your printer, affecting its performance and, eventually, even damaging it.

It's the paper. What you failed to consider is the choice of paper is so important to the quality of your prints that it's essentially *more important than the printer itself*! A handful of printers on the market can generate photo-realistic prints. But, unless you use quality paper, they will all disappoint you.

Which Paper Is Best

Unfortunately, choosing paper isn't easy, even if you know you want to get the best. There are a lot of choices, and it isn't generally clear which kind is best based on the name or description on the package. This is especially true for inkjet printers. I honestly don't know why paper manufacturers make this so hard; it seems counterproductive to sales.

As a general rule, you'll find store shelves stocked with paper divided into four quality levels: inkjet paper, high-quality inkjet paper, photo quality paper, and glossy photo paper.

So where do you start? Let's begin with daily use that doesn't involve printing photos—I suggest you use either plain paper or inkjet paper. Even when printing on plain paper, use quality stock because cheap paper can plug the nozzles and decrease the effective resolution of the printer. For general-purpose printing, you can use the same stock I recommend for laser printers. Of course, I'm assuming the majority of what you print is test prints, text, and other routine output. If every print you make is destined for the Louvre, then you might want to skip directly to the section where I talk about photo paper.

When you're ready to step up to some higher-quality printing, you have a number of choices on store shelves (see Figure 15-5). Here's a general overview of the various grades available.

- **Plain paper**   As I've already mentioned, this is good for general text and ordinary graphics printing. The paper is inexpensive, but the ink tends to absorb quickly into the paper and blur the image. The paper also curls and distorts.

- **Inkjet paper (and high-quality inkjet paper)**   This is a step up and embeds clay or some other ink fixture into the paper to stop the inks from spreading before they dry. For most printing, you won't notice a big difference, but this paper makes for better draft-quality photographic prints.

- **Photo paper**   A variation of coated paper, photo paper is generally bright-white coated paper that's designed explicitly for photographs. If you're looking for paper in an intermediate price range that can give decent results, try this stuff.

- **Glossy photo paper**   The best paper around, this stuff is expensive, generally costing about a dollar a sheet. Certainly you won't use it all the time, but if you

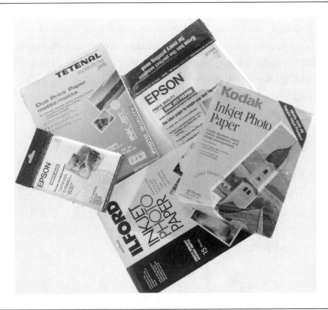

FIGURE 15-5   With so many choices on store shelves, it pays to experiment with a few to find the paper that delivers the best output with your printer.

plan to frame a picture or give your digital "prints" away to family or friends, definitely use the special photo paper. Note, you can only print on one side of photo paper; the back side looks like the back of a photograph and generally has a logo printed there (as the following shows). I don't recommend printing on the back of glossy paper, even on a laser printer.

Which Brand?

What brand of paper should you use? Should you use Epson in an Epson printer and Canon paper in a Canon printer, or should you buy paper from a company like Ilford—known in 35mm photography circles for their excellent paper—instead? This is a good question. Obviously, each printer company wants you to use its own brand of paper with its printer.

In truth, vendors like Canon, Epson, and HP go to great lengths to fine-tune their paper to match their inks so colors won't bleed and they'll be as vivid as possible. My own Epson Stylus Photo 1270 does best with Epson's Premium Glossy Photo Paper, and I tend to use that paper almost exclusively. When I first got the printer, I tried a dozen different kinds of papers, including paper from companies like Ilford and Tetenal, which came highly recommended by computer and photography store salespeople. After being disappointed with all those other brands, I tried Epson's own Premium Glossy paper, and was blown away—the results were dramatically better. I've had similar experiences with other printers, though I have to admit they weren't as dramatic as with the Epson printer, which was clearly engineered with specialty paper in mind.

So what should you do? If you have a few dollars to spare, buy a bunch of different paper packages and try them. Print the same image on different kinds of paper and lay them out, side-by-side, in good light. Determine which one is best, and then stick with that brand of paper.

Other Specialty Papers

In addition to ordinary plain, coated, and photo paper, printer manufacturers and paper vendors sell a variety of other specialty papers. You might want to investigate these papers because they can be a lot of fun and enable you to do all sorts of things with your printer that you never imagined possible:

- **Greeting card paper**   Greeting card paper and matching envelopes let you make your own greeting cards with your printer and some greeting card software.

■ **Transparency paper**   This clear film media is perfect for printing color overhead slides for business meetings. You can use this to print PowerPoint slides or any other kind of image or document.

■ **T-shirt transfer paper**   This special paper is an iron-on transfer that you can run through your printer, and then apply to clothing. When you print on T-shirt paper, be sure to use special T-shirt transfer software or just reverse your image before you print. (Create a mirror image of what you want it to look like.)

■ **Fabric sheets**   This unique kind of printing media is fabric that gives your prints texture. You can print on it just for its own sake or use the print to make cross-stitch designs and other craft projects.

Make a Print

Now that you have all the parts in place, it's time to print. I'll show you how to make a print of a specific size in Paint Shop Pro; other programs use a similar method. Of course, if printing the picture at a very specific size (like 5×7 or 8×10) isn't important to you, just click the Print button and get it over with. But, if you want to print your image so it fits properly in a traditional picture frame, here's how. Specifically, let's say we're going to make a print at 8×10 inches. Do this:

1. Load the paper in your printer. Make sure you put it in with the appropriate side set for printing, and only load a single sheet at a time.

2. Load the picture you want to print in Paint Shop Pro. The first thing we want to do is crop it to print at the right proportion. Click the Crop tool and drag it through the image, creating a rough crop of your image. At this point, it's not important to be accurate; just make a crop box.

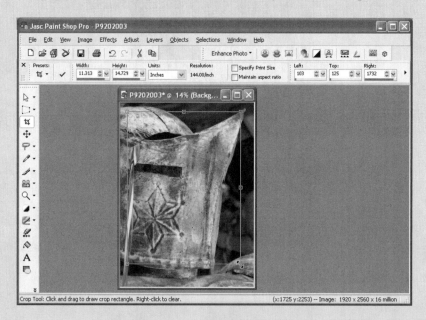

3. In the Tool Options toolbar atop the screen, set the Units to Inches, and then enter the dimensions of our print—width of 8 and height of 10. Click the checkbox for Maintain Aspect Ratio.

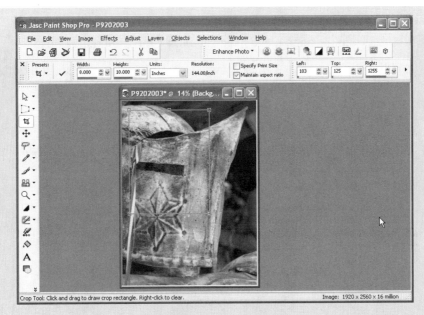

4. Now position the crop box precisely on the screen and resize it by dragging one of the corners. Because the aspect ratio is locked, it'll keep the proper proportions for our 8×10-inch print. When you're happy with the final result, click the checkbox to make the crop, and you'll get an image that's proportioned exactly right for an 8×10-inch print:

15

5. Now we're going to select the paper size and orientation. Choose File | Print from the main menu. You should see the Print dialog box.

6. Click the Portrait or Landscape button in the Orientation section of the dialog box to get the image oriented properly.

Which Side Is the Right Side?

Often, it matters which side of the page you print on. Plain-old laser paper is the same on both sides, so if you print on a laser printer or you use plain paper in an inkjet, it doesn't matter. But if you print on specialty paper in an inkjet printer, make sure you load the paper the right way. Keep these tips in mind:

- Usually, the brighter or shinier side of the paper is the printing side. Occasionally, it's rough, like sandpaper.

- If you're printing on photo paper, the back will probably have a company logo on it.

- Many paper types label the paper with small marks to indicate the proper print side.

7. Click the Printer button to open your printer's preferences and find the paper size selector. Choose 8.5×11, if it isn't already selected. While you're there, select the appropriate type of paper, such as inkjet paper or photo glossy. Click OK to close the printer dialog box.

CAUTION   *If you don't tell the print driver about the kind of paper you're printing with, the results will invariably be disappointing.*

15

Be sure you look carefully at the print directions the first time you try a new paper. Ink won't adhere well—or at all—to the wrong side of specialty papers, and you could end up with a real mess in and around your printer if the ink runs everywhere.

Can you print on both sides of the paper? I get that question a lot. And the answer is this: it depends. Don't ever try to print on the back of glossy premium paper, but you can usually print on both sides of inkjet and high-quality inkjet paper without any trouble. If I'm printing a newsletter or a greeting card, I might

8. If you click Fit To Page, the image is printed using all the available page space. Instead, click Center On Page.

9. Now specify the width of the image as 8 inches. You should see the height adjust automatically to 10 inches.

10. When the paper comes out of the printer, leave it there to dry for several minutes. Don't handle it until you're sure it's dry. Otherwise, you could smudge it.

print the pictures on one side and use a laser printer to add text to the back. You can also find paper that's intended for double-sided printing. Check the paper aisle of your computer or office store to see what's available.

Caring for Your Prints

All picture colors tend to fade over time, but inkjet photos tend to fade somewhat faster. In fact, inkjet inks are sensitive to ultraviolet light, and your images will fade faster if exposed to direct sunlight for extended periods. If you plan to frame pictures and leave them exposed to sunlight, consider using UV-shielded glass, available at some framing shops.

Keep original image files on your hard disk or archived on CD-ROM, so you can reprint them when the fading becomes noticeable.

Some newer printers are marketed specifically as models that create prints with more *lightfastness* than older printers. You can probably guess that *lightfastness* is a print's capability to resist fading when exposed to light. In particular, a number of Epson models offer a lightfastness of ten or more years—check out this chart of Epson photo papers, for instance:

Epson Photo Paper	6 years
Epson Premium Glossy Photo Paper	10 years
Epson Matter Paper Heavyweight Paper	25 years
Epson ColorLife Photo Paper	27 years

In addition, you can find some inkjet printers designed to offer extremely long resistance to fading, such as pigment-based inkjet printers, like the Epson Stylus Photo 2200. Intended for serious photo enthusiasts and professionals, pigment-based inkjet printers are a bit more expensive than dye-based inkjets, but they can deliver a print life of over 100 years. By comparison, 35mm prints tend to be lightfast for only about 50 years; so newer printers can create prints that last longer than traditional prints.

No matter what kind of printer, ink, or paper you use, you should protect your prints from fading from the moment you print them. Here are a few precautions you can take:

- Cover the print with glass or plastic as soon as it's completely dry (wait 12–24 hours after the print is complete). Contaminants in the air can fade a print quickly, but if you put it under glass or in a photo album, the print is no longer in direct contact with air and, thus, is protected. Some ink and paper combinations can cause a print to fade dramatically in a matter of days if left exposed to the open air.

- Keep the print out of direct sunlight, even when under glass. Hang the print where the sun doesn't shine directly on the wall.

- Avoid handling the print in such a way that you touch the ink with your fingers.

If you've spend much time in the world of 35mm photography, you might also be familiar with acrylic UV-blocking sprays that you can apply to prints. These sprays "fix" the print and give it a longer life before fading, especially when the print will be framed and hung where it could be exposed to direct sunlight. Can you—or should you—use these sprays on digital images?

Well, that depends. I'd avoid using a photo-fix product designed especially for traditional film-based prints. I've tried it, and it seems to work, but I've neither been able to test a wide variety of ink and paper combinations nor have my tests observed the prints for a long period of time. Indeed, I asked several printer companies what their opinions are of these sprays and, for the most part, they were all a bit wary. Epson, for instance, said this: "We recommend avoiding UV sprays since the effect on lightfastness of one color ink could be different than another ink, and may actually lead to the visual acceleration of fading or color shifting." On the other hand, a few companies make a special spray just for inkjet printers, and I think these "inkjet fix" sprays are a lot safer for your digital prints.

Calibrating Your Monitor

A lot of people run into a problem with their printers that can be summarized thusly: "I just printed a photo on good quality paper, and it doesn't match what's on the monitor."

This common problem stems from the fact that the two output devices—the printer and monitor—are calibrated differently. If you want what's on the screen when you edit a photo to exactly resemble what comes out of the printer, then you need to correct one or the other so they're in agreement. It's easier to adjust the output of the monitor (printers don't come with any sort of calibration tools), so that's what most people commonly do.

If you don't mind spending money, a few solutions are available that are designed to help you calibrate your monitor. OptiCAL, from Pantone (www.pantone.com), is a popular program—but, priced around $200, it's probably too rich for you unless you happen to be a true graphics professional. A lot of folks like ColorBlind Prove IT (www.color.com), which works with sensor (called a spider) that clips on to the front of your monitor to help calibrate it. Priced around $300 with the sensor, ColorBlind is also a bit pricey—but it's a good deal if you want the most accurate results for the least effort. Finally, Colorific (www.colorific.com) offers an affordable color-matching and monitor calibration system. It's priced at a reasonable $50, but the truth is it's possible to calibrate your monitor manually, without buying any software at all. It does take a good eye and some judgment, though.

Set Your Display Properties

If you're ready to optimize your monitor, the best place to start is with the Windows Display Properties. You can do a few things here to render images on screen more accurately and to improve the overall look of your display at the same time.

Right-click on a blank portion of the desktop and choose Properties from the drop-down menu. You should then see the Display Properties dialog box. Click the Settings tab to see the details about your computer's display settings. First, check the screen resolution. If should be at least 800 by 600 pixels, and higher is generally better. If the resolution is too low, you won't see as much onscreen and digital images won't look as sharp. Experiment by increasing the resolution and clicking the Apply button. Keep the resolution comfortable; if things get too small, revert to a lower resolution. I think 1024×768 is a good value for a 17-inch display, and try 1280×1024 if you have a 19-inch monitor.

Also, set the color quality. If it's set too low, then images will look dramatically different on screen than they do when printed. The best setting is 24 bit. For working with digital images, 32 bits doesn't really improve the look of images on the screen, and it can be a drag on your system's performance. After you choose 24-bit color and the resolution you like, click the OK button for the changes to take effect.

Print a Test Photo

The most important tweak we can make is to match the monitor's settings to a real print from your ink jet printer. So load a picture you like—choose a daylight photo that includes a person with natural skin tones—into your image editor and print it at highest quality on to a sheet of good, glossy photo paper. Let the picture dry out of direct sunlight for a few hours to let the colors set permanently.

Now we're ready to get to work. Make sure your monitor is set up the way you usually use it, with the same level of ambient light as you typically have when editing photos. Eliminate any harsh glare by closing window shades or angling the monitor.

Next, set the monitor's contrast and brightness levels to their halfway point. Most monitors have buttons or dials on the front of the case; you might need to experiment or check your monitor's user guide. Now open the image file on the monitor and set the picture you printed right next to the monitor, so you can look from one image to the other. From here, it's just a matter of adjusting the brightness, contrast, and color levels until the printed and onscreen images agree with each other.

Unfortunately, there's no magic bullet for monitor calibration. It takes a good eye to tweak the red, green, blue, brightness, and contrast levels to match a test image, like the one we just made. But tons of useful web sites are out there that can lend a hand with fine-tuning your monitor. If you want to read more, check out one of these web sites that offer monitor calibration tutorials:

- www.bryce-alive.net/calibrate

- epaperpress.com/monitorcal

Working with Printing Services

Do you have a great picture that you'd like to print, but you can't get the results you want with your own printer? You can always enlist the aid of a print shop or a service bureau. Such businesses are generally not cheap, but they might be able to take your image on disk and provide you with a high-quality image. And modern print shops aren't nearly as intimidating as they used to be because local copy centers have started offering similar services.

If you want a print shop to make prints for you, shop around and find out a few important things before you decide which one you want to use:

- What are their rates?

- How does the volume affect the cost? (If you want 50 copies, it might begin to get a lot cheaper on a per-image basis.)

- In what format do they require the image?

- How can you submit files—on floppy, Zip, or e-mail?

- What kind of paper do they use?

Most important, some local photo shops have started offering digital image printing. Visit your local photo finisher and see if it can make prints from digital images for you. Another alternative: some web sites have begun offering this service as well. One site I've tried and like is www.ezprints.com. This site can create prints as small as wallets or as large as 20×24 posters from digital images that you upload to the site. Photo sharing sites like ClubPhoto.com can also make oversized poster prints.

Chapter 16

Sharing Your Pictures

How to…

- ■ Send and receive images via e-mail
- ■ Choose the right file format for e-mailing pictures
- ■ Compress images for e-mail and disk
- ■ Prepare images for display on the Web
- ■ Choose a web design program
- ■ Store images on the Web without programming
- ■ Show off pictures on a Palm handheld
- ■ Display images on a digital picture frame
- ■ Create a video slide show with your camera and a VCR
- ■ Create a video slide show using PowerPoint on your PC

Taking pictures is one thing; sharing them with friends, family, and coworkers is something else entirely. Of course, this is one area where your digital camera has a leg up on 35mm cameras. To share traditional prints with someone, you need to physically give them a copy. That means visiting the photo finisher and having duplicates made. Or, you could scan the images and distribute them electronically.

Digital camera images are electronic to begin with, though, and that makes everything a whole lot easier. Want to share your images? E-mail them. Or, you can post them to the Web or show them off with a digital picture frame or a Palm handheld PC. In this last chapter of *How to Do Everything with Your Digital Camera,* I'll show you how to easily make your images available to other people.

Sending Images via E-mail

E-mail is perhaps the most common way to share digital images with people who live far apart. Not only is e-mail good for casually lending images to friends and family, it's also the medium of choice for professionals. When I create images for print in newspapers, magazines, and books, I typically send the files via e-mail unless they're so large that e-mail is impractical.

So how do you do it? Sending pictures within e-mail is simply a matter of including one or more images as attachments in your mail message. *Attachments* are binary files—as opposed to plain text—that your mail program can deliver to another person's mail system.

Most of the time, attachments work just fine. Occasionally, though, you'll run into problems sending images as attachments. That's because the original Internet wasn't designed to accommodate the sending of binary files like pictures via e-mail, and encoding schemes were "tacked on" after the fact. Here are some snags you might run into:

- *Beware of sending files that are too big.* Many e-mail systems can't deal with a single e-mail file that's bigger than about 2MB—a few older or "free" e-mail systems even have a 1MB limit. Personally, for most e-mail transmissions, I'd consider 1MB as your upper limit on file size, though broadband users (like cable modem and DSL) can often receive 5MB files without trouble. In any event, if you send a very large file to someone, it can get "stuck" in their mail server, clogging up messages that are trying to come in afterward. Check the file size of your attachments (see Figure 16-1) before sending them. I strongly recommend resizing images that you plan to e-mail down to around 640×480 or 800×600 pixels.

NOTE

When you attach a digital image to an e-mail message, the attachment usually ends up about 10 percent larger than the original image because of the encoding necessary to send it across the Internet.

- *Older versions of America Online can only receive a single attachment.* Even though most mail systems can accept multiple attached files in each

marin-matrix Properties

General

marin-matrix

Type: Corel PHOTO-PAINT 8.0 Image
Location: C:\My Pictures\karate
Size: 2.58MB (2,716,620 bytes), 2,719,744 bytes used

MS-DOS name: MARIN-~1.TIF
Created: Saturday, December 09, 2000 10:49:14 AM
Modified: Saturday, December 09, 2000 10:49:38 AM
Accessed: Sunday, December 31, 2000

Attributes: ☐ Read-only   ☐ Hidden
               ☑ Archive   ☐ System

OK   Cancel   Apply

FIGURE 16-1   This 2.7MB file is, for many folks, simply too large to e-mail effectively. Resize it or change it into another file format so it's under a megabyte.

16

e-mail message, if you know someone still using an old edition of AOL, their PC won't quite know what to make of that kind of message. Only one of the attachments will get to the recipient, and the others will simply disappear. On the other hand, the newest versions of AOL handle multiple files in a single message just fine— it assembles all the images into a single, convenient zip file.

■ *Not all mail programs are completely compatible.* You can send a plain text message between virtually any two Internet mail programs in the world, but if you want to send an attachment, on rare occasions, it won't work quite right. The solution? Your mail program might let you change the way your attachment is encoded. If that's the case, you could be able to experiment and send the file to the recipient anyway. The most common encoding schemes are called MIME and UUENCODE. If your recipient claims that an attachment came in all garbled—it looks like page after page of meaningless text instead of a picture—switch from MIME to UUENCODE or vice versa. Attachments should be icons you can click on to view, such as the one in Figure 16-2. If that doesn't work for other users, you can always switch back again. In Outlook, for instance, you can find these settings by choosing Tools | Options and clicking on the Mail Format tab of the Options dialog box (see the following). From there, click the Settings button and change the format.

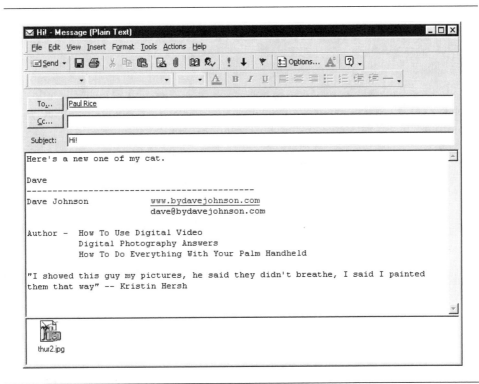

FIGURE 16-2   This is what an attachment looks like in many e-mail programs. Attachments that are decoded incorrectly by your mail program, instead, turn out to be page after page of gibberish.

Shrinking Images for E-mail

Having a lot of resolution is a good thing for printing, but two- and three-megapixel digital images are cumbersome to send through e-mail. You should resize pictures in your favorite image editor before attaching them to electronic messages (see Chapter 11). In general, e-mail-bound images should be cropped and/or resized down to 640×480 pixels and saved in JPG format. If you remember to do that, you'll never get any complaints from friends or family that your images are too big and are clogging their e-mail systems.

If you don't mind spending a few dollars, you can get a specialized program for cropping and resizing images as well. A Smaller Image, from TriVista (www.trivista.com) is a great little program for prepping your photos for e-mail.

View Images Someone Sent to You

In most e-mail programs (like Netscape Messenger, Microsoft Exchange, Outlook, and Outlook Express), your attachment appears as an icon that you manipulate like any other file icons. Here are your most common choices:

- With the message window open, right-click and choose the View option to see the image on the desktop without opening a large image-editing program.

- Double-click the image icon to launch a preview window or an image-editing program and display the image.

- Drag-and-drop the image icon from the message window to the desktop or another Windows folder for permanent storage.

This simple $15 program is designed from the ground up to crop and resize photos. After you drag an image into the application window, you can move a cropping frame around the screen until you've composed the picture just the way you want. The cool part is this: you can configure the cropping frame's proportion based on how large you want the resulting photo, so there's absolutely no guesswork. Set the end photo size to 640×480, for instance, and the cropping frame is proportioned exactly right for the job. You can also scale the cropping frame to include more or less of the original image in the new, resized photo. It's all very clever and makes you wonder why no one ever thought of that before.

A Smaller Image also includes sharpness, brightness, and contrast controls, an optional graphic border for your images, and a simple text tool for adding captions. If you frequently resize photos for e-mail, the Web, or printing, A Smaller Image is a handy tool.

Attaching Pictures in E-mail

Although the process varies from one program to another, attaching one or more images to an e-mail message isn't hard. The basic procedure is this: drag-and-drop an image file directly into your open e-mail message, or use a menu option to insert a file into the message. Almost all mail software uses the paperclip icon as a standard symbol to represent an attachment to your message, so look for that button and use it to specify files for inclusion in your e-mail (see Figure 16-3).

TIP *If you're sending an image to someone using Windows 95 or later, almost any file format is fair game (but JPG is probably best because the files are so small). I recommend that you send Mac users files in TIF or JPG format, and Windows 3.1 users should get BMP or JPG files. Because JPG is an efficient file format for sending photographic images, you're best off sending images in JPG format exclusively.*

Click this button to attach a file.

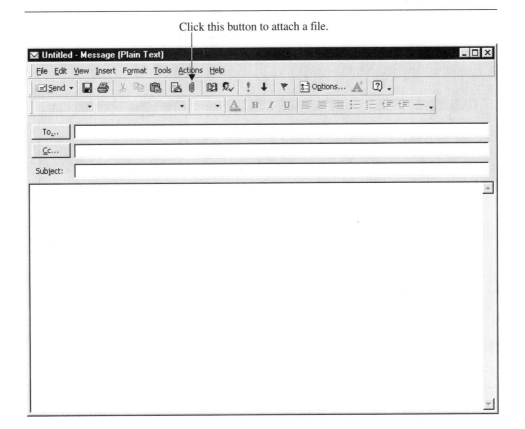

FIGURE 16-3   Use the paperclip icon to attach images (and other kinds of files) to your e-mail.

16

Send E-mail with Outlook

If you're a Microsoft Outlook user, here's how to attach a pair of images to an outgoing message:

1. Click the New button in the Outlook toolbar to create a new mail message. A blank, untitled message should appear.

2. Address the e-mail by typing the appropriate e-mail address in the To box.

3. Add a subject by typing in the Subject box, as the following shows.

4. Enter some message text. It's generally a good idea to write a personal, specific note rather than sending a blank message with attachments—that way the recipient knows it's not some sort of virus.

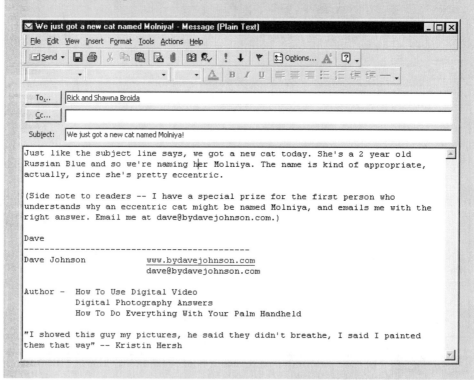

5. If you have a folder with pictures open on the desktop, you can drag an image file from that folder over the message window and drop it, as the following shows. You should see an attachment appear in the message.

6. To add another image to the message, choose Insert | File from the message window's menu, or click the Attachment button (shaped like a paperclip). You should see the Insert File dialog box.

7. Navigate to the appropriate folder and select the image file you want to attach. If you want to attach multiple files from the same folder, you can hold down the CTRL key while you click each image file.

8. Click the Insert button to close the Insert File dialog box, and then insert the images in the message.

9. When your message is complete, click the Send button to send it to its recipient.

16

Distributing Images on Disks

Because JPG images are so small, you can often copy a lot of images to a floppy disk and pass them around that way. After all, everyone has a floppy disk drive, right?

Even better, pretty much everyone can read PC floppy disks—even Mac users. The Macintosh floppy drive can read PC floppies. That means you can copy a few JPG images to a floppy and give it to a Mac user, and she or he will be able to read the images just fine.

One caveat, though—PCs can't read Macintosh floppies. So Mac users need to be sure the disk is formatted for a PC before doing the handoff. The same is true of Zip disks. A Zip disk made on a Mac can't be read on a PC. Instead, you'll see an error message saying the disk isn't formatted.

The New Floppy Disk: CD-R

Floppy disks have some important limitations, though. They don't hold much data, they're slow, and despite the fact that they've been around forever—or perhaps because of that—they're starting to lose popularity. Some new computers come without any floppy drives at all, in fact. The heir to the floppy throne? The CD. These days, many new PCs come with CD-RW drives (these are drives that can write data to blank CD-R and CD-RW disks), and you can add a CD-RW drive to a PC very inexpensively. I suggest using a CD to share images because a CD-R drive is readable by any CD-ROM drive, making it handy for sharing. For details on copying images to CD, see Chapter 9.

Strategies for Sharing Lots of Images

If you need to send someone a lot of images and you want to minimize the total file size, you have a few ways to get the data to the recipient. Often, you'll need to combine these techniques. Here are some things you can try:

- Use a compression program like WinZip (www.winzip.com) to shrink the images to a smaller size. You can see several images compressed into a single Zip file in Figure 16-4. If your image files are already compressed (such as if you use the JPG or compressed TIF formats), then Zip won't do much for your total file size, and WinZip can make JPG files larger! But if you're trying to send uncompressed images via floppy or e-mail, this compression program can be a lifesaver.

- Break the image collection into several e-mail messages, with each message weighing in at less than a megabyte or so.

FIGURE 16-4   WinZip is a great program for sending a bunch of images at once as a single, compressed attachment.

- Use the compression feature in the JPG format to reduce file size. With many images, you can compress the image significantly before you start to see any obvious degradation because of compression. This is great if you're just passing images around among friends, though I'd be more careful about images you're planning to print.

- Instead of e-mail, mail a CD-R disk. Because a CD disk holds 650MB of data, you have an awful lot of room to work with. It's certainly more efficient than using the Internet.

16

Creating Your Own Web Pages

The Web is a great place to store and share your digital images. Your pictures are probably already in a convenient Web format—like JPG—and most of your friends and family probably already own a computer with Internet access. If you have a web design program like FrontPage, FrontPage Express, or Netscape Composer, you can

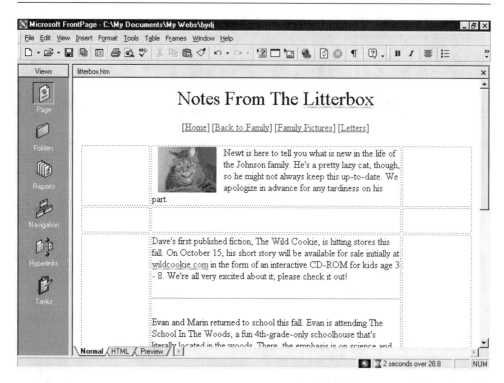

FIGURE 16-5   If you can handle programs like Publisher, PowerPoint, or Word, you can probably slap together a simple web site in a program like FrontPage.

drag-and-drop your way to a nice little web page with a minimal amount of effort. Figure 16-5 shows FrontPage 2000 being used to edit a typical web page. The learning curve is similar to what you might expect from a program like Microsoft Publisher.

Using a web design program, you can enter text, drag-and-drop graphics and pictures, and then edit and format the web site's appearance with simple toolbar and menu controls. Many good Web design programs are on the market. Some are free and some are retail products. Here are some of the most popular editors:

Editor	Where to Find It
Microsoft FrontPage	www.microsoft.com/frontpage
Sausage Software HotDog	www.sausagetools.com
Avantrix Koala HTML	www.avantrix.com
Netscape Composer	www.netscape.com
Macromedia Dreamweaver	www.macromedia.com

Also, it's worth noting that you can create web pages with some Microsoft products that aren't even designed specifically for the Internet. Publisher, for instance, has a feature that lets you publish documents to the Web. It's not a great web design program, but it'll let you get pictures up on the Web with a minimum of fuss and with software you already own.

Choosing an Image Size and File Format for the Web

Many digital cameras take pictures in resolutions as low as 640×480 pixels, but this can be too big for a web page. Not only does an image that big take a while to download, it consumes a lot of space on the screen. Instead, I recommend that you shrink your images down to about 500 pixels across. (Look at Chapter 12 for details on how to do that.)

Two file formats are commonly used on the Web: GIF and JPG. CompuServe originally developed the GIF format, which stands for Graphic Interchange Format (making the term "GIF format" somewhat redundant). *GIF* is a compact file format commonly used in web pages. The major disadvantage of GIF, however, is it limits images to just 256 colors (or less, depending on the settings you use when saving the file). That can affect the quality of the image on screen, though that's generally not too important.

Usually, web designers like to use *GIF format 89a,* which is the newest version of the GIF format that supports three important features:

■ **Transparency**   *Transparency* lets you specify a color in the image that will be treated as transparent. That way, you can make the image's background or border transparent. If you have an irregularly shaped image, like a diamond or an oval, this feature can look cool, as you can see here:

←——— No matter what kind of background you use, a picture with a transparent background will blend in.

16

■ **Interlacing** An *interlaced image* downloads to a web browser first as a chunky, low-resolution image, and then it increases in quality as more information is retrieved. Otherwise, the image would normally load a few lines at a time, so you'd see the top of the image display before the bottom. Interlacing isn't faster than the alternative, but it gives the viewer something to look at, and so it can seem faster. This is a good option to use when you know that people with slow Internet connections will be viewing your images.

■ **Animation** An *animated GIF* is just a sequence of individual images played one after the other. Not really fast enough to give a sense of cinematic motion with large images, animated GIFs are usually used to slowly display one image after another, like a slide show.

The JPG format was created by the Joint Photographic Experts Group to be a scalable file format that could be compressed to yield low file size or be left uncompressed for higher quality. Unlike GIF, JPG images can display a full 16-million-color palette. Depending on how much you compress a JPG image, however, the image quality can vary from nearly identical to the original all the way down to unrecognizable.

As discussed in Part III of the book, you can specify the level of compression to use when saving a JPG file. Most programs default to a fairly low compression level, preserving image quality. In reality, though, you can often compress the image much more aggressively than the default and still get adequate quality for a web page.

Which Is Best?

You can use whichever file format—GIF or JPG—that best suits your needs. It's perfectly all right to mix JPG and GIF images in a web site, even on the same page. This chart should help you decide which is the appropriate file format.

Use JPG:	Use GIF:
To display full-color photographs compressed to a small file size	To use a transparent background To interlace the display of an image To display an image with a few colors

Sharing Images on the Web Without Designing a Web Site

Certainly, you can design a web site that shows off your pictures to friends and family, and as I just mentioned, quite a few tools are around to help you do just that. If you aren't' thrilled by the idea of learning how to manipulate a web design program, though, there's an easier solution—one that requires no programming, no eye for page design, and no real Internet skills. The solution? A photo-sharing web site.

These sites take the arcane drudgery out of designing web sites from scratch and posting photos to the Internet by enabling you to upload images to a commercial site via a simple interface. The site itself arranges your images into an attractive layout, complete with thumbnail views (which you can click to see a full-sized version of the image), captions, and even printing services that can print your favorite images and mail the hard copy directly to you. These sites are a convenient way to publish your images online for friends, family, and strangers to browse, and you needn't learn anything about web site creation.

A year or two ago, as many as two dozen of these sorts of sites existed, and they all tried to deliver free photo-sharing services. I recognized at the time that this was a business plan disaster waiting to happen, and guess what? I was right! Most of them are gone now.

Of course, a few are left, and those that remain are excellent. ClubPhoto.com, for instance, lets you arrange your photos into albums and display them for visitors (see Figure 16-6). The site lets you drag-and-drop images from your desktop directly to the web browser—a convenient way to upload images. Some other excellent options include the following:

- **SmugMug**   www.smugmug.com
- **dotPhoto**   www.dotphoto.com
- **Shutterfly**   www.shutterfly.com
- **Ofoto**   www.ofoto.com

Another option is ofoto.com. This site has a clever image-editing tool built right into the web page. You can crop, rotate, and even remove red eye from your pictures right from an ofoto.com upload assistant program, which you can download and use to store images on the web site. And there's shutterfly.com, a nicely organized site that works with both digital and film pictures.

The bottom line is you can't expect sites like these to stay in business on advertising or good thoughts. If you find one you like, I highly encourage you

FIGURE 16-6 ClubPhoto automatically arranges your uploaded digital images in an elegant manner.

to pay the subscription fee and keep it in business. That's what I've done with ClubPhoto because I'd like my digital images to still be online six months, a year, and even two years from now.

 Even if you maintain your own personal web site, you can save yourself the time and trouble of arranging digital images on a photo page by linking from your own web site directly to your album on a photo-sharing site. That's what I do; to see it in action, go to www.bydavejohnson.com and click on the Photography link to see how I connect to the ClubPhoto site.

Showing Off Images on a PDA

A popular way to show off traditional 35mm pictures is by carrying them in your wallet. Wallet photos and digital imaging don't mix that well—or at least they didn't, until recently. Now you can transfer images from your hard disk and store them on your Palm OS handheld (like the Zire 71, Tungsten T, or Sony Clié) or

Pocket PC device. A typical PDA can store dozens of images on a memory card and let you display them a picture at a time or in Slideshow mode.

Applications abound for storing and displaying images on a Palm device. Here are some of the best choices (see Figure 16-7 for a glimpse of what some look like):

- ■ **AcidImage**   www.red-mercury.com
- ■ **SplashPhoto**   www.splashdata.com

Your PDA might come with image-viewing software. Sony often includes its Clié Viewer, for instance, and Palm bundles SplashPhoto with many of its devices.

FIGURE 16-7   A variety of photo applications let you display images and even videos on any Palm handheld.

16

If you have a wireless modem connected to your PDA or your handheld is a Smartphone like the Handspring Treo or Samsung i330, you can wirelessly e-mail pictures to other PDA users and ordinary desktop e-mail accounts as well. One way to do that is via a program called Pixer, from Electric Pocket (www.electricpocket.com).

Pixer is a program that mimics the European MMS experience. MMS enables mobile phone users to send digital images, hand-drawn sketches, and written notes between mobile handsets. It's quite literally a multimedia alternative to SMS text messaging, which is popular in the US. You might have trouble finding recipients for your Multimedia Messaging on a mobile handset in the United States right now, but Pixer lets you send and receive digital images on a Palm via e-mail—both between PDAs and the desktop.

Showing Off Images in a Digital Picture Frame

Another way to display digital images is in a digital picture frame. Digital picture frames are inexpensive LCD displays mounted in a picture frame shell. Equipped with a memory card, the picture frame can show digital images in a slide show format. Digital picture frames are readily available. Models include the Ceiva, the Digi-Frame, and Sony's Digital CyberFrame.

Sony's *CyberFrame* uses Sony's Memory Stick to display both still images and MPEG movies in a small LCD screen, which you can place on a tabletop like an ordinary picture frame. If you already have a Sony digital camera that uses Memory Stick memory storage, the CyberFrame is a good choice because you can simply remove the memory card from the camera and insert it directly in the picture frame to begin displaying images. The *Digi-Frame* is a similar product, though it uses both CompactFlash and SmartMedia memory cards, so you can insert the memory card from most digital cameras to view your images.

The *Ceiva,* which you can see in Figure 16-10, is unique in two ways: in addition to a small cache of internal (nonremovable) memory, it also connects to the Internet via an ordinary telephone jack. Using a built-in modem, it regularly connects to the Internet and downloads images you've stored on the Ceiva web site. With the capability to rotate among 20 images stored in the Ceiva's memory each day, you can have a constant supply of images on display with minimal effort. Likewise, Ceiva makes it possible to share images from your digital camera with other Ceiva picture frame owners. So you can establish a community of friends and family who exchange images among their picture frames via the Ceiva web site.

FIGURE 16-8   Digital picture frames put an always-changing slide show of your digital images right on a table top.

Here is a handy chart showing the digital picture frame makers and their web sites:

Digital Picture Frames	Find It At
Ceiva	www.ceiva.com
Digi-Frame	www.digi-frame.com
Sony CyberFrame	www.sonystyle.com

Showing Pictures on TV

No one likes to admit it, but we all spend the best hours of our lives in the family room within a stone's throw of the television. So while the Web and framed enlargements are two good ways to show off your pictures, nothing beats watching them on the familiar old television. Heck, I can even think of a non-couch-potato reason to show your pictures on a TV: it's the biggest screen in the house, so everyone can see your photos without craning their necks.

Thankfully, showing your digital images on television is easy. Most digital cameras have video-out ports built right in that can directly display the contents of your camera's memory card on a TV screen. Don't lose the video cable that comes

16

with your camera, though; one end is a standard RCA jack for connecting to the video-in port of a TV or VCR, but the other end is a specialized connector for your camera. It's expensive to replace and is' only available from the camera manufacturer.

Your camera is designed to take any picture on your camera—even big 3 megapixel ones—and fit them on the TV screen. That's fine, but it can be slow because the camera has to read a lot of useless data from the memory card, pack it down to a smaller image size, and, finally, pump it to the TV. If you want to make a faster slide show, use your PC to convert the images to 640×480-pixel images, and then copy them back to a memory card. Insert the card in your camera, and you're ready to rock and roll.

> **TIP** *You're not limited to showing pictures you took with the digital camera on the TV. Most cameras will output any image on the card to the television. This means you can convert PowerPoint slides, graphics, and other images to JPEG images, store them on a memory card, and display them on a TV. That makes your camera a portable general-purpose projector system.*

Creating a Slide Show on Videotape

Another way to show your images on TV is by making a videotape slide show that people can pop into their VCRs. This is a convenient solution for folks who might not own a computer. For years, photography stores have offered video slide show services for a fee: they'd copy your old prints, slides, and negatives to videotape with a musical soundtrack. Now you can do it yourself.

Record Video Directly from the Camera

You can make your own video slide show in two ways. If your camera has a video-out jack, you can do it quickly and easily without even using your PC. Here's what you can do.

1. Start by arranging the images you want to show off on your camera's memory card. Delete any images you don't want to show, for instance. You can also copy other images from your PC to the camera's memory card, and then insert the card in the camera. Also, make sure they're all oriented properly—sideways images taken by holding the camera on its side should be removed.

2. If your camera has the capability to display transitions between each image during playback, turn that mode on now.

3. Attach the video-out port of the camera to your VCR. If you want musical accompaniment, connect your CD player to the VCR as well, and queue up some music. Set the VCR on pause.

4. When your tape is ready to record, start recording, and then start the CD player and the camera's playback mode simultaneously. You should end up with a slide show of images with music recorded on tape.

Using PowerPoint to Make a Video Slide Show

Using the camera to create a slide show is easy, but it's fraught with compromises. Usually, there's no way to precisely time the transition from one image to another in your slide show, for instance, so you can't easily synchronize the images to music. Also, images tend to roll slowly onto the screen as they're read from memory. This might look cheesy, particularly if you're used to seeing pictures "snap" rapidly onto the screen.

Instead, you might want to try the second, though obviously more elaborate, solution if you have the necessary gear. For this approach to work, you'll need a PC, a program like PowerPoint (which you might already have, especially if you use Microsoft Office), and a video-out port on your PC that you can connect to a VCR or camcorder. Here's how you can do it:

To create a slide show using PowerPoint, do this:

1. Start by making sure all the images you plan to use are 640×480 pixels. If they're bigger, resize and save them using a different name. It's often easiest to create a special folder for all your slide show images, and then delete that temporary folder when you're done creating the slide show.

2. Launch PowerPoint and choose Blank Presentation from the New Presentation dialog box.

3. We need to choose a slide style—it doesn't matter which one, so pick the blank slide from the bottom.

4. Choose Insert | Picture | From File, as the illustration shows. Find the image you want to add to the slide.

5. When the image appears on your slide, resize it, if necessary, so it takes up the entire slide, from top to bottom and side to side, as the following shows.

16

6. Now add another slide. Click the New Slide button option in Common Tasks, and then add another blank slide.

7. Add another image to this new blank slide.

8. Continue this process until you've created a complete slide show.

9. To add a common transition to every slide in your presentation, choose Slide Show | Slide Transition. and then select a transition from the transition drop-down menu. The Dissolve transaction is a good choice. To apply this transition to every slide in your slide show, choose Apply To All, as shown in Figure 16-9.

TIP *You can apply transitions to a particular slide or apply them to all the slides at once. In my opinion, slide shows that use a different effect for every transition have a decidedly unprofessional look. I suggest you stick with a subdued, single-transition approach throughout the entire presentation.*

FIGURE 16-9   PowerPoint lets you add transitions between each of your digital images.

10. Save your presentation by choosing File | Save As.

11. When your slide show is complete, you can plug your PC into a VCR or camcorder, and then record the show to tape, using your own mouse clicks as timing for when to change the slides. You can also add a CD audio source to the VCR to add a soundtrack as you record the show.

If Your Camera Has No Video Output

Not all digital cameras have video outputs and, if you have one of those video-deprived models, showing your pictures on the big screen can be difficult. If this sounds like you, consider getting a stand-alone device that displays digital images on a TV without needing a camera with a video-out connector. Microsoft's *TV Photo Viewer,* for instance, is a cool little device that looks like an external floppy disk drive. It plugs into your TV's video port and displays pictures from a floppy disk.

The TV Photo Viewer comes with Windows software that lets you drag-and-drop images into a custom slideshow. You can arrange the images, rotate them, crop pictures, and even add captions. When you're done, the images are copied to a standard floppy in 640×480-pixel resolution, which you can insert into the TV Photo Viewer. If you give one of these guys to your parents, you can make slideshows on

16

floppy disks that you can mail to your folks. They can watch the pictures on their own TV at their leisure.

And Microsoft isn't the only game in town. The *SanDisk Digital Photo Viewer* (www.sandisk.com) is a similar box that connects to your TV, but it has an array of slots for inserting CompactFlash, SmartMedia, Memory Stick, SD, and MMC cards. The device is designed for no-nonsense simplicity. Just insert a memory card from your digital camera and use the bundled remote control to view, zoom, rotate, and step through photos. Or, there's the *eFilm Picturevision,* from Delkin (www.delkin.com), which also lets you insert memory cards from digital cameras and display their contents on a TV. Any one of these gadgets can bring back the old-fashioned experience of watching 35mm slides in the living room.

Index

INTERNATIONAL CONTACT INFORMATION

AUSTRALIA
McGraw-Hill Book Company
Australia Pty. Ltd.
TEL +61-2-9900-1800
FAX +61-2-9878-8881
http://www.mcgraw-hill.com.au
books-it_sydney@mcgraw-hill.com

CANADA
McGraw-Hill Ryerson Ltd.
TEL +905-430-5000
FAX +905-430-5020
http://www.mcgraw-hill.ca

**GREECE, MIDDLE EAST, & AFRICA
(Excluding South Africa)**
McGraw-Hill Hellas
TEL +30-210-6560-990
TEL +30-210-6560-993
TEL +30-210-6560-994
FAX +30-210-6545-525

MEXICO (Also serving Latin America)
McGraw-Hill Interamericana Editores
S.A. de C.V.
TEL +525-1500-5108
FAX +525-117-1589
http://www.mcgraw-hill.com.mx
carlos_ruiz@mcgraw-hill.com

SINGAPORE (Serving Asia)
McGraw-Hill Book Company
TEL +65-6863-1580
FAX +65-6862-3354
http://www.mcgraw-hill.com.sg
mghasia@mcgraw-hill.com

SOUTH AFRICA
McGraw-Hill South Africa
TEL +27-11-622-7512
FAX +27-11-622-9045
robyn_swanepoel@mcgraw-hill.com

SPAIN
McGraw-Hill/
Interamericana de España, S.A.U.
TEL +34-91-180-3000
FAX +34-91-372-8513
http://www.mcgraw-hill.es
professional@mcgraw-hill.es

**UNITED KINGDOM, NORTHERN,
EASTERN, & CENTRAL EUROPE**
McGraw-Hill Education Europe
TEL +44-1-628-502500
FAX +44-1-628-770224
http://www.mcgraw-hill.co.uk
emea_queries@mcgraw-hill.com

ALL OTHER INQUIRIES Contact:
McGraw-Hill/Osborne
TEL +1-510-420-7700
FAX +1-510-420-7703
http://www.osborne.com
omg_international@mcgraw-hill.com

Sound Off!

Visit us at **www.osborne.com/bookregistration** and let us know what you thought of this book. While you're online you'll have the opportunity to register for newsletters and special offers from McGraw-Hill/Osborne.

We want to hear from you!

Sneak Peek

Visit us today at **www.betabooks.com** and see what's coming from McGraw-Hill/Osborne tomorrow!

Based on the successful software paradigm, Bet@Books™ allows computing professionals to view partial and sometimes complete text versions of selected titles online. Bet@Books™ viewing is free, invites comments and feedback, and allows you to "test drive" books in progress on the subjects that interest you the most.